DATE DUE

7-23-92 ILL JUL 23 RECD			
DEC 14 2009			

The Politics of Harmony analyses how traditional ruling elites in Swaziland, as in other parts of Africa, use harmony ideologies to downplay and resolve land disputes. Such disputes could be used by foreign development agents or indigenous new elites as justification for implementing land tenure changes, including a reduction of traditional elites' power based upon land control. Swazi commoners accept the cultural value and legitimacy of most harmony ideologies, but they use strategies when disputing about particular land rights to produce more favourable outcomes.

This book is unusual in its focus on political rather than economic dimensions of land tenure and disputes. It searches for links between individual concerns with land use rights and national concerns with land policy. It also examines gender and leadership issues associated with land, showing how women and new elites threaten land interests of men and traditional leaders.

THE POLITICS OF HARMONY

AFRICAN STUDIES SERIES 69

Published in collaboration with
THE AFRICAN STUDIES CENTRE, CAMBRIDGE

A list of books in the series will be found at the end of the volume

An unmarried Swazi woman who struggled to acquire and retain her land plot, separates, with her children's assistance, maize kernels after the harvest.

THE POLITICS OF HARMONY

Land dispute strategies in Swaziland

LAUREL L. ROSE

The right of the University of Cambridge to print and sell all manner of books was granted by Henry VIII in 1534. The University has printed and published continuously since 1584.

CAMBRIDGE UNIVERSITY PRESS
CAMBRIDGE
NEW YORK PORT CHESTER MELBOURNE SYDNEY

Published by the Press Syndicate of the University of Cambridge
The Pitt Building, Trumpington Street, Cambridge CB2 1RP
40 West 20th Street, New York, NY 10011-4211, USA
10 Stamford Road, Oakleigh, Victoria 3166, Australia

First published 1992
Printed in Great Britain at the University Press, Cambridge

British Library cataloguing in publication data

Rose, Laurel L.
The politics of harmony: land dispute strategies in Swaziland. – (African studies series ISSN 0065 406X: 69)
1. Swaziland. Social conditions
I. Title II. series
968.1303

Library of Congress cataloguing in publication data

Rose, Laurel L.
The politics of harmony: land dispute strategies in Swaziland / Laurel L. Rose.
p. cm. – (African studies series: 69)
Based on the author's dissertation (Ph.D.) – University of California.
Includes bibliographical references and index.
ISBN 0 521 39296 9
1. Land tenure – Swaziland. I. Title. II. Series.
HD995.Z63R67 1992
346.6887′ 04′3 – dc20
[346.8870643] 90-2549 CIP

ISBN 0 521 39296 9 hardback

VN

To the memory of my grandparents,
Harold and Emma Rose

Contents

Figures, tables and maps

List of cases

5. Land dispute cases in the Swazi hierarchy

* Clan names do *not* refer to the actual disputants.

Disputant dyad: chief vs. subject

Disputant dyad: chief vs. chief

Disputant dyad: Central Authority vs. chief

6. 'A woman is like a field': Swazi women's land dispute strategies

Disputant dyad: family member vs. family member

Disputant dyad: subject vs. subject

Disputant dyad: subject vs. chief

Acknowledgements

Many people across three continents contributed ideas to the doctoral dissertation upon which this book is based. I am immensely indebted to my dissertation chairperson in the Anthropology Department at the University of California–Berkeley, Professor Laura Nader, for providing careful guidance during all phases of dissertation preparation and writing. She stimulated my interest in law and harmony, a subject which she has been researching for decades. I am also grateful for the assistance offered by Professors William Shack and Louise Fortmann who served on my dissertation committee. Professor Shack underlined the importance of land and suggested Swaziland as the location of my field study, while Professor Fortmann provided special support for my interest in women as disputants. Finally, I offer long-due thanks to a few of the many teachers, from the time of my secondary school years through university studies, who stimulated and propelled me along the long academic road: Shirley Kelly, George Horner, Susan Todd, Christina Reordan, Morris Freilich, Ruediger Schott and Alan Dundes.

Research grants from the Wenner-Gren Foundation for Anthropological Research, the Fulbright International Institute of Education and the University of California–Berkeley allowed me to carry out eighteen months of field work in Swaziland. A USAID contract through the Land Tenure Center at the University of Wisconsin–Madison, in association with the project 'Changes in Agricultural Land Use: Institutional Constraints and Opportunities', enabled me to analyse my research data and write a first draft.

My field work could not have been carried out without the cooperation of countless people who generously submitted their time to my unending requests for assistance. Members of the Social Science Research Unit at the University of Swaziland offered valuable guidance in archival research, help with permissions and introductions to people. John Daniel, as director of the Social Science Research Unit, supplied me with a dose of encouragement at the start of my research endeavour. Members of the Zombodze and Kwaluseni councils graciously allowed me to attend their meetings, in which they deliberated upon many of the cases described in this book. They also spent many hours explaining to me the fine points of Swazi customary land law. They may not fully agree with my accounts, but I thank them for granting me the opportunity to present the cases for scholarly consideration. Residents of my research communities opened their hearts and homes, making my stay a most memorable personal and academic experience. Lizzie Simelane assisted me in untangling the complex web of facts in court cases and introduced me to many women; Mponiswayini Sukati offered me delicious food after the long, tiring court sessions and taught me much about Swazi custom; and *Make* (mother) Motsa provided me a place to sleep in her house and demonstrated the domestic activities of a Swazi housewife. Josiah Sikhondze, Faith Masuku, Elijah Dlamini and Dumisa Matsebula assisted me as court interpreters on numerous occasions. Many other people, whom I cannot name for lack of space, offered me their only chair when I came to visit their homestead, fed me when I was hungry after a tiring trek along dusty country paths, and talked about their problems, fears and joys (or listened to my own) when I was in need of companionship.

My deepest appreciation goes to members of my family, especially my inquisitive father, for their encouragement throughout my research effort. To my grandparents, who continually supplied all their grandchildren with many material and intellectual tools of the scholarly trade, I dedicate this book.

Glossary

bandlakhulu – council of community elders
bandlancane – chief's inner council
bemdzabuko – true Swazi
emafikawuva – clans who 'came late'
emakhandzambili – clans 'found ahead'
imvimba – valuables paid to the father of a girl impregnated out of marriage
Incwala – celebration of kingship
Indlovukati – Queen Mother
indlu – house on a Swazi homestead
indlu yaka gogo – grandmother's house
indvuna (pl. *tindvuna*) – chief's deputy, governor chief, local commander of age regiments, head of *Inkhundla*
Ingwenyama – King of the Swazi
inhlanti – woman who marries the husband of her sister who could not have children
inhlonipho – respect for people, especially superiors
Inkhosi – King
Inkhundla (pl. *Tinkhundla*) – regional committee comprising several chiefs
insulamnyembeti – the cow paid to compensate the mother of a girl getting married
khonta – see *kukhonta*
kraal (Afrikaans) – livestock enclosure
kubekwa – placing of a person on land (or, installing of a chief or king)
kuboleka umhlaba – land loan from one individual to another
kukhonta – (noun) offering of allegiance to obtain land; *khonta* (verb) to offer allegiance to obtain land
libandla – council
libutfo (pl. *emabutfo*) – warrior regiment
lihambate (pl. *emahambate*) – sub-areas entrusted to a chief
lincusa (pl. *emancusa*) – representative
Liqoqo – inner council

lobolo – valuables transferred from a man's family to a woman's family at marriage
lusendvo – family pedigree (or council)
Mfecane – movement of clans during the nineteenth century out of present-day Natal to escape Zulu conquering armies
Ndabazabantu – official created by British bureaucracy who links chiefs to customary hierarchy of national councils
Ndvunankhulu – traditional Prime Minister
sikhonti – man who pledges allegiance to a chief, is accepted as a subject, and may receive land
sikhulu (pl. *tikhulu*) – clan chief
sisa – to lend out cattle
umgijimi (pl. *bagijimi*) – chief's runner
Umntfwanenkhosi (pl. *Bantfwabenkhosi*) – member of the royal family (may be allotted land and a following)
umnumzane (pl. *banumzane*) – homestead head
Umpakhatsi – a chief's or the King's homestead
umsumphe (pl. *imisumphe*) – long-term resident of an area
umuti (pl. *imiti*) – largest residential unit on Swazi Nation Land (homestead)

Introduction

Swaziland is an alluring place to do research. The tranquil beauty of green pastures and fertile farmlands mesmerizes the newcomer, yet scarcely hints that land disputes are boiling in many parts of the countryside. Such disputes are ripe for research exploration: they have been granted little attention in several major land tenure studies that have been conducted.[1] Even the customary legal forums in which land disputes are fought out have not been adequately described in the literature.[2]

Good fortune was with me during the early weeks of my anthropological field work when my research assistants unwittingly tantalized my curiosity with half-told tales of struggles over land. I seized the opportunity to redesign my planned study of Swazi customary law as a specialized study of land disputes. My luck continued when an unusually hospitable chief supported my interests, allowing me to attend public sessions of his court where land was a frequent topic of debate. Unfortunately, soon thereafter, when I began to attend such sessions, the promise of my early successes began to deteriorate: my Swazi hosts began to suspect and resist my research effort. Clearly, my probings were exposing some hidden and delicate developments in customary land law. As I gradually delved into the reasons for my hosts' resistance, I came to understand that their land disputes revealed much more than rules of land law; in fact, such disputes were an important although often cloudy mirror of the changing social and political order.

Confrontation with research difficulties

My research, which extended over eighteen months during three separate visits to Swaziland between 1983 and 1986, involved several activities: investigation of archival material; interviewing scholars, customary court members and government officials; attendance at customary court sessions; and analysis of a questionnaire. Despite the enormous possibilities of this exploratory research, I soon despaired that my research goals might not be met. I confronted many difficulties in data collection that are commonly described by field workers in Africa – such as comprehending indigenous concepts, locating reliable assistants and knowledgeable informants, and finding transportation to distant research sites. In particular, I confronted difficulties peculiar to anthropologists of law, who have noted that African informants are bothered by questions about disputing behaviour, and particularly by questions about land disputes (Brokensha and Njeru 1977: 2; La Fontaine 1979: 99; Richards 1939).[3] My difficulties in data collection were exacerbated by gender-related frustrations: as a woman, I had difficulties gaining full access to male-controlled Swazi institutions – in this case, to the Chiefs' Courts, in which men dispute about land rights (women are usually represented by a male agnate or affine), and to beer-drinking groups, in which men informally discuss land disputes.

Although my research difficulties had clearly been experienced by investigators in many parts of Africa, I gradually came to believe that my predicament in Swaziland was somewhat extreme. Local authorities refused to cooperate without government authorization, while government authorities either claimed ignorance about sponsorship requirements or referred me back to local authorities; I thus found myself uncomfortably wedged in a no-win situation. Swazi elders, who were my intended informants, admonished me that land disputes were no concern of 'outsiders'. Some potential informants even denied that land disputes existed, dismissing my inquiries with testy remarks such as: 'We Swazis are not permitted to fight over land because it belongs to the King!' The only persons who unreservedly aided me were members of the European-influenced legal system – lawyers, magistrates and prosecutors. Unfortunately, such persons played almost no role in Swazi customary land matters.

The reluctance of Swazi elders to speak about land disputes frustrated me, but I reasoned that the causes of my difficulties could be determined and resolved. I pinpointed two sources of difficulty. First, Swazis are generally reluctant to tell foreign researchers about any customary law matters; for example, a major foreign-funded customary law research project had been rejected by government officials shortly before my arrival. Consequently, I believed that if I wanted to investigate land disputes, I would have to inquire initially into related topics – for example, methods of boundary demarcation and fencing practices. Secondly, Swazis were particularly reticent to speak with foreign researchers at the time of my arrival since political circumstances in the country had deteriorated after King Sobhuza's death in 1982. Pamphlets and oral directives of uncertain origin were being widely circulated, warning Swazis not to speak to unknown persons or attend unauthorized meetings. As I was a newcomer, I needed to spend many months cultivating friendships with numerous people at different kinds of social functions, such as funerals, weddings and beer-drinking gatherings.

My primary investigative strategy evolved into a search for the deeper roots of my research difficulties than common cross-cultural constraints.[4] I realized that the widespread secrecy about land disputes presented a curious paradox: Swazis denied or downplayed the existence of land disputes when making ideal statements about customary law but nonetheless knew full well that land disputes constituted a major and prolonged type of litigation coming before customary legal institutions. I became convinced that denials about land disputes were a clue that important, although hidden, land tenure developments were occurring in Swaziland.

Exploration of the paradox posed by Swazi land disputes

By the end of my study, I concluded that my research difficulties, as in many parts of Africa, were linked to tensions arising from decades of stressful land relations between an indigenous African population and European settlers. At the same time, I believed that my extreme difficulties arose from the particular character of Swazi institutions – kingship and associated political ideologies – that have made Swazi sensitivity about and responses to land matters notable. Unlike other places in Africa, Swazi traditional authorities (members of the ruling Dlamini clan, dominant clans and chiefs) have not only succeeded in gradually augmenting their customary authority over land after colonial incursions, they have succeeded in expanding areas controlled by customary land tenure. My final analysis focused upon explaining why and how Swazis have protected and reinforced to an unusual extent their customary system of land law – even though it shares many rules and procedures in common with other African systems.

The answer to this question lies in an intriguing combination of geographical, historical and political factors. Swaziland, located next to the eastern edge of South Africa, was not significantly affected by land-hungry European settlers penetrating the southern part of the continent until the late nineteenth century, at which time the Swazi King granted land to the settlers. The Land Partition of 1907 interpreted these land transactions as permanent concessions rather than temporary loans, thereby granting Europeans about two-thirds of the territory and the vast majority of Swazis only one-third of the territory. A succession of Swazi rulers in the early 1900s reacted to what they perceived as outside land transgressions by several brilliant tactics: for example, by encouraging commoners to contribute wages obtained from migrant labour towards land buy-back efforts and by acquiring considerable control of government administrative organs which plan and implement land policy – the most significant manoeuvres occurring after Independence from Britain in 1968. Importantly, Swazi rulers persuaded commoners that all Swazis should display harmonious behaviour, and thus cooperative and conciliatory behaviour, if they, as Swazis, wanted to avoid further intervention in their affairs.

Following Independence, Swazi rulers wisely realized that if they were to expand customarily tenured land as well as augment their control over such land, they needed to ward off new and multiple threats to customary land tenure – namely, both foreign development agents/landowners, who threatened extensive changes, and those Swazi commoners (for example, an expanding group of new elites and increasingly dissatisfied women) who felt that national commercial productivity or social equity, among other things, were inhibited by such tenure. As in much of Africa, foreign and Swazi critics commonly argued that customary land tenure should be abolished or reformed in favour of freehold tenure. Swazi rulers, as a contrast, who were well aware that their hereditary power was closely linked to customary land control (see also Gluckman 1955, 1965b, 1969; Schapera 1938), rejected many land reforms out of fear that such reforms represented the first step towards abolition of customary land tenure and thus loss of their power-base. Nonetheless, true to their conciliatory philosophy, Swazi rulers voiced support for development initiatives when foreigners were their audience but often criticized such initiatives when Swazi ears were listening.

A significant threat to Swazi rulers' customary land control was posed by land disputes. Such disputes, which could easily be construed by critics as indications that customary land tenure was not working and should be replaced by freehold tenure, needed to be downplayed or hidden. To prevent unfavourable interpretations by critics, Swazi rulers effectively used harmony ideologies in public rhetoric to disguise the disruptiveness of land disputes for individuals and groups and to promote an image of unity. In their turn, Swazi commoners generally supported their leaders against a common enemy that was believed to have caused land shortages through the Concessions and Partition. The commoners widely acknowledged that harmony in behaviour, if not always in beliefs, would protect and enhance valued cultural traditions.

While Swazi traditional elites and commoners are in agreement about the need to maintain appearances of harmonious relationships in national land matters, they are engaged in a push and pull struggle in specific land cases: disputants are concerned with protecting or promoting their land use interests, and authorities are concerned with maintaining their relative power and control over subjects. Thus, disputants seek power to achieve favourable outcomes in individual land cases, whereas authorities seek to secure more general power in local and national legal processes. In an effort to promote their own interests, while simultaneously producing defensive images of harmony, both authorities and commoners involved in specific land cases develop disputing styles which are characterized by strategies. These strategies, derived from ideologies about harmony, are based upon their status and circumstantial opportunities relative to other participants in the land dispute process. The strategies maintain continuity of the customary land tenure system and associated social/political unity, although manipulating it to secure individual interests.

The strategic tug-of-war in land cases between litigants and between litigants and authorities continually moulds the pliable borders of land use rules and practices. Sometimes rules and strategies remain distinct; the rules define the established 'traditional', and the strategies mould the political 'situational'. At other times, rules and strategies merge; the strategies define ideologies underlying new rules. In the latter scenario, change in both the theoretical interpretation and practical implementation of customary law is achieved, even if 'reform' in the sense of change in a written legal code has not been achieved.

The irony about Swazis' defence of customary land tenure against external or internal incursions is that land disputes, which are commonly interpreted by both Swazi and foreign critics as indications that changes in customary land law are needed but inhibited, might also be correctly interpreted by all Swazis as indications that change is under way. Therefore, land disputes may inhibit change through reinforcing social boundaries and reaffirming traditional values, but they may also promote change through reforming old rules or creating new rules, devising new consensual understandings and adjusting interests between competing individuals and groups (see Coser 1956; Simmel 1955). This means that land disputes need not inevitably be interpreted by 'traditionalist' Swazis as a weapon which 'developers'[5] will use to foment change disruptively, but also as a tool which Swazis can apply to achieve change incrementally. In this way disputes, like the strategies used within them, have contradictory sides – both discouraging and encouraging change: Swazis may use disputes conservatively to stabilize customary law or innovatively to adapt it to changing conditions. But critics of customary land tenure seem more inclined to emphasize the change-inhibiting function rather than the change-producing function of land disputes.

In effect, land disputes can be either 'good' or 'bad' from the perspective of traditional Swazi elites, because elites can use them either positively to shore up their status positions relative to foreigners and other Swazis, or negatively to diminish such positions. Elites try to remove uncertainty from disputing processes, directing such processes towards fulfilment of their general administrative interests, by strategically propagating harmony ideologies. Elites allow deviations from procedural rules and new interpretations of practices when 'justice' would best be served and when their control is not threatened. At the same time, disputes can be either 'good' or 'bad' from the perspective of Swazi commoners, because they can be either empowering or disempowering in specific cases. Commoners strategically respond to customary land tenure rules, which elites have cloaked within harmony ideologies, with their own disputing strategies. Commoners' strategic deviations from 'recognized' procedures and rules solve their dilemmas and promote their interests on a case-by-case basis.

Despite common arguments in the Africa development literature that customary land tenure and authority structures inhibit change (at least changes sought by non-African development agents), evidence indicates that some Swazi land practices are slowly changing – in the direction of enhanced social equity and national productivity – under elite direction. In specific cases, Swazi dispute participants' strategic manipulations, which are both produced by and producers of Swazi customary legal rules, collectively provide a piecemeal momentum towards larger developments in customary land law. In each case, clever strategies preserve images of harmony and at the same time lead to new interpretations regarding, for example, rules about fencing, about women obtaining land through minor sons, or about elites collecting monetary tributes for performing land administration functions. Swazis share information across customary courts and territories about small rule interpretations effected in land cases, thereby contributing gradually to changes in shared beliefs and practices in land tenure.

In several of my cases, Swazi chiefs, similar to what Schapera (1970) has reported for Tswana chiefs, established new land rules or tentatively followed precedent reported elsewhere. For example, in one case a procedural rule of evidence was restated by the chief when a female disputant used documents from the 'modern' District Commissioner's office, rather than testimony from her in-laws, to substantiate her land request. The chief allowed this deviation, stating that justice would best be served. In another case, a customary rule regulating land access procedures was transgressed when a chief's council permitted a woman, who was severely disadvantaged by her inability to obtain land according to customary protocol, to receive land in the name of her infant son rather than a mature son. The chief based his action upon similar actions reportedly taken by chiefs elsewhere. From an analytic perspective, a problem arises in that such changes remained invisible to all but the closest observers due to the regionally variant, temporally incremental and uncodified nature of customary law. Compounding the 'invisibility' problem, Swazis did not report or even acknowledge such changes. When I asked people in interviews, for example, about women's land rights or about elites' acceptance of monetary tributes, they inevitably related conservative, ideal rules rather than actual practices, as I had observed.[6] Clearly, Swazis believed that land reforms were a cultural matter and should be directed and acknowledged solely within customary institutions.

Swaziland's customary land disputes: comparison with other African polities

As mentioned, Swaziland shares much in common with other African polities. As a result, investigation and comparison of similarities in land development practices and political responses can be enlightening. At the same time, investigation of apparent differences – such as the unusual continuity of Swazi customary land law and secrecy regarding land disputes – are instructive.

Swazi land disputes are analysed in this study according to contextual strategies rather than exclusively in terms of customary land tenure norms; this way, both individual and class interests that compete to define ideologies underlying these norms are explained. The disputes are also analysed as processes within which norms are not absolute 'givens' but rather continually evolving variables. Finally, disputes are analysed as personal and political struggles to define in theory and to convey in practice the ideological variables underlying norms – particularly the variable of 'harmony'. In effect, local land dispute processes are characterized by a 'politics of harmony' which influences the politics of the emerging Swazi state.

Swazi customary land disputes point to the interrelationship between geographical, historical, social and political circumstances and everyday manifestations of land tenure norms. They display theatrically the structural stresses in a customary system of land law that must accommodate an imposed foreign legal system and expanded commercial interests. At the same time, they demonstrate the growing confusion among Swazis regarding legal norms and institutional avenues of legal protest. Individuals can strategize to clarify or to use to their own advantage such legal (normative) and institutional confusion. In Swaziland, as elsewhere in Africa, nearly everyone is concerned about allowing a 'play' in the land tenure system which permits minor case-by-case adjustments and occasional major changes in land practices, but they are also concerned about how norms are played with: traditional elites are concerned that land disputes might produce changes which deprive them of some land administration prerogatives; new elites and women are concerned that changes must currently occur through disputing processes in a sometimes frustrating and hidden (strategic) manner; while 'developers' are concerned that changes occurring through customary institutional processes are not sufficiently rapid or certain to benefit national productivity.

Questions about land norms, interests and changes arise. One question about land norms asks whether land development can proceed within a customary normative and administrative structure and still successfully balance private use rights with development interests in national productivity. A second question about land interests asks whether development initiatives can be taken away from traditional leaders without such leaders moving against land reform, and whether development initiatives will not be promoted by such leaders if left under their control. A final question about changes in land law asks whether and how customary land norms can change through disputing processes in individual cases. It also considers whether land tenure changes can be sufficiently rapid, broad and open to satisfy both commoners, such as women and new elites who are calling for increased social equity, and developers who are calling for increased economic productivity. In addition, it debates whether the changes are slow enough to guarantee a peaceful, negotiated transition which does not rupture social and political relationships.

This study of Swazi customary land disputes does not provide definite answers to these questions, but it does offer Africanists, social scientists, legal specialists and development specialists a model for comparison. The Swaziland data indicate that land development is proceeding within a customary land tenure framework, that traditional leaders are promoting land reform within this framework and that land norms are changing within this framework. Contrary to expectations based on the literature, the data indicate that a customary legal system as apparently conservative and resilient as that of the Swazis is subtly adapting to changed conditions. Unfortunately, 'developers' – even when they recognize and acknowledge processes of change in customary land law – downplay or ignore such changes, in contradiction of their awareness that fundamental characteristics of customary land law are flexibility and adaptability. Many 'developers' also downplay 'certainty' and 'security' in customary law, arguing that customary law proceeds according to random, unpredictable processes. They promote legislation, as in other parts of Africa, in the belief that changes are too slow, uncertain and circumstantial (linked to particular leaders and regions) to satisfy many Swazis and foreign 'experts'.[7] Perhaps they fail to comprehend or they underestimate developments in Swazi customary land law when such developments conflict with their conceptual models and interests.

The model of Swazi dispute strategies presented in this book addresses inaccurate conceptions on a case-by-case basis. Thus, it demonstrates not only how traditional elites are directing adaptations of customary law according to recognized status relationships, but also how commoners are playing a role in developments. In other words, it shows how Swazi customary land law is ordered in a way which outside observers cannot easily recognize: a flexibility and adaptability that are perpetually caught in the tug-of-war between individual use interests and elite political prerogatives. But importantly, it argues that Swazi elites must judiciously balance competing interests; they maintain prestige, which blossoms from the seeds of hereditary power, through both command and consensus.

The development agent and legal specialist in Africa are advised to conceptualize multi-layered customary law processes according to cultural vocabularies embedded within indigenous analytic models. Regardless of one's perspective and goals in a land tenure study, the Swaziland data demonstrate that land reforms, in order to be widely accepted by an indigenous African population, must emerge from within, rather than parallel to, the octopus of customary law that extends its tentacles into all of life's arenas.

Chapter organization

The book is divided into two parts. The first part presents geographical, historical, political, social and legal data in the national and local settings, whereas the second part presents the theoretical model and data analysis (case studies). Some readers may find that there are a great many cases and that some cases are described in considerable depth. Nonetheless, the cases selected demonstrate both different and important principles of Swazi customary land law as well as associated patterns of social/political organization. In addition, the more lengthy case descriptions provide an important record of events for Swaziana specialists.

In Part I, Chapter 1 provides material on Swaziland's history, geography, political structure and social system. Chapter 2, which focuses upon the dual legal structure, describes Swazi customary disputing forums and associated personnel, illustrating how they operate according to dissimilar interpretations of political harmony. Chapter 3 describes the two primary research communities. In Part II, Chapter 4 develops the theoretical problem, which is characterized in terms of political harmony in land disputes. Chapter 5 provides dispute cases in the framework of several dyadic confrontations about customary land rights. All dyadic confrontations between disputants are characterized in terms of authorities' strategies of political harmony and litigants' manipulative disputing strategies. Chapter 6 focuses upon women's disputes about land use rights, and Chapter 7 focuses upon new elites' disputes about land administration rights. Women and new elites use disputing strategies which are shaped by gender or class interests. Chapter 8 offers conclusions about the nature of harmony, the ways in which harmony becomes political in Swazi land disputes, and the continually evolving role of harmony in Swazi land disputes processes.

Part I

National and local settings

1

Geographical, historical, political and social bases of customary land tenure relations

Land disputes in Africa arise in association with unique constellations of geographical, historical, political and social conditions. Geography provides Africans with the natural resource base for the exploitation of land, but differing geographical conditions also present individuals with various reasons for dispute. Historical circumstances determine which system of European law, including land law, will be introduced into a country, and how it will be meshed with customary law. Political structures provide the administrative framework for land control, including land dispute resolution procedures, but also the incentive for confrontations about land. Social organization provides the kinship and age class framework for realization of land rights. Patterns of organization prescribe how people are spatially arranged in homestead units, and thus the kinds of land disputes which arise between kin and neighbours. In Swaziland, as elsewhere in Africa, participants in land disputes strategize to achieve their best interests according to the limitations and opportunities posed by geography, history, political structure and social organization.[1]

Geography

Swaziland, a small, land-locked country of 17,364 sq. km, is perched on the edge of the Southern African escarpment. It is bounded on three sides by South Africa and on the fourth by Mozambique. Four distinctive north–south topographic steps largely determine the characteristics of its natural environment (see Map 1). First, there is the highveld which has grassy hills and averages 1,219 m above sea level. It has a cool, moist climate and soils not usually adequate for arable farming but well suited for forests and grasslands. Secondly, there is the middleveld which is also hilly and averages 610 m above sea level. It has a warm and sub-humid climate with palatable grasses suited for livestock and rich soils good for agriculture. Thirdly, there is the lowveld which averages 274 m above sea level. It has a hot, dry climate and tall grasses suited for grazing but usually not dry-land agriculture. Fourthly, there is the Lebombo mountain range which is a narrow plateau averaging about 610 m

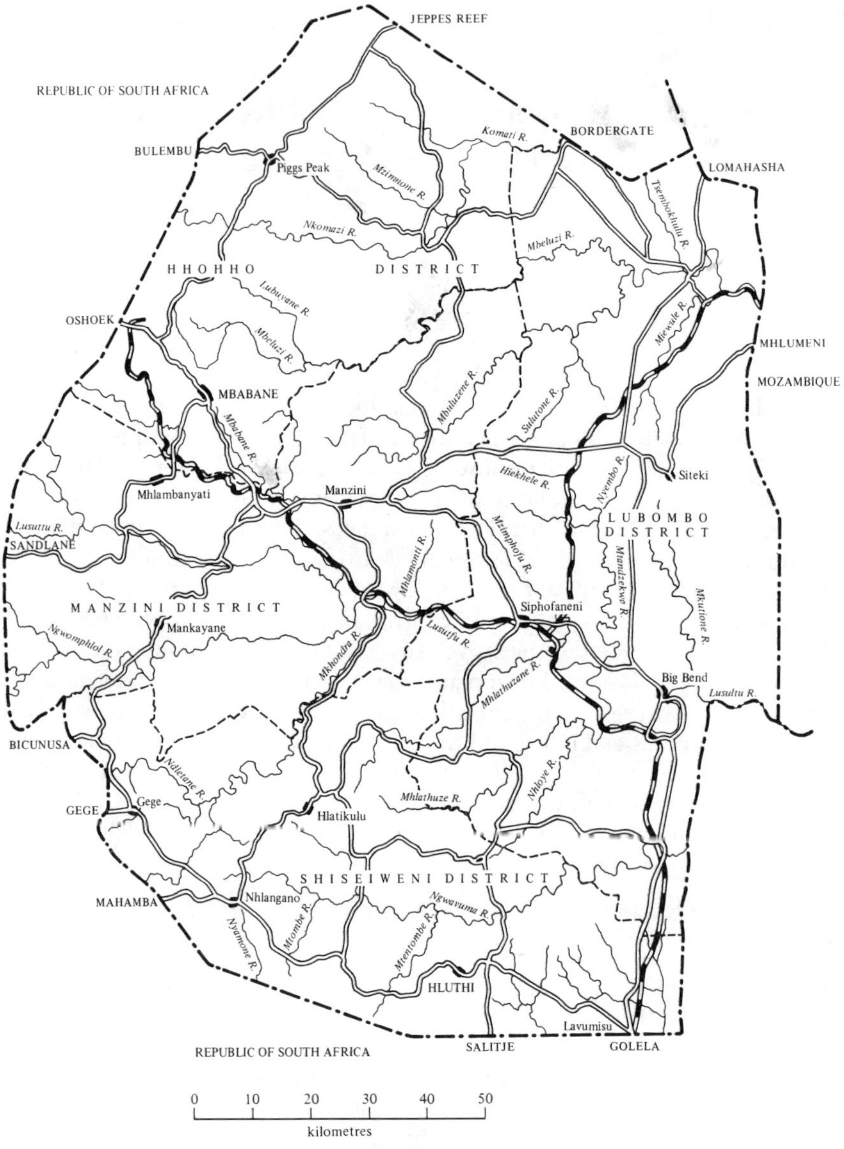

Map 1 Swaziland topography
Source: Third National Development Plan, 1978/9–1982/3, Government of Swaziland

above sea level. It has a warm, sub-humid climate and basaltic soils suited for arable agriculture.

Swaziland's potential for economic development, in terms of water and mineral resources, is considerable. Several rivers, the Mbeluzi, Ngwavuma, Great Usutu, Komati and Lomati, cut through the highveld, middleveld and Lebombo mountains. Although seasonal rains limit the potential water resources of these rivers, construction of hydroelectric storage dams encourages irrigation in the drier middleveld and lowveld. The main irrigated crop for export is sugar. Other major crops include cotton, maize, tobacco, rice, vegetables, citrus fruits and pineapples. Swaziland's mineral wealth consists of iron ore, coal and asbestos which have been mined for export.[2]

Swaziland's geographical features influence both population distribution and associated land utilization patterns, which in turn influence the nature and frequency of land disputes. A good example is provided by the physical and demographic characteristics of the middleveld, where the bulk of the present research project was conducted. In the middleveld nearly one-half of the Swazi population (estimated in August 1982 at 634,678; see Hutcheson 1983: 815) resides in a patchwork pattern; rural homesteads are interspersed with densely populated settlements around employment centres (average of 50 inhabitants per sq. km, rising to more than 200 per sq. km in some rural and in more developed areas). These employment centres, particularly the Matsapha Industrial Complex, and rich soils enhance employment opportunities and agricultural prospects. Unfortunately, high population concentrations reduce the availability of unused land and natural resources. Conflicts frequently arise over land allocations by family and chief's councils for residential and agricultural purposes, over boundaries, over fencing and cattle transit paths, over irrigation rights, and over exploitation of scarce natural resources such as trees. These conflicts and others appear in the sample of cases collected by myself in several middleveld research sites.

Land history

Hughes (1972: 33) has divided Swaziland's complex land tenure history into four phases: (1) the period of the clans and the emergent state (fifteenth century up to 1839); (2) the Concessions period until the Partition of 1907; (3) the post-Partition period until 1968; and (4) the Independence period after 1968.

During the first period of the clans, Bantu-speaking people, who were predominantly Nguni in language and culture, fled from invading Bantu and European armies and settled in present-day Swaziland under the leadership of King Ngwane III. Under the leadership of Ngwane's grandson, Sobhuza I (d. 1839), disparate clans were united under the dominance of the Dlamini clan within a stabilized and centralized Swazi state. The clans comprising members of the Dlamini clan, and several others pledging allegiance, became known as the *bemdzabuko*, or 'true Swazi'. The loosely organized groups of

Nguni and Sotho whom they incorporated became known as *emakhand-zambili*, or 'those found ahead'. Under the reign of King Mswati (1839–75), newly entering groups who were granted asylum became known as *emafikawuva*, or 'those who came late'.

During the second period, King Mbandzeni (1875–89) granted Boer and British concessionaries usufructuary rights to overlapping, extensive land areas for grazing and mining purposes in exchange for revenues. Unfortunately for the Swazis, the Europeans interpreted the temporary land grants as permanent concessions. According to Swazi customary law, land could not be bought or sold by Swazi rulers. As a result of the misunderstanding, a dual land tenure structure and associated dual economic, political and social systems emerged. Land disputes between Swazis and Europeans developed as it became clear that most land areas had multiple claimants.

During the third period, the High Commissioner's Partition Proclamation of 1907 served to give formal recognition by the British administration to the concessionaires' land claims but also to reserve approximately one-third of Swaziland's territory for occupation by the Swazi majority.[3] Colonial land policy arguably sought to impose a situation of land scarcity on Swazis in order that a capitalistic system of production, supported by cheap and plentiful local labour, would be possible.[4] Booth (1982: 35), suggesting that 'there is no clearer example of a calculated and meticulously planned strategy for land deprivation and surplus extraction aimed at proletarianization by a colonial state in early twentieth century Africa', cites Lord Selbourne's written words of 1906: 'We hope that the native settlement will be so devised that it will pave the way to [European] tenure and responsibility and the de-nationalization of the Swazis . . .' (Selbourne cited in Booth 1982: 38). In fact, the colonial land policy resulted in over-population, overstocking, erosion, child malnutrition and disease in the same areas which became the 'greatest generators of labour out-migration' (Booth 1982: 39). Predictably, many Swazis responded to the externally imposed land shortage and heavy taxation by migrating to labour centres (see Booth 1983b; de Vletter 1981: 2; Maasdorp 1976: 416).

Many conflicts about land rights arose following the Partition, requiring several legislative acts as attempts to clarify inconsistencies and contradictions: the Swazi Areas Proclamation No. 39 of 1910 which protected Swazi rights; the Swazi Areas Proclamation No. 41 of 1916 which described the areas set apart for Swazi use; and the Control of Land Purchases Proclamation of 1915 which controlled the purchase of land for Swazis. Other pre-Independence land legislation included the Swazi Land Settlement Proclamation of 1946 which provided for the establishment, control and development of land settlement schemes for the Swazi, and the Acquisition of Property Act of 1961 which provided for property acquisition and payment of compensation.

When Sobhuza II was made King in 1921, he was so influenced by the Concessions legacy that he immediately initiated a long series of protests aimed at regaining land which Swazis believed had been improperly expropriated from them. The hard realities of the Concessions had persuaded him and other Swazi leaders to forge a conservative land policy which aimed to adjust modern-day land developments according to the structure provided by customary land tenure arrangements, rather than the reverse situation, as in many parts of Africa. Swazis never accepted the validity of Partition, and they thus took many legal actions, according to European protocol, to recover alienated land (for example, the 1891 High Court inquiry, 1922 deputation to London, and 1924 petition to Special Court of Swaziland). Their efforts were in vain. By the late 1920s, they were reconciled to the option to buy back the land: petitioning to British officials had been futile and military revolt would be suicidal (Youe 1978: 67). Thereafter, their efforts at land recovery focused upon buy-back programmes (e.g. Lifa Fund of the 1940s; Matsebula 1972: 175) (see Maps 2 and 3 and Figure 1).

Since the beginning of the fourth period, or Independence (1968), when the Constitution vested Swazi Nation Land in the King, buy-back initiatives have continued rather than expropriation of European-owned farms (Jones 1977). The Swazi rulers' land policy had become established as 'retribalization' rather than 'detribalization' (Hughes 1964b: 4; Hutcheson 1983). In 1972, the Land Speculation Control Act controlled speculative land transactions involving non-Swazi citizens (Amoah 1978: 31–4). At the present time, Swazi Nation Land comprises about 60 per cent of the Kingdom. Nearly 70 per cent of the population reside on Swazi Nation Land, and about half of the people depend directly on traditional agriculture. Individual Tenure Farms account for the remaining 40 per cent of land in the Kingdom. At the time of Independence, the Individual Tenure Farms were owned almost exclusively by foreigners and companies, but foreign ownership has been reduced to about 17 per cent of the land, largely as a consequence of the Land Speculation Control Act of 1972. The remaining 23 per cent of the land is currently taken up by publicly owned modern farms, which are run by governmental bodies such as the Ministry of Agriculture, the Prisons Department and the Defence Force as well as by the government corporation, Tibiyo Taka Ngwane (Booth 1983a: 90–1). The Individual Tenure Farms are generally highly productive.

Government land policy, since 1966, has focused on improving Swazi Nation Land quality and productivity through the Rural Development Area programme. The Rural Development Area scheme incorporated large tracts of land covering 60 per cent of Swazi Nation Land area and involving about 200,000 people. The government's purpose in implementing this policy was to redress the post-war imbalance between the dynamism of the commercial sector and the stagnation of the rural sector. In general, the policy aimed to improve the quality of rural life, and thereby reduce the flow of capital and labour to urban-industrial areas. According to Booth, the scheme specifically aimed at 'land development, intensive farming, and the creation of improved communications, marketing, and social services. Those were to include agricultural supply, storage, and marketing depots; pools of mechanical

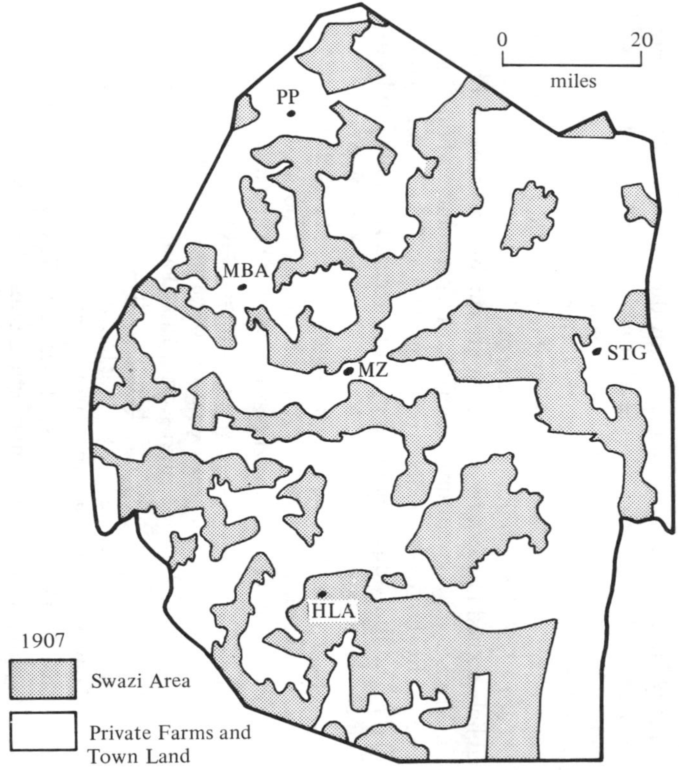

Map 2 Land apportionment 1907
Source: Based upon Fair *et al.* 1969: 26–7

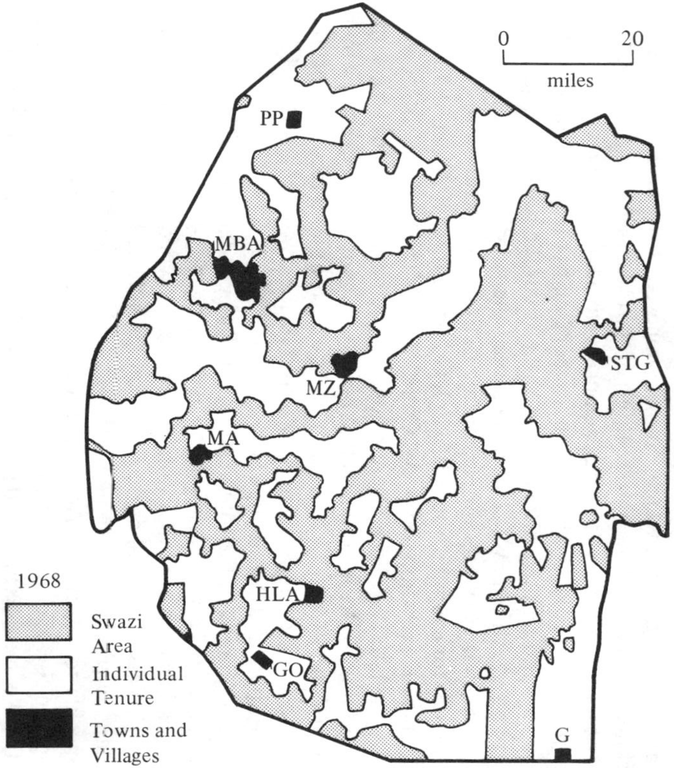

Map 3 Land apportionment 1968
Source: Based upon Fair *et al.* 1969: 26–7

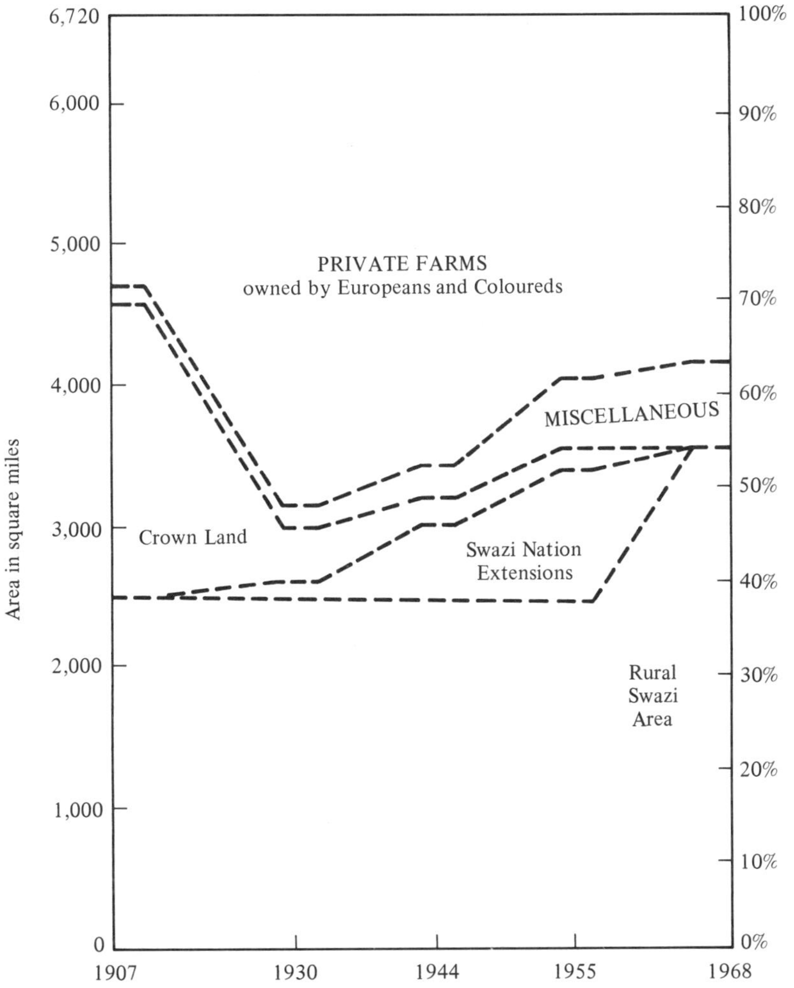

Figure 1 Land ownership from Partition to Independence
Rural Swazi Area in 1968 should strictly be termed Rural Communal and National land as it includes about 140 square miles of cattle-holding grounds, agricultural research stations and game reserves.

Swazi Nation Extensions by 1955 comprised 580 square miles of Native Land Settlement and 340 square miles purchased with the Lifa Fund (a cattle levy: Lifa means Heritage)

Miscellaneous (with 1968 areas) × Commonwealth Development Corporation 380 square miles, urban and periurban land 110, private farms owned by Africans 70 and religious mission land 40 square miles.

Source: Based upon Murdoch 1968: 43

equipment for hire; portable water supplies; "appropriate technology" schools; and health clinics' (1983a: 94). Unfortunately, the Rural Development Area scheme failed to achieve goals of self-sufficiency, increased commodity cropping and decreased rural–urban migration. As has been the case throughout Africa, the blame for failure of such development policy has been attributed to the socio-political basis of customary land tenure; in essence, it is argued that as long as chiefs have the power to withdraw land rights, thus contributing to a sense of insecurity, development policy cannot be effective.

Political structure

Dualism of national land tenure administration

On the one side of Swaziland's dual land tenure system, land is held by customary tenure and regulated by customary law which is administered by customary Chiefs' Courts/the King, and, on the other side, land is held by freehold tenure and regulated by Roman-Dutch law which is administered by the Deeds Registry Office. In the more precise legal terms of legislation passed at the time of the infamous Concessions, there are three types of land tenure in Swaziland: Private Tenure Land, Crown (Government) Land and Swazi Nation Land. Private Tenure Land may be held by freehold title or by concession. Crown Land is land owned by the government, but technically speaking, also by the King. Swazi Nation Land has never been defined by legislation but consists of the former 'Native Areas', i.e. 'Swazi Areas', of the colonial era (refer to Maps 2 and 3 above; see also Figure 1).[5]

A 'Swazi Area' has been defined in the Natural Resources Act No. 71 of 1951 as follows:

> 'Swazi Area' means any land set apart for the sole and exclusive use and occupation of Africans under the Concessions Partition Act No. 28 of 1907 and land set aside for African land settlement in terms of the Swazi Land Settlement Act No. 2 of 1946, and shall include any land registered in the name of the Ngwenyama in Trust for the Swazi Nation.

The term 'Swazi Area' is no longer used, and has been replaced by the term 'Swazi Nation Land'. The latter was introduced into common usage through Hughes' doctoral land tenure study (1964c). Some confusion arises regarding the current administration of Swazi Nation Land. It may be administered by chiefs in a traditional manner, by chiefs as repurchased land, and by national organizations controlled by the royal family, Tibiyo and Tisuka,[6] or government agencies as agricultural projects. As Armstrong writes:

> The confusion arises because under the 'Lifa Fund' and under the British Land Transfer Program (which still continues and is administered by the Ministry of Natural Resources), the Swazi Nation has purchased more than 1/2 of the land lost to concessionaires in the 19th century, and this repurchased land is registered in the name of the Ngwenyama in Trust for the Swazi Nation.

> Sometimes this land is given to chiefs and administered by them according to Swazi law and custom. More often, the land is used by Tibiyo or Tisuka as agricultural projects, industrial projects or housing projects. The land may also be administered by the Ministry of Agriculture as an agricultural project. Working farms acquired in this way generally remain farms, worked by hired labour, rather than reverting to the traditional tenure commonly considered synonymous with Swazi Nation Land (1985: 5).

In this research project, two types of Swazi Nation Land were considered: land administered by chiefs on the basis of long-standing hereditary rights, and land administered by chiefs under recently acquired rights, such as through repurchase schemes. Despite differences in administration, the King controls all kinds of Swazi Nation Land on which land disputes arise.

Hierarchy of political authority for Swazi Nation Land

Customary land law applies to Swazi Nation Land. The basic principle underlying customary land tenure on Swazi Nation Land is embodied in *kukhonta* bonds, i.e. bonds of allegiance which tie chiefs to the King and commoners to chiefs (Kuper 1947a; Rosen-Prinz 1976). Similar bonds between rulers and their subjects have been described elsewhere in Southern Africa: Gluckman (1940, 1943, 1955) for the Barotse; Krige for the Zulu and Lobedu (1936, 1943; also 1938); and Schapera (1953, 1956) for the Tswana (see also Sansom 1937). The *kukhonta* bonds entail reciprocal rights and obligations. Thus, the chief must demonstrate allegiance to the Dlamini rulers by performing in national ceremonies and attending meetings of the national council. He, in turn, has the right to exact tribute labour from his subjects, but he has the obligation to control political, economic and ritual matters in his community as well as distribute land among his subjects. The subject (customarily a male), in turn, has the right to receive a land allotment from the chief as well as the protection and representation of the chief, but he has the obligation to respond to the chief's and King's formal summons to work in fields or build/repair royal homesteads. Although the King is said to 'own' the land, chiefs exert a certain degree of autonomy in their areas. They are entrusted by the King with the day-to-day maintenance of law and order, including the distribution of land to headmen and the resolution of land disputes.

Over the course of history, three types of chiefs acquired control over land: *indvuna*, the governor of a royal village; *Umntfwanenkhosi*, the prince who is allotted an area and following of his own; and *sikhulu*, the clan chief.[7] In essence, historic differences in clan incorporation within the Swazi state influenced the types of chieftaincies which developed.

Hughes (1964c) states that the first type of chief, governors, are technically appointed as deputies of the Swazi King but are never supposed to be members of the royal family. They are given administrative control over royal homesteads and the territories attached to these as rewards for their special abilities and loyalty. Governors receive different kinds of territorial placements and consequently serve a variety of functions: they may take charge of each of the current national capitals, or of the capitals of previous rulers, or of lesser royal homesteads and cattle posts. Swazis usually state that the land supervised by governors is more directly under the control of the King than the land in other chiefdoms. In fact, it is known that some chiefdoms currently under minor governors will be reassigned to a section of the royal lineage. At that time, the former governor chief will become the chief deputy of the newly placed royal chief.

Royals, the second type of chief, are known literally as 'children of the King'. Nowadays, the term has expanded to include many members of the Dlamini clan such as persons who are genealogically far removed from the senior line but who have obtained important positions. Royals (usually princes) may be granted land either as an apanage[8] or as a reward. They are placed in apanages around the country for the purpose of supporting and extending the monarchy's control, symbolizing royal authority and diffusing potential rivalry for central control. Royals tend to consider themselves superior both to neighbouring clan chiefs and to governor chiefs.

Clan chiefs, the third type of chief, obtained their positions in several ways: by being placed under the early Swazi rulers; by being eventually incorporated under the Dlamini rulers (e.g. Sotho groups); and by being incorporated under the Dlamini rulers after their later migration into the territory. Clan chiefs claim a significant degree of independence from the Dlamini overlords (e.g. distribute land and perform clan ritual), but they must recognize the King as the ultimate owner of the land. Some clan chiefs may hold their own rituals of 'kingship' and may execute customary law without close supervision of the King. For example, Hughes (1964c: 156) mentions that the powerful Mamba chief formerly had the power of executing his subjects without reference to the 'Central Authority'.[9]

Because each type of chief (governor, prince and clan) maintains a unique relationship with the monarchy, he exercises land rights in a slightly different way. Thus, a strong clan chief, as head of a clan which entered into an early treaty relationship with the Dlamini monarchy, is more likely to exercise control over subjects without appeal to the monarchy (e.g. in land banishment cases) than a governor or prince, who as an appendage of the monarchy is more likely to defer continually to the monarchy. As indicated on Map 4, governors and royals are concentrated within this study's research area near Manzini (MZ) (refer to Map 7, p. 61).

In exercising their land administration duties, chiefs necessarily delegate responsibilities to others. A chief may entrust his deputy (*indvuna*) and council of elders with the supervision of minor land matters. At the lowest level, he entrusts individual male homestead heads with the reallocation of family holdings to individuals, usually married sons. Wives of the sons, including wives of polygamous men, will be granted access to common land.[10]

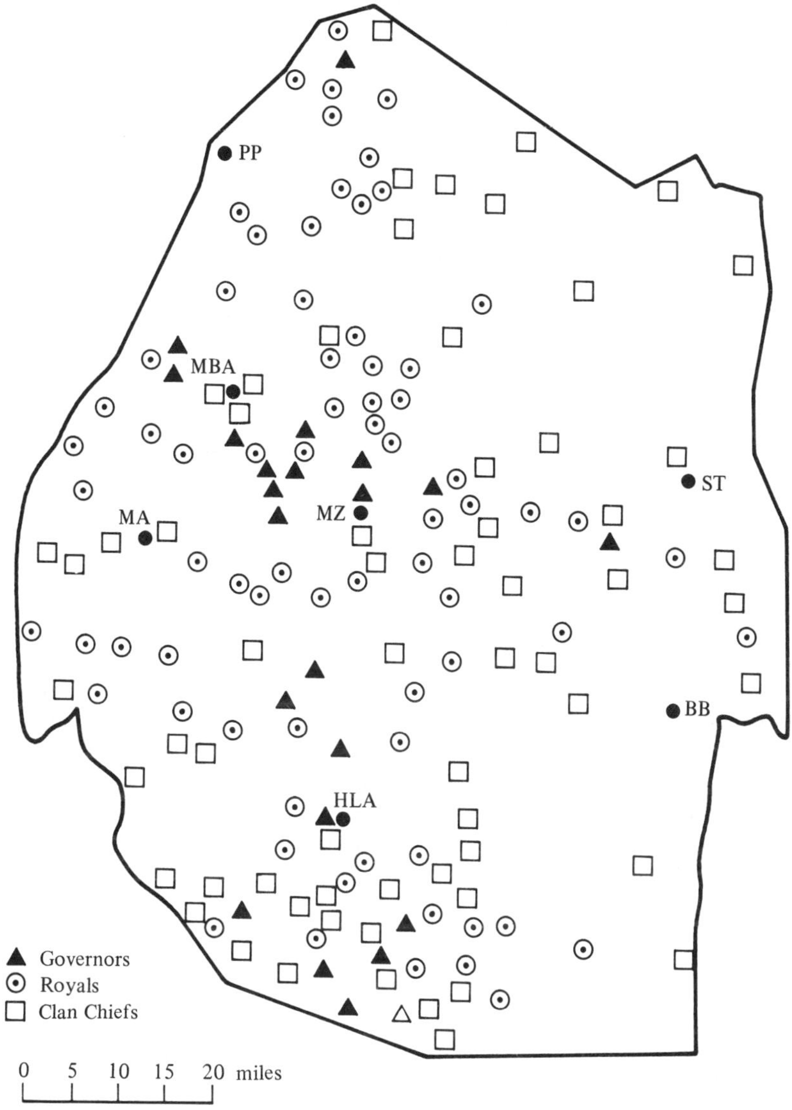

Map 4 Distribution of chiefs
Source: Based upon Hughes 1972: 181

Allocation of Swazi Nation Land

Legitimate patterns of allocation on Swazi Nation Land differ radically from those patterns prevailing on freehold land in the juxtaposed Roman-Dutch system: land is not a saleable commodity. Land access rights on Swazi Nation Land are held by the community as a whole, and the King, representing the entire Swazi Nation, is responsible for its allotment. In effect, as has been described for land in many parts of Africa,[11] land rights on Swazi Nation Land are derived more from a political than an economic basis: rights in land against or with persons rather than things. Such rights are commonly classified according to four types: (1) rights of *access* to land; (2) rights of ritual or political *control* over land; (3) rights of *allocating* or distributing land; and (4) rights of *settling disputes* over land. The first type involves rights of usufruct (i.e. accommodation and use, including rights to arable land, grazing land and natural resources), whereas the latter three types involve rights of administration. In other words, the first type represents a person's rights, whereas the latter three types represent a ruler's rights. A subject's rights are commonly held securely as long as he is a respectable member of the community, pays taxes, pledges allegiance to the chief and uses land in a customary fashion, thus actively cultivates.

The land allocation methods practised in a Swazi chiefdom must be analysed within the context of national and local political communities; membership in a political community underlies land access. The national political community involves a bond between rulers and chiefs, and the local political community involves a bond between chiefs and their subjects. Both local and national political communities are incorporated within a complex spatio-political pyramid consisting of ruler–chief–subject relationships. At the apex of the pyramid begins the land allocation process: rulers distribute land and associated responsibilities to chiefs. At the middle level of the pyramid, chiefs distribute land to subjects, while at the lowest level of the pyramid, subjects, usually male homestead heads, assign plots to members of the homestead.

There are standard, normative methods (according to customary law) by which a Swazi subject can pledge allegiance to a chief and rulers and thereby obtain rights to land. The basic land acquisition methods, which may vary in different types of chieftaincies, are: (1) direct grant by the chief; (2) direct grant by another individual; (3) inheritance; and (4) being 'lent' land by another individual. These methods are familiar to specialists in African land law, although variations are common.[12] According to Hughes (1972), the first three methods lead to 'ownership'[13] rights, whereas the last leads only to the right of use (Hughes 1972; see also Doggett 1980: 34).

The first method comes into play when a newcomer approaches a chief seeking acceptance in the area. This newcomer is described by Swazis as a 'man', *sikhonti*, who wants to *kukhonta*, thus offer allegiance and be accepted as a subject. Ordinarily, a close relative or friend residing in the new area and pledging allegiance to the chief will introduce the newcomer to the chief's deputy. The deputy will then take the applicant and his envoy to the chief who will inform his council of the application and further present the newcomer to the community at a public meeting. The next step is for the chief to assign his own envoy to go to the present chief of the newcomer and investigate his reputation. If his reputation proves favourable, then the applicant will be accepted and will formally 'bid farewell' to his present chief. Initially the applicant may be given a temporary residential site. When he is formally placed, the boundaries of the homestead site and the arable land will be indicated. Sometimes he receives an additional land grant from the chief at a later point in time.

The second method, a land grant, usually involves a land transfer within a kinship group; this process is known as *kubekwa*, 'placing'. According to Nkambule (1983: 42), placing methods are commonly relied upon when a new settler in a chiefdom has been allocated insufficient land or completely virgin land and his relatives compensate for the deficiency with an additional grant. In both situations, the grantor forfeits all usufructuary rights over the land. A land grant may also be made to current residents of a chiefdom; however, my data, which were obtained in a densely populated area, indicate that land holders prefer not to give away land. In addition to land grants made to newcomers and neighbours, a land grant may also be made within a single homestead group, although such a grant represents a division of labour more than a land alienation exercise.

The third and most common method, inheritance, occurs when a homestead head dies and land rights are normatively passed down in the male line. When the family council of agnates (including full- and half-brothers of head, his own and brothers' senior sons, etc.) discuss the disposal of a man's estate upon his death, it primarily considers the household divisions prevailing within the homestead group during the life of the homestead head as well as the land allocations made by the head during his life. In monogamous families, the largest land allocation and administrative responsibilities usually go to the oldest son, whereas in large polygynous families, the largest land allocation and administrative responsibilities usually go to the oldest son of the senior wife.

The fourth method, a land loan from one individual to another, i.e. *kuboleka umhlaba*, serves to supplement an insufficient land grant awarded to a newcomer in a community. A land loan may also take place between community members when one party, the borrower, wishes to expand his subsistence farming or to engage in cash crop farming. The borrower requires a land loan because he cannot obtain additional or suitable land from the chief for any one of several reasons: land shortage in the area; no available land in the immediate vicinity of his homestead; disinclination of authorities to grant land to a man who has sufficient land for subsistence needs. More research needs to be done on why land is loaned (particularly under circumstances of land shortage), but it appears that the lender may want to aid a relative or neighbour, to repay or incur a debt, or to receive some compensation – such as part of the harvest from loaned land.

In Part II, discussion will focus upon disputes involving land that was obtained by each of the four acquisition methods. The dispute cases bear close resemblance to disputes about title to arable and residential land, land inheritance and land loans, as described elsewhere in Africa – notably by Simon Roberts (n.d.) for Botswana. In Swaziland, as in Botswana, dispute severity and frequency has been influenced by increased individual initiative, whether achieved when a person privately allots himself/herself land, privately conducts land transactions with other individuals, or privately approaches officials with land requests. Discussion in Part II will also focus upon disputants' strategic manipulations, which are partially determined by their *perception* of rights associated with each land acquisition method.

Promotion of individual land tenure

The emphasis upon individual land tenure in Swaziland must be explained within the wider African context, in which foreign-backed land reform movements encourage conversion from customary land tenure to individual land tenure in order to promote development (see Bishop 1979: 2; Whittington and Daniel 1969). In contemporary plans envisioned by various African movements, land tenure reform would involve changes in possession rights, use rights (e.g. suppression of 'communal' land rights), redistribution of land and alteration of agrarian practices (e.g. farming methods, granting of credit, technical services) (Jeppe 1980: 205–18). Policies designed to promote such reforms are, for example, land registration/title and restructuring of land administration.[14]

Arguments in favour of various African reform policies, primarily promotion of individual land tenure practices, cite national concerns such as economic integration and less uneven development (Uchendu 1971: 17) as well as local or individual concerns such as simplication of land transactions, increased land security, decreased land fragmentation and fewer land disputes (Jeppe 1980: 241). At the same time, advocates of reform policies acknowledge that reforms sometimes result in disruptions to traditional social organization, including reduced legitimacy of traditional authority structures and rejection of new structures.[15]

Land reform rhetoric in Swaziland envisions tenurial changes for Swazi Nation Land similar to those described elsewhere in Africa (see Magagula 1982: 15–16; Amoah 1982: 11–12). Customary land and freehold land are compared in terms of input technology, production techniques (e.g. cropping patterns), farm size, geographic location of production, nature of output, income levels, consumption patterns and demographic patterns (see de Vletter 1981: 6; Dlamini *et al.* 1984: 2; Maasdorp 1976: 412; Matsebula 1982b: 2). Swazi Nation Land, which falls under customary control of the King and chiefs, has primarily been criticized by 'developers' on the basis of production factors. They argue that only 10 per cent of Swazi households produce for the market and that agricultural production on Swazi Nation Land, which accounts for only 12 per cent of GDP, cannot keep up with growing population. They also note that Swazi Nation Land holdings are too small and fragmented, tenure is insecure, land is left fallow by migrant workers, serious erosion results from overgrazing, and modern innovations such as fencing and credit are discouraged. Most important, they argue that Swazi attitudes against individual experimentation on land and profiting from land inhibit efforts to alleviate customary tenure problems.[16]

Individual Tenure Land in Swaziland currently consists of commercial large-scale estates, medium-sized farms and urban areas (municipalities, towns, company towns and private townships) (Butler 1974: 170) and covers about 34 per cent of the country's land area. Individual Tenure Farms consist of about 850 farms and estates, averaging 800 hectares, but ranging from 20–30 hectare family farms to huge agro-industrial estates such as the Usutu Forest and the sugar plantations. Commercial activities are primarily carried out on estates – cropland, livestock ranches, timber and fruit plantations, and mining concessions (Magagula 1982: 6). Individual Tenure Farms are praised by foreign and local 'developers' because they generate about 31 per cent of the GDP, contribute to over 70 per cent of the country's export earnings and provide up to 75 per cent of employment for Swazis. They also contribute to about 60 per cent of agricultural production in Swaziland (Doggett 1980: 32). The estates are mostly foreign owned, but smaller Individual Tenure Farms are owned by both Swazis and Whites (Doggett 1980: 32; Magagula 1982: 6). In effect, Individual Tenure Land is evaluated in superior terms that are now litany: better technology, larger land areas, and greater output and income generation.[17]

Many Swazis report in interviews that development objectives, particularly those which promote increased agricultural productivity, are desirable.[18] Such a position was taken up by the Swaziland Department of Agriculture in the 1960s when policy innovations were introduced, for example, through rural development programs (Gina 1983: 2). Nonetheless, policies have been conservative since most Swazis argue that development objectives are not desirable if they could incur considerable economic or social costs.

This conservatism is clearly demonstrated in a study by Hughes (1962), in which fourteen Swazi Land Utilization Officers wrote essays about their perceptions of relative advantages and disadvantages of individual land tenure as opposed to customary land tenure. The essays indicated that even these 'progressive' respondents envisioned dire consequences should the customary land tenure system be radically altered or eliminated in favour of individual land tenure. The Officers wrote that widespread conversion to individual land tenure would result in the emergence of a landless group, a demise in the great national ceremonies and a loss of power by the traditional Swazi political authorities, including the King and local chiefs. Hughes concluded from the responses that Swazis anticipate with fear a wide range of changes – encompassing national and local political organization, the economic system and social 'neighbourliness' at the local level – if land tenure and associated land control should be transformed.[19] It would seem that Hughes' essayists remembered well the Concessionaires' 'Paper Conquest', which demonstrated, from the Swazi perspective, that Europeans were interested in alienating Swazi-occupied land for their own commercial interests. They were also persuaded by further ideological manoeuvres that Europeans were interested in promoting a national economic system associated with individual land tenure – even at the expense of Swazi economic, social and political (power of chiefs) structures (see also Doggett 1980: 37; Kunene 1982b: 15).

Regardless of the validity of arguments against freehold tenure, they have had the consequence that fundamental policies of customary land registration and title-granting, which have been promoted in many parts of Africa, are not generally accepted in Swaziland.[20] Antipathy towards freehold tenure, based on Swaziland's Concession experience, continues to be widespread (Riddell and Dickerman 1986: 6).

Social organization

The homestead

The ordinary Swazi derives land access and use rights by virtue of his/her residence or membership in a particular homestead, *umuti* (see Sibisi 1980 and Ngubane 1983). Currently, the homestead, *umuti*, is defined as the largest residential and distinct socio-economic unit on Swazi Nation Land (estimated number of homesteads is 45,000; de Vletter 1981: 6). Many disputes about land access and use rights arise between households within a homestead or between neighbouring homesteads.[21] For this reason, the Swazi homestead is a critical unit for analysis of customary land disputes; land disputes involving women (see Chapter 6) usually involve land allocations on a homestead and are resolved at the homestead level, while land disputes involving new elites (see Chapter 7) involve power plays for administration of homestead units. From a cross-cultural perspective, the Swazi local homestead group is an important analytic unit for comparison with village groups in other Southern African societies, such as the Sotho or Tswana (see Sansom 1937; Silitshena 1979): different patterns of social organization and physical settlement in homestead groups arise from variant ecological adaptations, and in turn, differently influence both the causes of land disputes and authority patterns for land dispute resolution.

Origins of the Swazi homestead

Very little information on the origins of the Swazi rural homestead exists, but Kuper's (1947a) and Marwick's (1940) observations in the 1940s provide a useful backdrop for recent developments. The homestead was the major social and productive unit. It was patriarchal, with a male homestead head, *umnumzane*, assuming primary powers, but the position of the main wife was important in family life. The homestead head determined resource allocation such as land distribution, made major decisions regarding both production (ploughing and types of crops grown) and economic expenditures, and mobilized homestead labour. He also had primary responsibility for consulting the lineage council, *lusendvo*, a council comprised of clan or lineage members, when members needed assistance in resolving internal problems such as land disputes between households or with neighbours. The homestead head was charged with suppressing conflict, including over land, in the interests of harmony.

Swazi homesteads focused on agricultural activities – primarily the cultivation of maize, sorghum, beans, groundnuts and sweet potatoes. Maize had been essentially unknown until the mid-nineteenth century, at which time it was introduced and gradually replaced sorghum as the staple crop. Despite the growing importance of agriculture to homestead economy, cattle continued to be considered the basis of wealth and status.

The traditional Swazi homestead was circular in shape; the dwelling-huts and cooking-huts were built around the circumference of a circle, forming two 'horns' embracing the courtyard and partially enclosing the cattle-byre. Members of the homestead had access as individuals to arable land and as members of the larger community to communal pasturage. Within a complex homestead were households – each household (*indlu*) consisted of one nuclear family (a man, his wife and their children), whose members shared agricultural tasks and ate from one kitchen. When there were several households on the homestead, each consisted of a simple polygynous family, an extended agnatic family or a complex family grouping (Hughes 1964c: 127). Sometimes a wife had an attached co-wife, *inhlanti*, who, along with her children, would form part of the same 'house'. A married son and his wife and dependants would occasionally form another house within the wider 'house' of his mother. After the death of the homestead head, the homestead frequently split into several homesteads, following divisions which already existed between 'houses' on the homestead. A factor which encouraged homestead contraction was land requirements, and a factor which encouraged homestead expansion was labour requirements (Russell 1984).

Changes in the Swazi homestead

In the late nineteenth century, a series of disasters (drought, locusts, scurvy epidemic and rinderpest) brought about significant changes in Swazi rural areas. An even more profound impact, as in much of Africa, was felt after the arrival of Europeans. Europeans introduced a monetary economy and promoted cash crops, thus providing new routes to status. They supported the idea of political pluralism in the context of the modern nation state. They conveyed European ways to indigenous elites, who educated their children for entry into a formal bureaucratic administration and wage labour. They introduced Christian beliefs which, among other things, suppressed witchcraft and discouraged polygyny, thus disrupting traditional beliefs and altering the family unit. Significantly, they expropriated land in many territories, thereby dislocating people or at least altering their means of livelihood.

Throughout Africa, European land expropriations brought about changes in customary land rights. Although land had once been held by unwritten, customary rights of use and administration that were flexible and adaptable to changing conditions (Gluckman 1944), following the European conquest of Africa, land rights became increasingly confused. Europeans successfully introduced changes within many African countries – other than Swaziland – regarding customary land use and administration: frozen boundaries, land consolidation, land adjudication and private titles (see Meek 1946; Mifsud 1967). Land became increasingly scarce and valuable as populations expanded and migrated, resulting in changes in socio-political organization (Bohannan 1964; Shipton 1984) and in local groups' control over land (see Gulliver 1958, 1963 and Moore 1986 on East Africa).[22] Chiefs' administrative powers were often reduced or transferred, and women's and new elites' use rights were newly granted or restricted.

Unlike in many parts of Africa, customarily tenured land in Swaziland did not come to be viewed as a commodity which could be bought, sold, rented, alienated and 'owned' by title. Swazi leaders successfully warded off social and political impacts upon customary land rights, although they could not prevent some undesired changes in land tenure from occurring – customarily tenured land was reduced in area, fragmented and taxed as a result of European incursions.

The European presence in Africa was strongly felt on the Swazi rural homestead. New agricultural methods, new hybrid seeds and fertilizers, and new technologies were introduced within homesteads. Although agricultural productivity was sometimes boosted, there were calculated (from the European perspective) side-effects. In particular, efforts to enhance agricultural productivity usually brought about greater leisure time and an emphasis upon cash within a homestead – both factors encouraged men to migrate within Swaziland or to South Africa in search of income. As a consequence, many homesteads experienced the following: prolonged absence of men and thus the assumption of agricultural and decision-making roles by women; subversion of elders' authority by younger men who had wages at their disposal; and loosening, or at least altering, of family ties as men migrated and children went to school or work for wages. In sum, from the Swazi perspective, labour migration often resulted in reduced labour power, altered sex roles, removal of the locus of decision-making, reduced agricultural productivity, or domestic disharmony on the Swazi homestead.

Changes in homestead production activities occurred together with changes in the social composition and physical organization of homesteads. Hughes

(1964c: 122) notes that most modern-day homestead groups tend to divide earlier in their life cycle than did larger homestead groups of the past (sons often set up their own homesteads after marriage) and the homestead is no longer inevitably divided into separate 'houses' (polygamous marriages have been on the decline). As an illustration of a change in physical organization, the homestead has abandoned the old circular pattern, although the majority still have a 'Great Hut' which faces the cattle byre. Swazis attribute changes in composition and physical organization to a preference of the modern Swazi man for independent decision-making, to an increased economic independence of individuals, and to a reduced need of homestead groups for physical defence.

Socio-economic differentiation among and within Swazi homesteads

A major study of modern-day Swazi rural homesteads, which emphasized socio-economic characteristics, was undertaken by the University of Natal in 1960 (Holleman 1964a, 1964b). A later study, the Swaziland Rural Homestead Survey, was conducted by the University of Swaziland, Kwaluseni, between 1978 and 1983 (de Vletter 1984; see also de Vletter 1981).[23] Based on the results of these surveys, a profile of the modern Swazi homestead can be constructed. The average Swazi homestead consists of about ten members of whom eight are resident. Almost one-third of the adult labour force is absent while a further one-tenth is present but normally engaged in wage employment; this leaves only slightly more than one-half of the adult work force (including the old and infirm) available for full-time agricultural work. Women tend to put three times as many hours into agricultural labour as men.

Several researchers (see Booth 1983a: 55; de Vletter 1984: 23) have observed that when homestead profiles are contrasted, greater socio-economic differentiation than in the past is evident. Socio-economic differentiation in Swaziland took root after Partition, which created a class of 'haves' (foreigners, Swazi farmers who own private farms, and post-Independence Swazi government officials) and a class of 'have nots' (Swazi farmers on Swazi Nation Land) (Barnes 1979: 31; Daniel 1966a: 506). Unlike in many parts of Africa, 'have not' in Swaziland refers more to type of land holding (including opportunities) than to landlessness, since all Swazis have a right to land use.[24]

Swazi individuals or classes are socio-economically differentiated not only on the basis of land holding type (i.e. customary or freehold), but also on the basis of homestead resources: size (physical and demographic), assets, location and human potential. Sixteen per cent of the Swazi population have landholdings of more than 5 ha, constituting 41 per cent of the Swazi land area. Larger homesteads can pool resources (money, credit, labour) for the purpose of generating greater assets through, for example, larger cropping areas or bigger cattle holdings. Wealthier homesteads, which are built out of better materials and possess ploughs, sewing machines, stoves and radios, comprise one-tenth of all homesteads and yet are responsible for 50 per cent of the total income points. Wealthier homesteads are often built near employment centres, where members can derive income from wage earnings rather than, or in addition to, cattle. Wealthier homesteads generally count educated members holding lucrative jobs within their ranks (de Vletter 1984: 14–19).

Socio-economic characteristics of Swazi homesteads influence women's opportunities. With the migration of men to urban labour centres and the South African mines, many women have attained *de facto*, if not *de jure*, control over the rural household. Women on all homesteads, but particularly poorer ones, have considerable responsibilities: performing domestic duties and agricultural tasks; managing livestock; caring for children and the elderly; and earning most, if not all, of the money needed to pay for their children's education. Those women, who are unable successfully to reproduce the household through subsistence production, enter wage labour, creating hardships for dependants left behind on the homestead (McFadden 1982). Although 'modernizing trends', for example the introduction of labour-saving technology and Roman-Dutch law, broadened the opportunities of those women who have the socio-economic possibilities to take advantage of costly agricultural technology (e.g. ploughs or maize-grinding machines) or of lawyers, such trends left untouched most women who are poor and unconnected. Women, unlike younger men who can acquire land upon marriage, can never, in theory, acquire and hold customarily tenured land except under male guardianship. Nor do many women have sufficient money to purchase freehold land. As the cases in Chapter 6 demonstrate, women learn to be resourceful in overcoming their dependency upon men.

Socio-economic characteristics of Swazi homesteads have also produced a new class of elites. Such elites emerged following the Second World War, when the primary homestead expenditure, particularly on wealthier homesteads, went towards educating children. The resulting 'new' elites were educated, ambitious and affluent, although they encountered barriers to upward mobility. These barriers were presented by several groups that aimed to maintain or attain power and resources: the European managerial class, coloureds (children born of unions between Africans and Europeans) and Swazi royals. New elites experienced tensions in relation to the European managerial class because they were not able to pass successfully through mid-level management in multinational corporations, although they had permeated all levels of the government bureaucracy and civil service. They also experienced tensions in relation to coloureds who were granted privileges during the colonial years, such as access to separate schools. These privileges enhanced the power and prominence of coloureds disproportionately to their numbers. Finally, new elites experienced tensions in relation to the Swazi royal elite who enhanced their political and economic control by successfully banning political parties, a channel for middle-class aspirations, by suppressing the labour movement, by defining government structure in accord with royal prerogatives, by controlling mineral royalties, and by securing independent control and tax-free status of the national corporation, Tibiyo (Booth 1982; Daniel 1982; Fransman 1982). Importantly, traditional elites retained control over land administration. Unlike in many parts of Africa (see Vincent 1971; Hammond-Tooke 1975; Fallers 1956), Swazi traditional elites neither experienced significant changes in their base of power nor were they significantly threatened by new elites.

The land disputes described in Chapters 5 to 7 demonstrate tensions between Swazis occupying both different structural statuses (ascribed) in the traditional political hierarchy and different personal socio-economic statuses (achieved). Such tensions have emerged, in part, through socio-economic changes on Swazi homesteads, which have altered women's opportunities and given rise to a new class of elites. Women potentially challenge the customary power-base of men on the rural homestead, whereas new elites potentially challenge the customary power-base of hereditary elites in local and national councils. In the discussion of land dispute cases, precise socio-economic profiles of all disputants and their homestead groups cannot be drawn, but basic data is given to illustrate structural and personal aspects of their relative statuses and thus their disputing opportunities.

Kinship and age grades

Kinship and age-grade membership are important determinants of rank in hierarchical Swazi society. Consequently, they form the fundamental structure from which emerge individual and organizational opportunities for disputing about customary land rights. This structure influences the form which the politics of harmony takes.

The clan

At the centre of each Swazi homestead is the biological family, which is established by marriage but dependent for its continuity on the concept of 'one blood'. Swazis believe that a child is of 'one blood' with its father and mother. The blood group is extended through classificatory kinship from the immediate biological family to maternal and paternal groups, the largest of which is the clan. The clan, which is the furthest extension of kinship, contains a number of lineages in which direct descent can be genealogically traced over three to eight generations. Despite the pervasive idiom of blood ties, daily contact and custom primarily determine the kinship system; sometimes people with remote or even fictional genealogical ties to a person may be described as being of 'one blood' (see Kuper 1947a: 105–6).

Clanship is important in regulating marriage and succession. Marriage with a person of one's own paternal clan is prohibited (although permissible for the King) but with a woman of the maternal clan is allowed. A woman retains her paternal clan name upon marriage, but her children acquire at birth their father's clan name. Paternal rights are acquired by the man's family through the transfer to the woman's family of *lobolo* (bridewealth), valuables such as cattle. Marital residence is virilocal; the bride goes to live with her husband and in-laws. In polygynous marriages, the type of marriage contracted with each wife is important in determining succession and inheritance, including land administration duties; the relative rank of the women – particularly in terms of clanship – influences selection of the successor who is also the main heir.

Because clanship regulates marriage and succession, it also influences how land rights will be exercised on the homestead and by whom. When disputes about land rights arise between homestead members, clan membership may form a basis for alliance and production of harmony. Thus, disputes between men of the same paternal clan would constitute an intra-clan matter, but disputes between husbands and wives or between unrelated wives of the same man could become an inter-clan matter – if the members of the woman's (women's) clan/s decided to support her/them.[25]

Clanship is also important in determining political status, which, in turn, is important in defining rank, including the privilege to control institutions which produce harmony (see Chapter 2). Although different clans served as dominant political units in themselves in the past, in recent times they have become important determinants of national political structure. Clans are graded in a rough hierarchy, and the rank of each clan is measured according both to the relationship it has with the kingship and to the position its members have attained in the national structure.[26] At the apex of the hierarchy is the Dlamini clan, in which the lineage of the ruling King is pre-eminent. In each lineage within the Dlamini clan, members are graded by their distance from the lineage head, and lineages are graded by their closeness to the senior lineage. Second in rank are clans which have provided Queen Mothers. Third in rank are clans which have their own 'kingship' – rulership by a well-defined lineage – and which maintain semi-independent political status (see discussion of clan chiefs above). Fourth in rank are clans which once had great power but were reduced in stature by the Dlamini conquerors. Fifth in rank are clans which have no local centre, no recognized national representative, no claim to national ritual and no effective relationship with any powerful groups (see Kuper 1947a: 111–13). The dominant Dlamini clan defines harmony ideology, and the remaining clans subscribe to it according to rank. The lowest ranking clans and those clans that desire to move up in the hierarchy are arguably most likely to resist prevailing harmony ideologies. Such clans and their members use land as an avenue of protest (see Cases 2 and 19 in Chapters 5 and 6). The clan members' disputing opportunities are determined by their clan affiliation; therefore, they decide how to dispute based, in part, upon their rank relative to their opponent(s) and the number of fellow clan members to whom they can turn for assistance. When disputes about land rights arise between members of different homestead units, numerous allied clans may take sides.

Age

Besides being bonded by kinship, men and women are bonded within age grades, or age regiments. Age, like clan membership, is an important determinant of status, and therefore control over land. Hilda Kuper took the perspective in the 1940s that age classes 'inhibit the development of an hereditary class with permanent privileges, since every individual can anticipate that, in the normal span of life, he or she will pass through every age class and its associated status activities' (1947a: 133). Nonetheless, aristocratic pedigree (lineage and clan membership) is arguably a more important determinant of status than age.

All regiments of men are headed by the King – no matter how young he may be. Men of the same age and training form a *libutfo* (pl. *emabutfo*), regiment (Kuper 1947a: 120). Although warfare, which was essential to the functioning of age grades in earlier phases of nation-building, is no longer practised, *emabutfo* continue to function as labour battalions for the aristocrats. Such labour may involve performing agricultural duties, building, fetching materials, serving as messengers or attending royals. When disputes between age members arise, the age regiment may assume responsibility for mediating a settlement.[27]

Summary

Geography, history, political structure and social organization have influenced land tenure developments and have moulded the types of land disputes which have arisen in Swaziland. They have also provided the natural and human resource foundation upon which individual and group interests in both harmony and conflict, associated with land disputes, could be expressed.

2

The legal structure for customary land tenure relations

This chapter discusses Swaziland's history of land legislation, Southern African land law developments and Swaziland's dual system of land law. On the one side of Swaziland's dual legal structure are 'traditional' courts, in which procedures are not controlled by legislative enactments or by codified legal rules. These courts include family and Chiefs' 'Courts' (councils) at the lowest level. On the other side of Swaziland's dual legal structure are 'modern' courts, or the colonial/post-colonial system of courts which have been formalized by national legislation. These courts consist of both Swazi and European-influenced courts at lower levels. As will be explained, customary land matters cannot be processed by either the Swazi Courts or Subordinate Courts, so that land matters that are not successfully resolved through private negotiation or settled by chiefs' councils must be either appealed to higher levels in the customary system or handled by one of the modern administrative agents, for example *Ndabazabantu*. At the same time, decisions in the Swazi or Subordinate Courts regarding matters related to land can influence disputants' opportunities in customary land cases. Disputing forums and authorities in each system influence the production of harmony.

Legislative history of Swaziland's dual legal system: the basis of a parallel system of land law

A convenient starting-point for discussion of Swaziland's dual legal system is 1894 when Swaziland became the centre of negotiation between European powers. The Convention of 1894 between Britain and the Transvaal provided that Swaziland be administered by the Transvaal, although incorporation was not to occur; and the Protocol of 1898, which was added to the Convention of 1894, provided for the trial of all serious crimes by the protecting power and forbade Swazis to pronounce sentence on a number of offences. At the conclusion of the South African Anglo-Boer war in 1903, Britain took over direct control of Swaziland. In 1906, when Britain granted self-government to the Transvaal, the administration of Swaziland was transferred to the High Commissioner for South Africa who was resident in Pretoria. The volleying back and forth of administrative powers over Swaziland created an unusual situation, unlike what occurred in most other former British dependencies: Swaziland received the Roman-Dutch common law plus some statutes of the Transvaal as its general law (Crawford 1969–70; Matsebula 1972: 137, 150–1).

The European-influenced court system in Swaziland consists of Subordinate Courts (first, second and third class), which were defined by the Magistrates' Court Act No. 66 of 1938, and the High Court, which was defined by the Swaziland Constitution Order. The Magistrates' Court has jurisdiction over the general Swaziland population, as does the High Court, but it may not try offences of treason, murder and sedition, which must be tried by the High Court. The High Court has unlimited jurisdiction.

Although Swazis long resisted foreign legal impositions (Amoah 1978; Armstrong and Nhlapo 1985; Bonner 1983), Swazi customary legal procedure has been increasingly drawn into the more formal structure of the West. While the Swaziland Order-in-Council of 1903 declared that the High Commissioner must respect native laws or customs, the General Law and Administration Proclamation No. 4 of 1907 made Roman-Dutch common law (including legislation) the general law of Swaziland. This meant that chiefs and other traditional leaders could hold courts and administer customary law among their people as they had done for centuries, but they had to do so in the shadow of a legal system which applied to the general population, not just Swazis.

With the passing of the Native Courts Proclamation No. 80 of 1950, now the Swazi Courts Act, the foreign legal presence became even more evident. This act provided for the formal composition of customary courts (for example, clerks provided for but lawyers excluded), the type of law they may apply (customary law), the procedure to be followed, and the limits of the courts' jurisdiction over persons. In terms of jurisdiction over causes of action, the Swazi Courts (currently more than twenty-five), two Courts of Appeal, and Higher Swazi Court of Appeal, all of which were instituted by the 1950 act, were ordered not to administer any Swazi law or custom which is 'repugnant to natural justice or morality . . .' such as witchcraft, not to apply Roman-Dutch law and not to hear any matters originally contracted under Roman-Dutch law such as a civil or Christian marriage (Butler 1974: 168; Matsebula 1972: 176; Nhlapo 1982, 1986).

Customary land law has been kept so exclusively within the jurisdiction of the customary legal structure that even the Swazi Courts, which were formalized by the 1950 statute for the purpose of administering Swazi customary law, may not hear land matters. Rather, only chiefs together with their *libandla* (council) hear such matters. If a chief reaches an impasse in a land matter, he can appeal directly or through messengers to the King and his council. A chief's control over land matters is regulated by the Native Administration Act No. 79 of 1950 (the act also provides that the King may appoint or revoke appointment of chiefs); but since the terms of this act are vague and incomplete, the nuts and bolts of a chief's land administration are left to his own interpretation of unwritten customary law provisions.

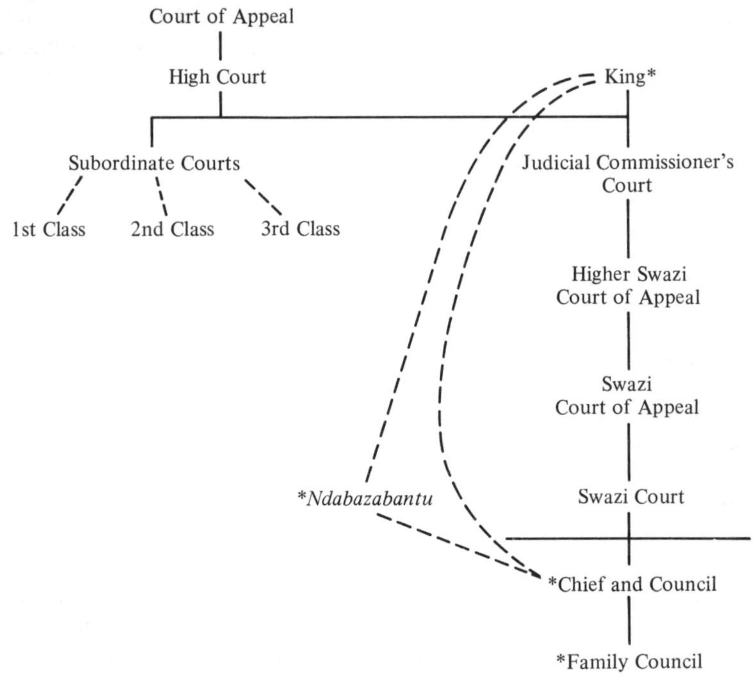

*Agencies responsible for customary land dispute management

Figure 2 Swaziland court structure

Since cases involving customary land law may not be referred to the European-influced court system, the practice of 'forum shopping', which has been observed in dual legal systems in other parts of the world[1] as well as in regard to other domains of Swazi law such as marriage law, rarely occurs with regard to land law. Nonetheless, as will be argued in later chapters, disadvantaged parties in land disputes strategically manoeuvre in customary courts, and they sometimes strategically use European-influenced courts to achieve indirectly their goals[2] (see Figure 2).

Developments in land law in Southern Africa

Swaziland's customary land law does not share its conservatism with customary law systems in the other two former British protectorates, Lesotho and Botswana. The governments of Lesotho and Botswana are currently more like one another than like Swaziland in terms of legislation that promotes changes in land tenure rules, practices and administration. The governments of Lesotho and Botswana have passed Land Acts which codify customary land law.[3] As a contrast, the government of Swaziland has introduced no statutory innovations of fundamental nature (see Amoah 1978:

41 on customary law in general). Swazi customary authorities have discouraged research and codification of customary rules, including those concerned with land tenure.[4] Secondly, the governments of Lesotho and Botswana have passed legislation which aims for significant land reforms (see Doggett 1980). For example, in Lesotho reforms encompass: increased crop outputs, improved marketing channels, improved land use planning, offering of government subsidies, taxing of land and crops, and removal of bad farmers (Bishop 1979; see also Hamnett 1973). Evidence indicates that common land tenure practices are changing. As a contrast, in Swaziland land tenure practices are changing slowly,[5] and customary norms and practices remain relatively intact. Thirdly, the governments of Lesotho and Botswana have passed legislation which displaces much land administration from customary chiefs' councils to Land Boards (see Frimpong 1986 on Botswana).[6] Chieftaincy Acts have also been passed to clarify chiefs' general administrative responsibilities, including powers over land.[7] As a contrast, in Swaziland, Land Boards do not exist, and the administrative powers of chiefs have been only vaguely defined in the Swazi Administration Act No. 79 of 1950.

An important change in land tenure administration concerns land dispute resolution. In regard to the Land Boards of Botswana, Werbner maintains that ordinary citizens question their authority and legitimacy to hear land matters, including disputes (1980: 149). Wynne (1985) argues that Land Boards in Botswana have spurred on land disputes by granting people a forum in which they could strategize to advance spurious claims to land or collude with neighbours to challenge rightful claims of others. Moreover, Land Boards give chiefs who are members a new vehicle for augmenting land control and disputing about land (Grant 1980).[8] In Swaziland, however, people are not presented with a new disputing forum because land disputes continue to be handled by chiefs and their councils in a traditional setting.

Although Swaziland, Lesotho and Botswana share many common rules, practices and administrative features of customary land tenure, Swaziland presents many anomalies. In Swaziland, indigenous authority successfully reinforced legal authority and norms, particularly concerning land, in a situation of colonial legal imposition. Peter Takirambudde explains how this happened:

> Whereas legal imposition in the Third World and elsewhere weakened indigenous authority and radically altered the normative content of such key legal areas as the indigenous proprietary rules, owing to a combination of factors peculiar to the Swaziland colonial situation and social structure, normative imposition did not lead to the wholesale suffocation of indigenous authority and legal values as was largely the case in other instances of colonial intrusion. On the contrary, the Swaziland case is a unique illustration of the relative triumph of indigenous authority and a substantial subordination and/or containment of alien legal norms... [The] indigenous authority [was able] to retain its control over land as a base of power, to control the post-colonial state apparatus and subordinate the technocrats and the acquisition of equity interest in the commanding heights of the Swaziland economy (1983: 209–10).

Takirambudde asks an important question: 'What strategies did the Swazi traditional authority use to achieve [triumph over and subordination of alien legal norms]?' (1983: 210). One step towards answering this question lies in analysis of land dispute strategies.

Research methods for investigation of Swazi customary law and legal forums

Swazis' conservatism regarding customary land law persuaded me to undertake a diversified archival, interviewing and observational research approach. During the early phases of my study, I conducted an archival investigation and preliminary interviewing of scholars, government officials and members of customary and European-influenced courts about Swazi customary land law. My topics of investigation were the historical and political background of Swaziland's customary land tenure system, the structure and organization of Swazi customary courts responsible for land dispute management, and the general content and outcome of land disputes heard in the above courts.[9]

During later phases of my research, my social network had expanded considerably as a result of persistent visiting and interviewing at locations all over Swaziland, and I was able to conduct unstructured interviews in twenty chiefs' areas. Thereafter, I focused my efforts on observing dispute resolution processes of the customary courts in Zombodze and Kwaluseni, communities near my university residence. As many kinds of land disputes came before these courts, my data base grew considerably. Unfortunately, since few land disputes were recorded, I could not profit from a wealth of public[10] and written court case summaries, as have legal researchers in other parts of Africa (see Bruce 1976 and Moore 1986). I opted to collect observed cases, memory cases and some hypothetical cases (see Nader and Todd 1978: 6). The cases were trouble cases (Llewellyn and Hoebel 1941: 21, 29), which I analysed as extended cases (Van Velsen 1967) in disputant dyads.[11] A typology of disputant dyads provided structure to my data, while simultaneously revealing systemic stresses and change (Moore 1986: 329).[12] In particular, the dyads clarified the political relationships of disputants in each case (status and power differentials in the Swazi hierarchy – for example, subject vs. chief or chief vs. chief).

While observing land dispute cases, I conducted supplementary interviews with residents (members of chiefs' councils and case litigants) of Zombodze and Kwaluseni regarding the following: land acquisition procedures; land use patterns; the nature (origin and subject matter) of specific land disputes; the political relationships (in Swazi hierarchy) underlying land disputes; the authorities' methods for land dispute processing and resolution; and disputants' interpretations of land dispute outcomes. In addition to my court visitation and interviewing activities, I analysed a questionnaire, entitled 'Women and Land Tenure in Swaziland', which had been developed and administered by University of Swaziland Law lecturer Alice Armstrong in the summer of 1984. The 67 respondents to the questionnaire (44 women and 23 men), representing all age groups, had been selected from nine chiefs' areas in central Swaziland. The 44-item questionnaire provided supplementary data on the land access process and inheritance, land disputes, land loans and land development (see Appendix).

Traditional forums

The traditional side of Swaziland's dual legal system consists of the family council, the Chief's Court, the Swazi Court, the Swazi Court of Appeal, the Higher Swazi Court of Appeal and the Judicial Commissioner's Court (refer to Figure 2).

Family council (lusendvo)

At the lowest level of the traditional hierarchy is the family council, *lusendvo*, which comprises members of the clan or, nowadays, the lineage. Specifically, the council consists of the homestead head, his brothers, his adult sons and brothers' sons, among others. It meets to discuss matters such as marriage, inheritance and family disputes. When it hears land disputes, the cases normally involve members of the same homestead unit. Such cases concern inheritance rights to land, rights of avail to land or common resources, and land rights of women who have married a member of the homestead unit. The cases are discussed and resolved by the family council, particularly in larger homesteads, within the central 'grandmother's house', *indlu yaka gogo*.

One informant described the operation of the family council in a land case:

> if only a family is involved [in a case], then the case doesn't go to the chief at all. The members of the family just discuss it... All the family and maybe the neighbours, i.e. neighbours who are relatives, are called... The case is heard and the homestead head tells the people what they should do.

In theory, the family council should hear a case arising between its own members before the Chief's Court will entertain it; if a litigant brings such a case to the chief's council before the family council has attempted a settlement, the litigant will be instructed to return to his/her family elders. The family and chief's council encourage dispute containment at the homestead level because they believe that family members better understand family relations and are better equipped to define and promote harmony. Female disputants who have married into the homestead indicate that harmony will be defined according to gender and kinship interests (refer to Cases 17, 19 and 23 in Chapter 6).

Chief and councils

As far as customary legal procedure is concerned, the literature, although generally incomplete, is most explicit on the structure and operation of the Chief's Court (see Fine n.d.; Green 1984; Kuper 1947a; Marwick 1940). This

Court will be discussed at length since most of the land disputes heard by myself were handled by a chief and his council.

Procedure

Chiefs' Courts are usually recognized as administrative organs rather than 'courts' even though they handle essentially the same body of customary law as the Swazi Courts. Unlike the Swazi Courts, the composition and procedure of the Chiefs' Courts have not been formalized by legislation. The following description of court procedure is based on my observation of three Chiefs' Courts in the middleveld and interviews with court officials from areas throughout Swaziland.

A chief may summon any subject pledging allegiance to him to a court session (usually on a weekend), and any subject may report a grievance to his chief. Customary matters such as marital disputes, land disputes, land requests, minor assaults and theft constitute common cases. Matters involving serious injury/death, witchcraft or marriage not contracted under Swazi law and custom are excluded from both the Chief's Court and the Swazi Court by virtue of the 1950 legislation.

A person with a grievance usually reports to the chief's deputy (*indvuna*), although occasionally he/she reports directly to the chief, to the messenger (*umgijimi*), or to the secretary. The number of parties who become involved in a case depends on its complexity. The chief's deputy tries to deal with a problem himself, but if he fails, he reports to the chief's *bandlancane*, inner council of advisers which consists of approximately ten to fifteen male homestead heads of the area. They discuss the matter among themselves, and if warranted, report to the chief that a formal case should be brought before him and the assembled *libandla*, senior men of the chiefdom. The chief's messenger then summons the parties and witnesses to a public meeting. All personnel act on a voluntary basis.

On the appointed day of the meeting, the chief, his assistant, messenger, clerk (recent addition), inner council and citizens of the area assemble at the designated spot. They usually seat themselves in a circle on the ground under shady trees. The atmosphere is leisurely in that people chat vigorously before the meeting with their friends and wander about fairly freely. After the meeting is called to order, someone is asked to pray for harmonious dispute outcomes. The proceedings are not characterized by the outer trappings familiar to formal courtroom settings, such as uniformed police officers and national banners. However, the procedure does follow certain guidelines. SiSwati is the only language spoken.[13] The complainant is called by the chief's assistant; he rises and stands before the chief and his council who are seated at one segment of the circle. After he has explained his case, the respondent steps forward and presents his side of the case. They reply to one another before the members of the *libandla* are entitled to cross-examine them. Other witnesses are then heard, and each witness is liable to cross-examination.

Several procedural guidelines which are common to more formalized courts are absent in the Chief's Court. First, there is no sworn testimony, so that cross-examination must be relied upon to sift truth from lies. Secondly, there are no rules of evidence, so that hearsay and irrelevant evidence may be tendered with little objection being taken. Evidence is obtained under cross-examination, and each person is allowed to tell his story almost uninterrupted until he talks himself out – or until members of the *libandla* halt his long-windedness.[14] Thirdly, there are no advocates, so that each party must rely on his own wits and those of his witnesses. Any person in the *libandla* may become an advocate of any party. The role of the chief and his assistant vary from court to court; either one may take a predominant role although both usually attempt to maintain impartiality. They continually remind disputants of their duty as Swazis to behave harmoniously.

At some point during a case discussion, the chief or his assistant proclaims that a case is concluded, and the parties and their witnesses withdraw. After all the cases for the day have been heard, the *libandla* is temporarily dispersed while the chief and his council privately discuss possible solutions for each case. After about fifteen to forty-five minutes – the exact duration depending on the number and complexity of cases heard that day – the *libandla* is recalled. The chief (or his assistant) sums up and pronounces judgement, frequently condemning certain kinds of behaviour as undesirably contentious and admonishing various parties that they should behave harmoniously. Occasionally a party is fined a beast or instructed to undertake some action. At other times, the police or Regional Administration officials are called in to enforce compliance with instructions ordered by the Chief's Court.

Structure

Councils: At the apex of the formal political structure in a chiefdom is the chief. He usually assumes his position through hereditary right, although, as my interview and court data indicate, succession formulations are not always clear and heated disputes arise. All my informants state that a chief is the ultimate authority in a chiefdom, but he may not rule as an autocrat. He usually plays a peripheral role as grievances escalate, but when his court meets, his pronouncements define the content and actualization of harmony (see Cases 3 and 26). As mentioned, he usually encourages family members to settle their disputes at home, and he attempts to contain at the chiefdom level disputes between homestead groups.

There are two important councils which assist a chief: the great council (*bandlakhulu*) and little council (*bandlancane*). The former is an open forum where every adult in the chiefdom is entitled to attend and express his/her views. The latter is a smaller, select council consisting of ten to fifteen influential men whom the chief has chosen from among his subjects to serve as his personal advisers. The members of *bandlancane* may consist of the chief's brothers, princes resident in the area or accomplished commoners.

One informant described the differences between the *bandlancane* and *bandlakhulu* as follows:

> *Bandlancane* [little council] is the most important council of the chief's. A chief can't take any case without *bandlancane*. He needs this council for everything. This council can deal with cases in the absence of the chief and then report to him. It can handle *kukhonta* [land acquisition]. A person consults with the *bandlancane* about land; the *bandlancane* can even give a person a right to *khonta* in the absence of the chief and then report back to the chief.
>
> *Bandlancane* is responsible for the whole area – how many people in the area, newcomers, people with trouble or sickness, schools for children.
>
> *Bandlakhulu* (big council) consists of every man and woman under a chief. They [council members] are supposed to bring all complaints to the chief. For example, they may complain about the [operation] of the *bandlancane*. They could also complain that there are no clinics in the area. The chief knows where he stands [i.e. job evaluation] by the continual report of [individual members of] the *bandlakhulu*.

Most of my informants initially stated that the influential *bandlancane*, which is headed by the chief's deputy, only debates issues and cannot reach decisions without the formal ratification of the *bandlakhulu*. However, after extensive questioning, these informants indicated that minor matters will be disposed of privately by the *bandlancane*. Some chiefs with whom I spoke – particularly if employed at a distant centre – said that they relied upon their *tindvuna* (deputies) or influential council members to dispose of matters at their own discretion. All informants agreed that the chief must be informed about the operations of the *bandlancane*.

A member of a chief's *bandlancane* described the procedure followed after a case has been initially heard by the *bandlancane* and subsequently brought before *bandlakhulu*:

> After the *bandlancane* has had a preliminary discussion about the case, it meets with the community, *bandlakhulu*, to talk over the problem. The chief and *bandlancane* will (privately) reach a decision as to who is right and who is wrong. If the chief or a faction of the *bandlancane* are dissatisfied with the proposed solution, they send representatives to the area to investigate further [particularly true in a land case]. Then, the case must be heard again. The chief is not involved in the [initial private] *bandlancane* discussion about the case but is involved in the [public] *libandla* meeting and [subsequent private] decision-making and sentencing by *bandlancane*.

Chief: Most observers of Swazi customary land tenure comment that a chief is the ultimate authority on land policy in his area – whether the matter involves land distribution, land utilization or land dispute adjudication. His authority derives from the powers entrusted to him by the King.

One well-educated, young chief emphasized to me that his primary roles do not centre on land matters *per se*. Nor, in his view, should a chief be mainly concerned with administrative matters, such as collection of taxes. Rather, this chief believes that the most fundamental duties of the modern-day chief centre on the implementation of development initiatives, thus land utilization policies which will better his subjects' standard of living. As he explained:

> The most important [role] of the chief is to look after the welfare of his people. Welfare means a lot of things. It means making sure that your people have

> enough land to plough, making sure that development is taking place... The chief must look after social services which are required generally – roads, schools, etc. A chief must be forward thinking in regard to his people... He follows the wishes of his people.

A chief exerts considerable control on policy formulation and implementation by virtue of the fact that he selects the members of his influential *bandlancane*. In essence, he is expected to implement policy after consensus is reached by his *bandlancane* and general approval is granted by his subjects. His office is hereditary, but his powers are exercised according to prevailing realities, such as development interests of area residents, population pressures and land availability. Many chiefs commented in interviews that they do not receive salaries but nonetheless feel compelled and honoured to perform duties.

Deputy: When one chief was asked to state who has more contact with the subjects of a chief – the chief or his deputy – the chief responded immediately by saying 'the deputy'. He claims that this structure of power delegation is traditional:

> According to Swazi law and custom, only very important cases are to be reported to the chief or King. Most of the cases are reported to the deputy. Even when the chief comes in, he will assign the deputy things to do on his own initiative. That way the deputy has more direct contact [with the subjects of the chief] than the chief. According to Swazi law and custom, the chief should not have to handle every petty thing. If he had to, there could be negative effects. If things go through the deputy, people will feel freer to say whatever they want to say. If things go through the chief, people are bound to be a bit reserved. The deputy [is assigned] important responsibilities in order to protect the chief's time but also in order to give room for the democratic process.

Since the deputy must be selected from a clan other than that of the chief, an important check on the powers of the chief and his agnates is provided. The deputy's duties are varied: he assists the chief in ruling in chiefdom; he attends and organizes all meetings and courts; he screens all business, complaints and requests that individuals wish to bring to the chief. Clearly, the deputy's role in land disputes, in particular, is significant: he hears the initial complaints; he chairs the *bandlancane* debates about the merits of a case; he schedules a land dispute for hearing before the *libandla* (community council); he chairs or co-chairs, along with the chief, the public hearing of the land dispute; he leads the *bandlancane's* decision-making process regarding the outcome of the land dispute, providing the chief with background information to the case and emphasizing salient points.

Secretary: The secretary assumes an important role in some customary courts. In connection with land matters, he provides records which are used by the chief or council members to verify disputant/court actions or case circumstances. Until the recent past, such actions or circumstances were only supported by witnesses' memories or conjecture: for example, regarding placement of boundaries at an initial land allocation or regarding a decision reached in a land dispute.

In several cases in my sample, court secretaries aided in land disputes by reading to the assembled *bandlakhulu* documents which verified that the King had granted individuals permits to build at specified locations in their respective chiefs' areas. At other times secretaries read letters from the District Commissioner which verified circumstances in question, for example the marital status of a woman (whether her separation from her husband was official and, consequently, whether she had the right to obtain land without his authorization).

A well-educated, influential secretary in one chief's area, which was recently engaged in a heated land dispute with a neighbouring chiefdom, took a very important role in handling paperwork generated by various court sessions (the Chief's Court, King's Court and High Court). This secretary, who takes his responsibilities as secretary very seriously, describes the role of the chief's secretary in sophisticated terms:

> The chief's secretary must receive correspondence. The chief will inform the *libandla* about the correspondence. The chief responds to some letters directly, but the secretary drafts all correspondence. Circulars coming from ministries are read by the secretary since they are written in English.[15] He interprets for the chief. Government gazettes about new laws would be read by the secretary. He prepares statements by the chiefs and also special announcements – these are signed. The secretary prepares documents for projects – drafting and presenting to the chief for work with the *libandla*. If approved, the documents are given to a representative of the chief to *Tinkhundla* – this regards a proposed project. Through *Tinkhundla* the projects are directed to the Regional Administrator and on to the appropriate ministry.

Messenger: One chief's *umgijimi* (messenger) told me that his responsibilities primarily involve announcing meetings to the subjects of a chief and summoning disputants before the chief's council. In the situation of a land dispute, the messenger might act as a local police officer by separating disputants, by dissuading disputants from violent measures, by summoning the police if violence erupts, and by informing higher authorities such as the chief or deputy and the officials of the Swazi Nation Court about the situation. Once the land dispute has become a formal case before the Chief's Court, the messenger may be asked by the chief and his council to investigate boundaries or other dispute-related problems.

One messenger explained his reasons for assuming his unpaid position:

> I am *umgijimi* because I am proud of the job. The only times I am paid are when I provide a service like taking someone to town. Then I get a gift for my services. In the old days the *umgijimi* didn't pay taxes but now he must pay. He used to be excused from them because of this service to the community.

Lincusa: One informant stated that the *lincusa* assists in land allocations by approaching the chief or *indvuna* on behalf of a *sikhonti* (man who wants to pledge allegiance to a new chief and obtain land). The *lincusa* informs the *bandlancane* and *libandla* that the newcomer is a good person and should be accepted in the area. Sometimes a *lincusa* conducts investigations on behalf of the chief regarding the character of a *sikhonti*.

Several influential citizens said that they would not serve as a *lincusa* in land allocations. One man said that he would be put in a difficult position should a land dispute arise:

> There can be problems. If the person whom you help to obtain land causes a dispute about the land or otherwise misbehaves, then the council [*bandlancane*] will come to you and blame you. They ask, 'Why did you say that this man would be OK?' The problem is that you can never know a person well enough. Even if you think you know someone well, he can still act up in ways you didn't expect.

An important elder said that the *lincusa* of a newcomer must be brought to him, and therefore he himself cannot serve as *lincusa*:

> When there was no royal kraal here, our family was in charge. My grandfather was chosen by King Mswati to look after the area . . . [Nowadays] mostly those who come to me want help to *khonta*, but I cannot be a *lincusa*. If I were to present a person to the [chief's council], then I would be told to find a place for that person to stay since it's believed that I've accepted the person [as resident of area]. Normally, when someone comes to *khonta* – even before [Chief] Mandanda died, Mandanda could only give him a place in the royal kraal. If the newcomer wanted to settle outside the royal kraal area, then Mandanda had to consult with me about finding a place.

Imisumphe: A very important role in land disputes – albeit an informally defined one – is played by *imisumphe*, the long-term residents of an area. Most *imisumphe* are elders, but young men who arrived early in a recently settled area could be *imisumphe* (particularly in the absence of older men). The *imisumphe* of an area may be called upon by the chief's council to testify at a public meeting about boundaries or about the nature of land transactions, i.e. they serve as 'expert witnesses' in land cases. They are believed to be knowledgeable about land matters by virtue of their residence in an area dating back to the days of its original (or earlier) settlement.

The most interesting question in regard to *imisumphe* concerns the impact of their *imisumphe* status upon their recruitment to a chief's *bandlancane* (inner council). As recognized *imisumphe*, they can indirectly influence the outcome of land disputes by 'restating' history in accordance with current political realities, but as members of a chief's council, they can directly decide upon land matters, including land utilization policy and land dispute resolution. *Imisumphe* who want to influence land policy directly will desire membership on a chief's *bandlancane*.

All my informants stated that any long-term resident of an area may be asked to testify before the community about land matters – his memory serving as a substitute for or complement to written land records. These informants also indicated that only those long-term residents possessing exceptional abilities and high social standing will be asked by a chief to serve as members of his council. One chief explained:

> If a person is appointed to *bandlancane*, he can be an *umsumphe*. But it doesn't stand to reason that if a person is an *umsumphe*, he is on *bandlancane*. It might be advisable that the *umsumphe* should participate in proceedings.

King and councils

Structure

The literature on Swazi customary land law says very little about the procedures followed by the King and his council in processing land disputes. My own investigations were only minimally successful since national officials either were unfamiliar with some new procedures introduced following the former King's death in 1982 or were knowledgeable but unwilling to divulge 'state secrets'.

Several anthropologists (Hughes 1972; Kuper 1947a; Rosen-Prinz 1976) state that the national administrative structure is headed by a dual monarchy – the *Ndlovukazi*, Queen Mother, and the *Ngwenyama*, King. The two figures ideally try to operate in harmony with one another, reaching decisions which are mutually acceptable. The Queen Mother's centre is the larger national headquarters where ritual matters are handled. The King's centre is the seat of the principal traditional court where the semi-traditional Higher National Court of Appeal has now been established. Both capitals, as part of the central Swazi political organization, are herein referred to by Hughes' term – the 'Central Authority' (1972: 161).

Royal villages (e.g. Lozitha, Lobomba, Zombodze) serve as centres for the coordination of national activities and as 'referral agencies'. In other words, they serve as important gateways for directing disputes to different levels of the hierarchy, thus determining *how* disputes will be contained and *who* will have authority to define inter-personal and community harmony. By means of the royal villages, information is channelled up and down the authority structure. For example, a land dispute between chiefs or between persons belonging to different chiefs may be referred to the *indvuna* at the linking royal village who will hear initial complaints and refer the case either to a local council or to one of the high courts at the national capital. The *indvuna* in all cases acts as a mouthpiece of the King. Informants report that in the past the *indvuna* at a royal village heard land cases between chiefs, but now he only hears land disputes between sub-*tindvuna* under his own jurisdiction (for explanations of royal villages and *tindvuna*, refer to Chapter 1).

Hughes describes in some detail the national administrative structure which is controlled by the Central Authority through various councils – some of which are responsible for land dispute management:

> there is an entity known as the National Council (*libandla lake Ngwane*) which, together with the Monarchs, is the supreme indigenous ruling body. In theory this consists of two parts, the General Council (*libandla lomkhulu*) and the Executive Committee (*libandla lencane*), while the older Inner Council (*liqoqo*) is available to deal with specialized problems. The last mentioned may also play the role of a 'party caucus', as it were, which can influence the decisions of the Executive Committee. In practice, it is the Executive Committee which is recognized as the 'Council' by the central government. Nevertheless, the members of this Committee are well aware that many Swazi regard the General

Council as the superior body; as *the* National Council. They are, therefore, careful to avoid taking any action which might unduly antagonize the latter.

Swazi informants (particularly if they are of the Dlamini clan and closely connected with the National administration) usually argue that land matters such as boundary disputes between Chiefs, do not strictly fall within the purviews of any of these bodies; but should be settled by the *Ngwenyama* (King) himself, in consultation with yet another Council (or selected body of advisors). However, as we shall see, 'land matters' impinge on many fields in which these Councils, and the local-governmental authorities in the Chiefdoms are concerned (1972: 166–7).

Procedure

A case goes to one of the royal capitals for trial when a chief's subject wishes to appeal his case, when subjects of two chiefs have a case which their chiefs will not hear, or when two chiefs have a case against one another. A man who wishes to appeal against a chief's judgement, ordinarily goes to the royal villages to which his chief is attached. He should be accompanied by the chief's messenger, who gives details of the case and the judgement of the Chief's Court. Cases at the royal villages are heard by the *indvuna* of that village. The conduct of the trial is similar to that in the lower court, except that the King (*Inkhosi*) or Queen Mother (*Indlovukati*) are not usually present. When the counsellors at the royal capital have come to a decision, it is confirmed by either the King or Queen Mother. If the case is an important one, the King or Queen Mother may participate in the trial or at least be present during the hearing of the evidence. Judgement debts are executed by a messenger (Marwick 1940: 285–7).

When informants were asked about the procedure for appealing land cases from a Chief's Court to national authorities, the role of *Ndabazabantu* was usually mentioned (see following section for an explanation about the origins and functions of *Ndabazabantu*). *Ndabazabantu* is an official created by the modern bureaucracy introduced by the British, but he serves to link customary Chiefs' Courts to the customary hierarchy of national councils.

When a case between a chief's subjects is transferred to the national authorities, a chief must provide authorization. When a case between chiefs is transferred, one chief must either refuse to meet with *Ndabazabantu* (usually at Regional Administration offices) or otherwise refuse to accept the recommendations of *Ndabazabantu* after a hearing. In most situations, an appellant will be assisted by an official who acts as his *lincusa*, official representative. Sometimes *Ndabazabantu* is bypassed and the King's counsellors are approached directly.

One chief described in theoretical terms how a land dispute between subjects might be appealed to higher authorities:

> After a [chief] has heard a dispute, he may [authorize that it be taken] to *Ndabazabantu*. After the matter has gone through all the [required stages – like a preliminary hearing before *Ndabazabantu*], then it will go to Lusaseni [King's royal kraal]. The two disputing parties will be called.

> The case is heard for the first time when everybody is present ... all persons who are knowledgeable may be present. [On the Lusaseni side], the counsellors will be present. Maybe not all of them will be there. Those present sit together with the King's *indvuna* [deputy] and exchange opinions. The *indvuna* and counsellors are all [equally] the King's advisers, but the *indvuna* assumes the role of chairman.

Another chief who recently appealed his own land dispute with another chief described how a land dispute between chiefs might be appealed:

> If I were to have problems with a particular chieftaincy, I would approach the other chief. Let's say I have land but there is no river, trees or stones which are the boundary. Somebody messes with, say, boulders which are serving as the boundary so that he can claim the area as his. The procedure would be for me to lodge a complaint against this chief at his royal kraal. We would sit down and discuss the matter.
>
> Usually the chief and his closest family members will first discuss the case. There has to be someone listening to the case when it is discussed. If the two chiefs and their groups fail to reach an understanding about the matter, then they approach *Ndabazabantu*. It is possible that the two chiefs would expand their private meeting to include members of whole communities; but if one of them just doesn't want to listen to [preliminary discussions], then the two chiefs and their followers – about thirty or forty – are called before *Ndabazabantu* [at the district offices] who acts as chairman. The chief brings people who have knowledge of the area ... that is, where the boundaries should be. Everybody will listen to the discussions and there should be some kind of verdict reached either for one or the other chief.
>
> Say *Ndabazabantu* decides for one chief and the other thinks the decision is unfair. The [latter] will go to the King – actually the King's *indvuna*. *Ndabazabantu* must first [authorize] him to take the dispute on to the King. The King's *indvuna* will set up a date for the hearing, and both chiefs as well as *Ndabazabantu* will be present.
>
> [On the assigned day], *Ndabazabantu* will state the case. [The disgruntled chief] is allowed to stand up and explain his case. He states that he is dissatisfied with the decision of *Ndabazabantu* and that the proper outcome should be [otherwise]. He also says why he thinks the land is his. Then the other chief is called upon to give his side to the story. The counsellors ask questions. Everyone asks questions [of opposing parties].
>
> When all has been said to the satisfaction of the *indvuna* and his counsellors, they send everyone away while they decide the case. Or, maybe they will tell everyone that they must come back another day. When the King's counsellors announce their decision, they may go along with the earlier finding of *Ndabazabantu* or they may come up with a new decision. They will give reasons why the land belongs to one party or another.

Modern forums

The modern side of Swaziland's dual legal system consists of District Commissioners, *Tinkhundla*, *Ndabazabantu* and the Swazi Courts. As mentioned above, the 'European-style' Subordinate Courts, High Court and Court of Appeal do not ordinarily hear customary land cases.

District Commissioners, *Tinkhundla*, *Ndabazabantu* and Swazi Courts were introduced or otherwise assumed new administrative powers during the late colonial era (the 1930s to the 1950s). These agencies, which were and still are associated with the modern political/bureaucratic order, have had an impact upon customary land administration. When created, they functioned in a dual system of administration: first, a team of expatriate officials headed by a commissioner appointed by Britain, and secondly, a tribal administration appointed by and functioning under the control of its acknowledged leader, the Swazi King. The latter operated under traditional Swazi law and custom. Following Independence in 1968, a complex administrative system was fused together from parts of the dual system. Thus, in Swaziland the colonial local administrative structure continues to function, and administrative procedures and legal authority continue to be based on procedures defined during the colonial period (Dening 1969; Picard 1983: 10).

A fundamental problem concerns, on the one hand, the powers of chiefs and their councils over customary land matters, and on the other, the impact which modern administrative officials have on chiefs' and councils' authority over customary land matters. Many Swazis state that they are not clear regarding the origins of various modern authorities as well as their current roles and functions.[16]

District Commissioner (regional administrator)

District Commissioners were established at seven administrative centres for the purpose of administratively linking the central government and the rural population (section 4 of Chapter 20 of Laws of Swaziland). After Independence in 1968 the number was reduced to four districts and two sub-districts. The roles of District Commissioners in Swaziland, typical of the British colonial model throughout Africa, were administrative and legal in nature. Since the early 1960s, they have performed increasingly less court and legal work and more work with *Tinkhundla* and rural development committees.

One of the important functions of a District Commissioner, now known as a 'regional administrator', is to work in conjunction with a *Ndabazabantu* in attending to inter-chieftaincy land disputes. In addition to peripheral involvement of customary land matters, he acts as a chairman of the farm dwellers tribunal (founded under Act No. 21 of 1967), authorizes buildings in rural areas (Building Act No. 34 of 1968) and controls all government (formerly crown) land, including the sale of stands in townships (Crown Land Temporary Occupation Proclamation). Moreover, except for the provisions in the Building Act, the District Commissioner has no authority over freehold land (see generally Butler 1974; Hitchcock 1985).

Ndabazabantu

As discussed above, a *Ndabazabantu* was appointed in the pre-Independence period to each district office. A *Ndabazabantu* represented the King in his district and acted as a liaison officer between the District Commissioner or

District Officer (currently titled 'Regional Administrator') and the chiefs in the district whom he had the power to summon to his presence. As Europeans had little understanding of Swazi customary law, a *Ndabazabantu* was charged with hearing criminal and civil cases involving Africans – particularly those who lived in town and were outside the jurisdiction of chiefs. Although *Ndabazabantu* could hear complaints between Swazis on his own, he heard complaints against a European by a Swazi together with the District Commissioner. Many of *Ndabazabantu's* duties were transferred to the Swazi Courts when these were constituted (see generally Butler 1974).

A *Ndabazabantu* continues to find support in the post-Independence Swazi government because of his earlier role in advising management about labour disputes; the current Swazi government is strongly resistant to trade unions (see Maasdorp 1976: 421). Some of the labour-related duties of a *Ndabazabantu*, who is appointed by the Swazi National Council, are described by the Council in an official paper:

> He will encourage the workers and build a sound sense of responsibility, respect and discipline – inspire the workers with a feeling of regarding the Industry in terms of a partnership – teach the workers to realize that any realization of profits will result in better wages and better social conditions in their villages ... He will advise Management on all matters pertaining to Swazi law and custom and usages and cultivate a spirit of co-operation and belonging which is conducive to economic progress by affording the workers equal opportunity in order to narrow the gap between the haves and have-nots. To fight against and wipe out any idea that there is what is termed 'cheap labour' in the Territory ... (quoted in Winter 1978: 38)

Today, a *Ndabazabantu* exercises many roles, such as settlement of quarrels involving customary marriage or loaned money; but his most important and confusing role is that of messenger between chiefs and the King in land dispute situations. A subject involved in a land case may be reported to *Ndabazabantu* by his chief when he fails to answer the summons of the chief. *Ndabazabantu* informs the police, and a message is sent to the chief's messenger, who orders the subject to report to the royal residence. When a chief refuses to report to *Ndabazabantu* (or the Regional Administrator or a *Tinkhundla* meeting), he may be brought before a traditional court by *Ndabazabantu*. *Ndabazabantu* has the power to fine or imprison a resistant chief, but in practice, *Ndabazabantu* cannot easily enforce compliance, even with police assistance, when the chief is evasive and is supported by many followers. Chiefs commonly state that a *Ndabazabantu* is inferior to a chief (without the backing of tradition and followers) and that only the King may summon a chief.

Although *Ndabazabantu's* role in land disputes was often mentioned by informants, an urban land supervisor in a regional administrator's office minimized such a role:

> *Ndabazabantu* doesn't deal with land disputes; this is the King's responsibility. He has no involvement with affairs of rural land. Chiefs can talk about minor land cases with *Ndabazabantu* – like where boundaries are supposed to be

> located. *Ndabazabantu* is not a part of the traditional court of law. *Ndabazabantu* is supposed to be like a chief in the urban areas. He handles cases of people in town who owe allegiance to different chiefs. He hears civil cases like the chief does in rural areas. In the rural areas, criminal cases – like theft and bloodshed – can be reported to the police [who report to *Ndabazabantu*], and the chief takes no role at all.

Inkhundla

Another modern forum, the *Inkhundla* (pl. *Tinkhundla*, regional meeting places), was first officially mentioned in colonial government annual reports in 1954, although archival evidence suggests that *Tinkhundla* are a pre-Second World War system. The word *Inkhundla* originally referred to the area in front of the cattle *kraal* where men would meet and talk. Under the new administrative system, the proposed *Tinkhundla* served as primary units of government, administrative agencies which linked modern and traditional sectors of government. Currently, forty *Tinkhundla* are organized nation-wide at the district level for the purpose of grouping chiefs into administrative units. The leader of an *Inkhundla* is called the *Indvuna* of the *Inkhundla* and, like *Ndabazabantu*, has the power to summon chiefs to meetings; however, the duties of the two officials are dissimilar (see generally Kuper 1978: 185; Levin 1985: 190–8; Shongwe 1983).

In some ways *Tinkhundla* resemble the royal homesteads in that *tindvuna* are appointed by the King to oversee their operations. However, the comparison is limited since no territories are under their jurisdiction and no subjects come under their direct control. They are in a peculiar, awkward position, argues Fine (n.d.: 5), because they are hierarchically superior to chiefs, but in practice, chiefs exercise real power in communities.

Although the *Tinkhundla* were originally not granted executive authority and served as convenient organizations through which District Commissioners could meet and talk to chiefs (see 'Tinkhundla System of Government Guidelines' n.d.; Ministry of Local Administration 1978), it appears that they, again like *Ndabazabantu*, sometimes have assumed roles in land dispute situations which are not considered legitimate by either the involved parties or traditional authorities. *Tinkhundla* occasionally refer land disputes to proper authorities or handle minor land disputes; however, no data are available on the nature of the disputes, the type of proceedings followed or the disposition of the disputes. Chiefs state that they are confused about powers which *Tinkhundla* may assume over land matters (particularly land disputes), about types of land control which they (chiefs) retain, and about the role to be played by the Central Authority.

In addition to playing a minor role in land disputes, *Tinkhundla* serve a variety of other functions – some of which involve land matters. According to Hitchcock:

> The *tindvuna yetinkhundla* had a number of different functions, including mobilizing local labor for various activities, providing a liaison between local

> people and government departments (e.g., the Ministry of Agriculture), and arranging for social service provision (e.g. schools and health facilities) in their areas.[17] In contemporary Swaziland, the *tinkhundla* serve as the foci for the announcement of many development projects, as well as being the organizations from which members of Parliament are drawn. (1985: 2)

Swazi (Nation) Courts

The Swazi Courts, currently numbering approximately twenty-five throughout the country, were formalized by the Swazi Courts Act of 1950. A Swazi Court President presides over cases, assisted by two assessors. Other personnel include a clerk who records cases in siSwati, and court officers who handle routine administration, such as bringing accused criminal offenders into the courtroom and maintaining order. Lawyers are not permitted to participate in proceedings, so that the Swazi Courts are accessible theoretically to any Swazi, regardless of economic resources. The Swazi Courts hear minor civil and criminal cases, similar to those heard by the Chiefs' Courts; but the presence of paid personnel, among other things, renders the proceedings more formal.

The Swazi Courts are not expressly prohibited from hearing land disputes, but most Swazis state that these courts may not play a direct role in land disputes. The Swazi Court can only handle land cases on other pretexts; for example, a person may destroy the crops of a person who he claims is improperly using his land (see Case 20 in Chapter 6), or he may assault this same person. In these situations, the case must go before the Swazi Court as either a destruction of property case or an assault case. Questions about customary land rights cannot be heard.

Although the Swazi Court may not decide upon land cases *per se*, it does have an impact upon land matters heard by other customary law forums. Therefore, when questions about land rights are heard by other forums such as the chief's council, following a judgement which the Swazi Court has pronounced on a matter unrelated to land, chief's council members may be influenced by the Swazi Court's earlier interpretations of case merit and disputant reputation. In any case, the Swazi Court does not have overlapping jurisdiction, along with the Chief's Court, and does not serve as a court of appeal in land cases.

One informant, a formally educated chief, explained why *Ndabazabantu* but not the Swazi Court may handle land disputes:

> I don't know if there is an [official] reason [for the separation of powers regarding land control], but I do know what makes sense to me. *Ndabazabantu* has no authority to judge a case but can reach an opinion [about a land case]. He must report to that person who has authority to judge on land issues ... the King. If you got the Swazi Nation Court mixed up in these [land] matters, there would surely be a lot of confusion because they [Swazi Nation Court Presidents] are used to judging. The law agrees that they should judge, but on this matter [land], they have no jurisdiction [are not supposed to reach a verdict]. They

cannot even try it [land matters] as a case because it is a dispute. *Ndabazabantu*, being used to listening to and looking into [land matters] as a neutral person on behalf of the King, can give an objective opinion on what he has heard about the dispute.

The dual legal system and harmony

In Swaziland's traditional and modern legal systems, due process or rule of law mean different things. Officials within the traditional system are constrained neither by written rules of procedure and evidence nor by written legal codes, as are officials within the modern system. Consequently, the former officials have considerable leeway to interpret rules in each land dispute case. They are constrained primarily by public opinion regarding their performance and judgement.

Harmony also means different things within the traditional and modern legal systems. In the customary system, procedural and substantive rules aim to achieve harmony through balancing, at least in appearances, the disputants' specific case interests with the officials' interest in general political control. Harmony emerges through political manoeuvrings – a situation which encourages all participants to behave according to concrete, contextual rules defining the social and political order. Every participant acts according to his/her hereditary position relative to all other Swazis. Therefore, customary processes are responsive to the nuances of individual cases, although the political 'order of things', rather than individual rules or cases, assume primary importance. Harmony is achieved, from the authorities' perspective, when disputes are contained at the lowest level of the political hierarchy; progression of a case through customary courts potentially poses political challenges at each level. In sum, harmony is best viewed as a component of relationships within an entire legal, social and political system, and disputing strategies are geared towards manipulation within that total system.

In the modern system, rules aim to achieve harmony through balancing disputants' differences. Court officials, as modern bureaucrats, have little political stake in specific case outcomes. Modern administrative agents, such as the Regional Administrator or *Ndabazabantu*, who administer customary law but within the context of a modern bureaucracy, are not fully legitimate representatives of either the customary or modern system. Consequently, they cannot effectively produce either customary political harmony or modern disputant-oriented harmony. In modern courts and administrative agencies, harmony emerges through adherence to formal protocol – a situation which encourages participants to behave according to rules defining the legal order relative to their immediate adversary. Modern court processes are primarily concerned with achieving disputant acquiescence in each case and with adherence to bureaucratic formalities, rather than ideologically supporting the larger social and political order. Therefore, harmony can be achieved either in a court of first instance or an appeal court, since movement of a case through different forums in the modern system does not affect officials' authority (dispute containment within the court of first instance is an economic rather than a political issue). In sum, harmony is best viewed as a component of the relationship between two disputants within a single case, and disputing strategies are geared towards manipulation within the microcosm of that case.

Careful examination of each traditional and modern forum, including officials' responsibilities within each forum, indicates varying ideological conceptions about and behavioural manifestations of harmony. On the traditional side of the dual legal system, family councils at the lowest level encourage reconciliation and compromise between homestead residents (brothers, fathers and sons, or uncles and nephews). Family councils are likely to put women who have married into the homestead at a disadvantage. Such women cannot freely dispute about their perceived land rights.

Chiefs' Courts seek dispute containment at the family or chiefdom level, thus encouraging compromise but resorting to adjudicated decisions when litigants are recalcitrant. During meetings, chiefdom authorities speak about harmony during initial prayers, throughout case arguments and when pronouncing judgements. Their arguments about the reasons and methods to act harmoniously reach a wide audience since representatives of nearly all homesteads attend at least several times a year. The chief propagates harmony primarily in oratory at formal proceedings, whereas his deputy perpetuates harmony both in daily interactions with residents and in oratory at formal proceedings. The chief and his deputy enforce behavioural compliance through formal sanctions (fines or police) and informal sanctions (ostracism or ridicule). A *lincusa* is responsible for maintaining harmony between neighbours and may be blamed for disruptions caused by a person whom he once represented at a land request hearing. An *umsumphe*, who has intimate knowledge of land affairs in the chiefdom, defines ideal rules of land tenure and ideal relationships of social and political harmony. The messenger and secretary perform administrative duties on behalf of the Court but ordinarily have little influence on decision-making procedures, including enunciation of harmony (an exception is Case 16 in Chapter 5). The messenger, acting as a traditional policeman, enforces behavioural, if not attitudinal, harmony between disputants.

The King's Court, which sometimes hears disputes between chiefs' subjects on appeal, relies upon the testimony of chiefdom officials. More often it hears land disputes between chiefs, relying upon the testimony of King's counsellors and witnesses. National authorities have the greatest and most encompassing power to produce harmony throughout the traditional hierarchy, and yet they usually promote attitudinal harmony but do not enforce behavioural harmony. They are extremely careful in voicing opinions so as to understand local affairs, to secure national unity and to bolster their own control and ideological interests. The King, as the head of the Swazi Nation, has the ultimate power to define harmony ideologies and to make decisions.

On the modern side of the dual legal system, a *Ndabazabantu* at the lowest level encourages, in theory, reconciliation and compromise between disputants who come before him. A *Ndabazabantu* makes utterances about harmony in proceedings, thus stating how people are to live together 'peacefully'. A *Ndabazabantu* has broad authority to resolve disputes between chiefs' subjects and between chiefs; however, he cannot easily produce harmony because he derives powers from and is ideologically linked to the modern system.

A District Commissioner offers new opportunities for 'unconnected' persons in the traditional sector – often women – to advance strategically their interests. District Commissioners assumed new responsibilities in connection with *Tinkhundla* and rural development committees following Independence, making their role in harmony production *potentially*, if not actually, greater than pre-Independence days when Europeans rather than Swazis performed duties as District Commissioners, and when the Commissioners had fewer important roles to play in the customary sector.

Tinkhundla, in theory, could promote or restore harmonious relationships between traditional and modern political systems; however, they fail to do so because their roles are unclear. Their ineffectiveness is particularly evident in land dispute cases. The *tindvuna* in the *Tinkhundla* are hierarchically superior to chiefs; but because they have no subjects directly under them, they are probably less able to produce harmony in the chiefdoms under their jurisdiction than are chiefs.

Swazi Nation Courts cannot effectively produce consensual harmony, even though they base their decisions upon customary law, because they received power and legitimacy in the modern sector during colonialism. Many cases come before Swazi Nation Courts after containment in traditional forums has failed; other cases come before Swazi Nation Courts because legislation provides that they are no longer within the jurisdiction of Chiefs' Courts. Swazi Court Presidents use the police power of the modern state to enforce adjudicated decisions.

In summary, traditional forums, which were assigned narrower jurisdiction during the colonial era, have lost some opportunities for harmony production, and modern forums, which have received new or additional jurisdiction, have gained possibilities for harmony production. As a consequence of changes, forums may produce more or less harmony, and they may produce different kinds of harmony, as will be discussed in Part II.

3

Two communities: arenas for land disputes

Selection

Several months of unstructured interviews with people in all districts of Swaziland persuaded me to concentrate on court visitation and extended interviewing in two communities sharing jurisdiction within the Swazi customary political hierarchy – Zombodze and Kwaluseni. The two communities, which lie in the western periphery of Manzini town, are in one of the most densely populated regions of Swaziland (see Map 5; Gina 1984). The natural resource base is limited, but good soils allow for agricultural development. In addition, industry is highly developed (see Map 6), and commercial establishments are numerous.

Although my selection of Zombodze and Kwaluseni was initially influenced by the cooperativeness of local councils as well as the close proximity of the communities to my part-time residence at the University of Swaziland (see Maps 7 and 8), I eventually realized that the communities presented fascinating anomalies within Swaziland. Zombodze is unusual as one of several prominent royal kraals (spiritual capitals) of the former Queen Mother, Labotsibeni, and as home to the recently deceased (1982) traditional Prime Minister, Mandanda Mtsetfwa. Kwaluseni is unique as the only semi-urban, industrialized area on customarily tenured land. While the uniqueness of the communities obviated many possibilities for representativeness in a national context, important research possibilities were presented. Zombodze offered outstanding prospects for data collection since its status as a royal village brings many kinds of land disputes under its jurisdiction, whereas Kwaluseni offered unusual research prospects since its proximity to the newly developing Matsapha Industrial Site, and its experience of rapid demographic growth, give rise to intense and new varieties of land disputes.

Zombodze and Kwaluseni are interlinked in the complex political hierarchy described in Chapter 1. Mandanda Mtsetfwa, as former governor of the royal village at Zombodze, was responsible for the affairs of Kwaluseni. In the 1950s, King Sobhuza took over direct control of Kwaluseni, while appointing a local council to assist him. Ultimately, a complex, heated dispute about

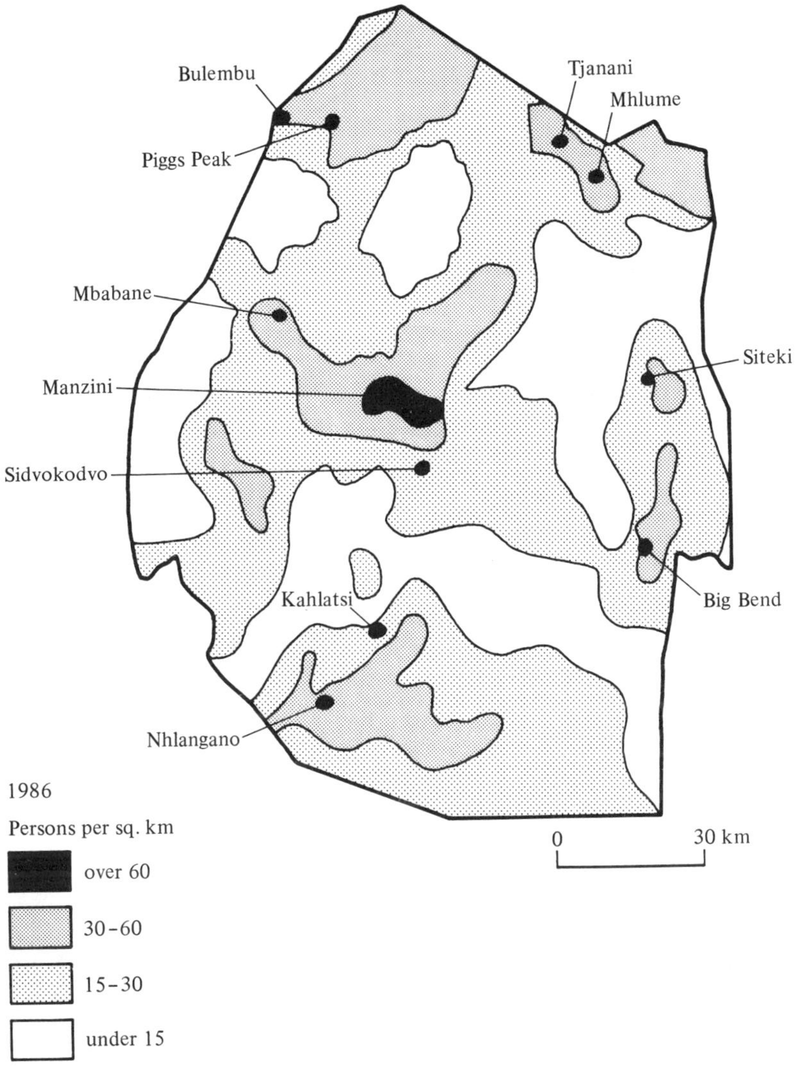

Map 5 Swaziland population
Source: Based upon Macmillan 1986: 12

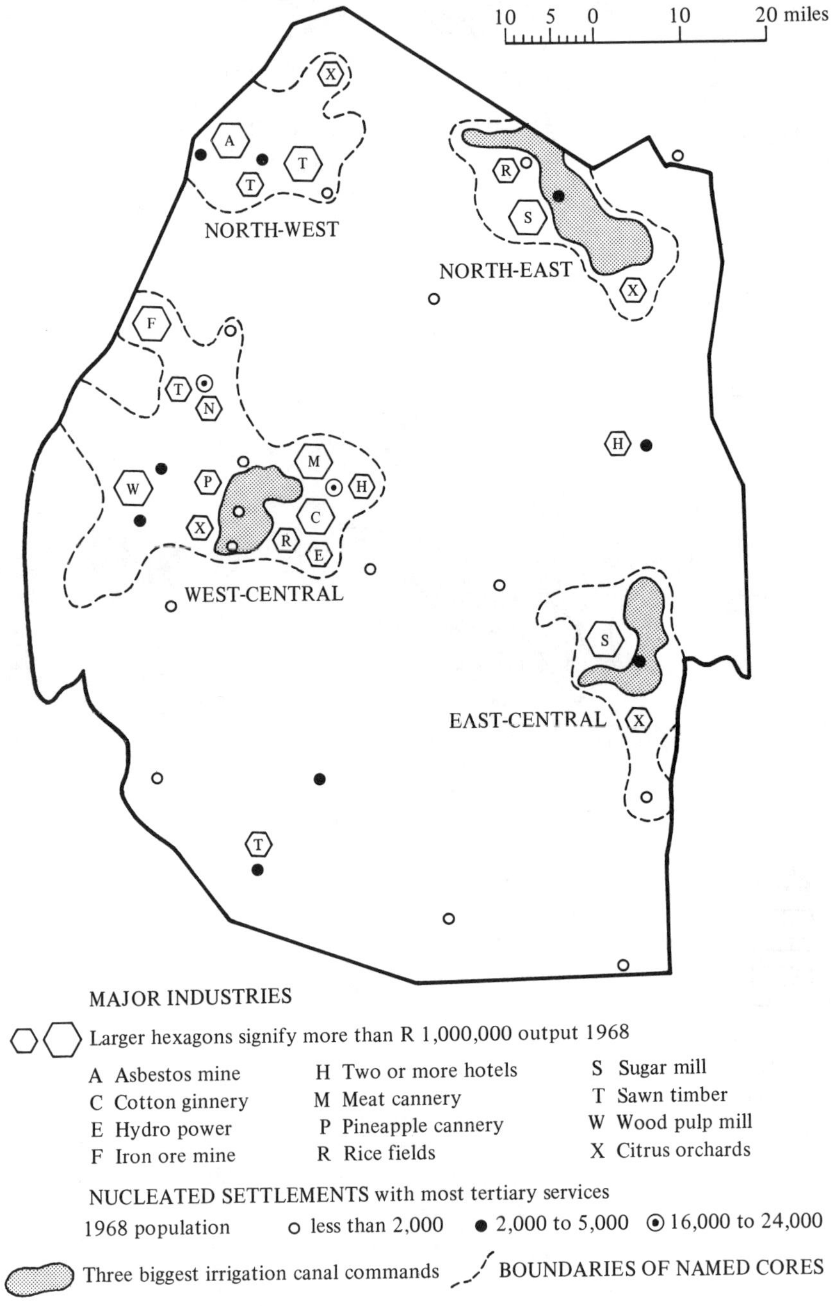

Map 6 Economic activity
Source: Based upon Murdoch 1968: 67

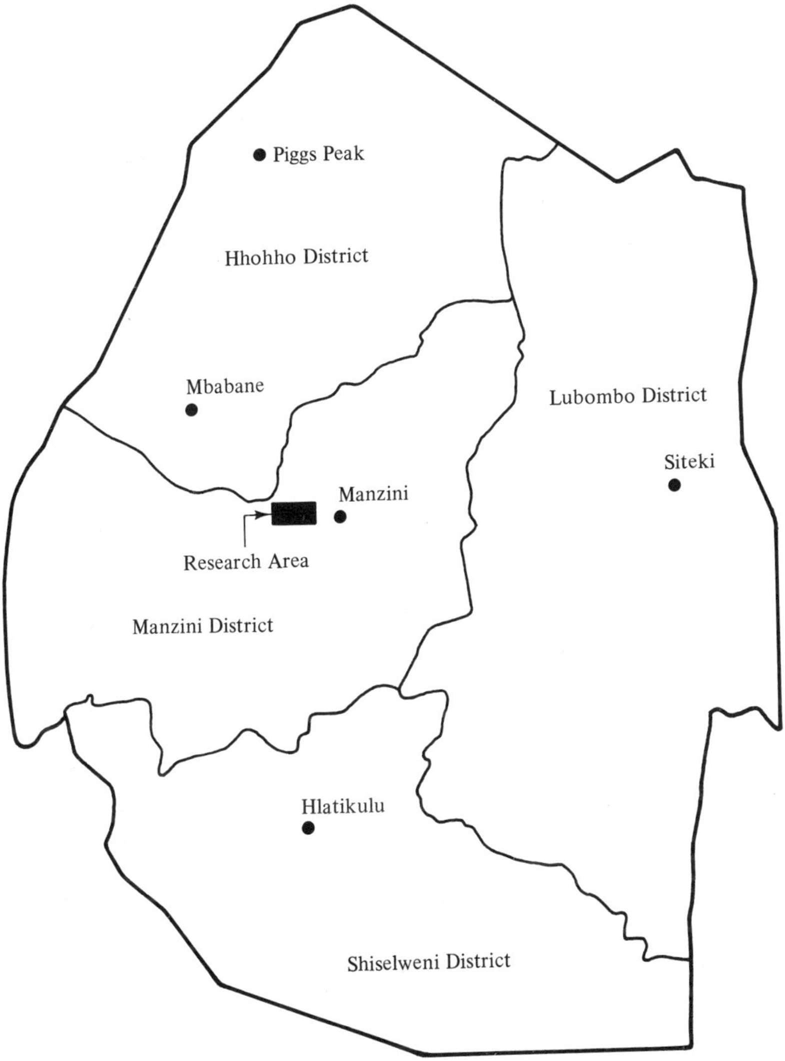

Map 7 Research area (Swaziland)

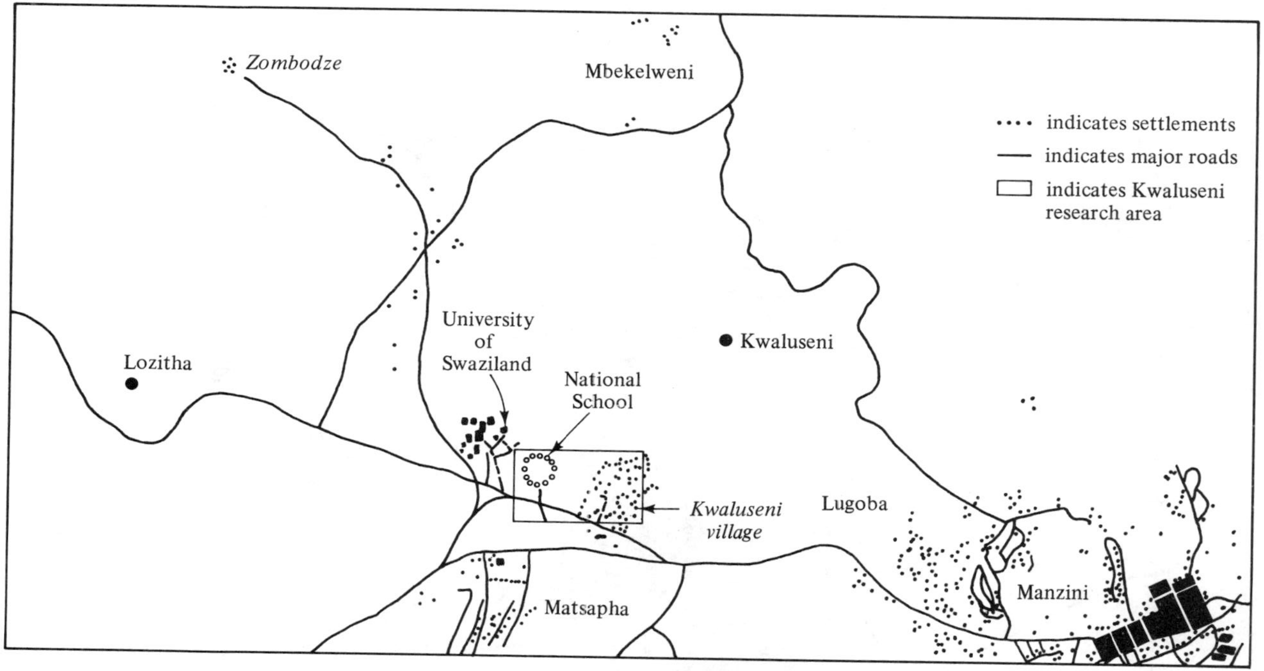

Map 8 Topography of research communities

jurisdiction developed; members of the Kwaluseni community disagreed about the constitution of the local council as well as the role Zombodze should play in community affairs. This dispute and the implications it has for the production of harmony will be given special attention in Chapter 7.

Zombodze

History

The history of Zombodze village must be comprehended in terms of royal village development. This history begins during the late eighteenth century, when two royal villages, one for the Swazi Queen Mother and another for the Swazi King, were established for the purpose of integrating dispersed patrilineal kin groups within large, dense settlements. Such villages, which were organized for self-protection and defence, ensured survival in the early nineteenth century when Europeans were penetrating the interior and clans were dispersing out of Zululand in present-day Natal. By the mid-nineteenth century, conditions had stabilized but land had become scarcer; territorial chiefs had disbanded from concentrated settlements and returned with their followers to those areas held traditionally or granted them by a Dlamini King.

With the dispersal of chiefs, two problems were created: communication in an extensive, topographically forbidding terrain, and maintenance of earlier national loyalties. The creation of a network of royal villages within a complex hierarchical political system proved to be the solution. Consequently, two new royal villages were established in the reign of each newly appointed Queen Mother and King. The network of royal villages served to link territorial chiefs to the national capitals; even the most distantly located chiefdoms were bonded within the national network. Ordinary homesteads were usually attached to royal villages through their chiefs.

As more villages were created, the functioning of the system diversified. The primary capital, the *Umpakhatsi* of the Queen Mother, served as the spiritual centre and location of major national ritual events. The other capital, the *Lilawu* of the King, served as the administrative centre and location of the highest court. Meetings of the national council (*Libandla*) were held in the cattle-byre of the Queen Mother's village, while those of the *Liqoqo*, an administrative council, took place at either one of the two capitals. In essence, the two capitals served as a focal point for a variety of national activities, such as exchange of goods, discussion of cases and celebration of festivals.

While the capitals of the current monarchs were vital centres, minor royal villages, i.e. those established during the reigns of previous monarchs, continued to serve important functions as administrative nodes. For example, they acted as focal points where participants in national activities, such as military or ritual, could gather. They also hosted customary courts where disputes which had not been satisfactorily handled by a chief's council, or disputes between chiefs, or disputes between persons belonging to different chiefs, could be reported for settlement or referral to one of the high courts at the capitals. Importantly, the governor of a minor royal village, who assumed various responsibilities such as dispute settlement, was not a member of the royal Dlamini clan and was not considered superior to other chiefs. In his capacity as link between chiefs/commoners and the monarchs, he primarily achieved unusual status through personal achievement (see Map 9).

Sobhuza II (*Ngwenyama*, long-reigning and influential King of the Swazi people from 1921 to 1982), was born in 1899 at Zombodze, then the spiritual capital of the nation and residence (*Umpakhatsi*) of his paternal grandmother, Queen Mother Labotsibeni Mduli (*Ndlovukati*). The national capital had been shifted from Nkanini to Zombodze following the death of Sobhuza's paternal grandfather, King Mbandzeni, in 1889 and the subsequent appointment of Labotsibeni as Queen Mother and her son Bhunu (Sobhuza's father) as King. The Zombodze capital was rebuilt in 1910 at a nearby site after a fire destroyed the original village.

Hilda Kuper, in her biography of King Sobhuza II, describes the importance of the court at Zombodze village for the education of the young prince:

> The court of Zombodze was a school of rich experience. There were always people coming and going, and under the large fig tree outside the byre the elders sat and debated, and eloquence and skill were applauded. Sobhuza heard Swazi history not in neat chronological sequence but episodically, often dramatically, listening to people who were living records of unwritten events. In cases of clan disputes, they would refer to early migrations and ancient settlements, and when dealing with rival claimants for succession and inheritance old and intricate family connections would be recounted, genealogies and marriage alliances traced in detail. Memory was an asset, and he remembered well; this served him in later years when many of the cases came before him under new disputants. (Kuper 1978: 45)

By the early 1980s, Zombodze had become a minor royal village. Residents told me many stories about the governor of the village, Mandanda Mtsetfwa. Mandanda's grandfather, a man who reportedly possessed great military skill and knowledge about medicines, had forged a close relationship with the Swazi Kings. In 1898, when King Bhunu was accused by the British of having ordered the murder of Mbhabha Sibandze, the governor at Zombodze, Mandanda's father was asked to fill the post.

Mandanda filled the post of governor of Zombodze royal village (*indvuna*) from 1916 until his death in 1982, while also serving as governor of the Swazi Nation (*Ndvunankhulu*). As governor of Zombodze village (*indvuna*), Mandanda represented the first of three types of chieftaincy, as discussed in Chapter 1. In this capacity, he was responsible for overseeing local affairs. As governor of the Nation (*Ndvunankhulu*), he was entrusted with national rituals and coordination of national political activities: looking after the royal cattle; organizing tribute labour for the King's fields; and arranging the national rituals such as the celebration of kingship (*Ncwala*) (Kuper 1947a: 61).

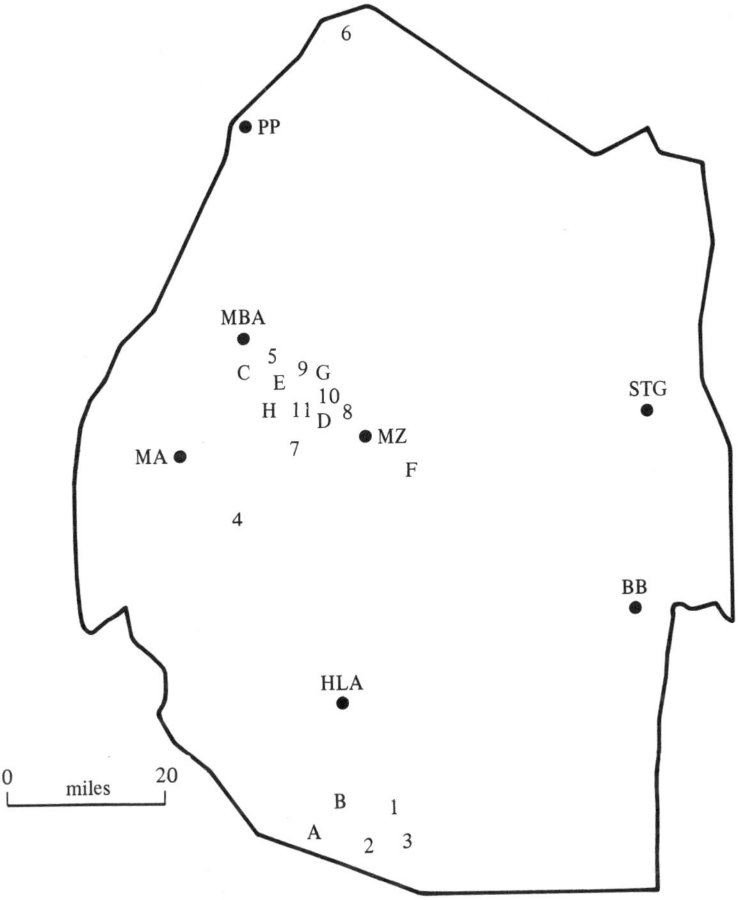

King's Place*

1. Old Hhohho 1750–80
2. Omcinsweni 1780–1815
3. Shizelweni 1815–20
4. Qaboneni 1820–3
5. Langeni 1823–42
6. Hhohho 1842–50
7. Kufinyeni 1850–67
8. Embekelweni 1874–89 (Mbandzeni)
9. Mampondweni 1889–94
10. Zabeni 1894–1900 (Bhunu)
11. Lozita 1922–82 (Sobhuza II)

The dates are approximate.

Queen's Place*

A. Old Zombodze 1750–80 (Ngwane I)
B. Old Lobamba 1780–1824 (Sobhuza I)
C. Ezulwini 1824–36 (Somhlolo)
D. Dzidzini 1836–67 (Mswati)
E. Nkanini 1867–74 (Mbandzeni)
F. Gundwini 1874–89
**G. Zombodze 1889–1925 (Bhunu)
H. Lobamba 1925– (Sobuza II)

*Name in parentheses refers to the King in whose reign they were founded.

**Royal village where most of the research described in this book was conducted.

Map 9 Royal villages
Source: Based upon Fair *et al.* 1969: 22, and Rosen-Prinz 1976: 67

Mandanda's reputation was so considerable that he was ranked above all chiefs, despite the customary practice of ranking the governor of a royal residence founded during the reign of previous rulers (minor royal village; in this case founded by King Bhunu) lower than the governor of either the present Queen Mother's residence (*Umpakhatsi*) or the present King's residence (*Lilawu*).

One of Mandanda's important responsibilities involved presiding over and judging, along with his council of elders, many types of land disputes. He played a role in an inter-national land dispute in that he was an instrumental member of the Swazi delegation which travelled to London in 1923 to protest land expropriation. Regarding local and inter-chieftaincy land disputes, Mandanda's responsibilities were diverse since he had to hear disputes between subjects, between sub-chiefs and between chiefs who were affiliated with Zombodze royal village. The 'sub-chiefs' under Zombodze's jurisdiction were actually *tinvuna* of approximately twenty-four *emahambate*, areas which were under the King's control but entrusted to the care of Mandanda.[1] A lack of clarity about the delegation of authority for *emahambate* gave rise to many land disputes – some of which reappeared during my research stay (see Case 5 in Chapter 5 and Case 23 in Chapter 6) (see Map 10). After King Sobhuza's and Mandanda's deaths – both in 1982 – new royal villages were established, and many important land disputes were directed to centres other than Zombodze.[2]

Chief's Court

At the time of my first visit to Zombodze in 1983, one of Mandanda's many sons, Timothy Velabo, former Commissioner of Police, was acting as governor of the village. He granted me permission to attend sessions of the Zombodze Court, where litigation arose between disputants occupying various dyadic configurations within the hierarchical political structure: at the family level, between brothers and between women and their affinal and agnatic kin; at the chiefdom level, between subjects resident in the immediate Zombodze area, between chiefs' subjects in areas under the jurisdiction of Zombodze, and between sub-chiefs under the jurisdiction of Mandanda (in *emahambate*); and at the national level, between chiefs who chose to go to Zombodze before approaching the national capital.

The Zombodze Court can be described according to general and specific features. The general features are standard for most Swazi Chiefs' Courts: personnel (chief, deputy, messenger and secretary) and procedural format (presentation of argument by litigants, discussion by public, decision-making by chief's council and enforcement of decision). The specific features are peculiar to the Zombodze Court, although some features might be similar in other courts: public attendance patterns; characteristics (socio-economic) of court personnel; litigant relationships; and case content. Features of public attendance patterns and characteristics of court personnel are discussed in this

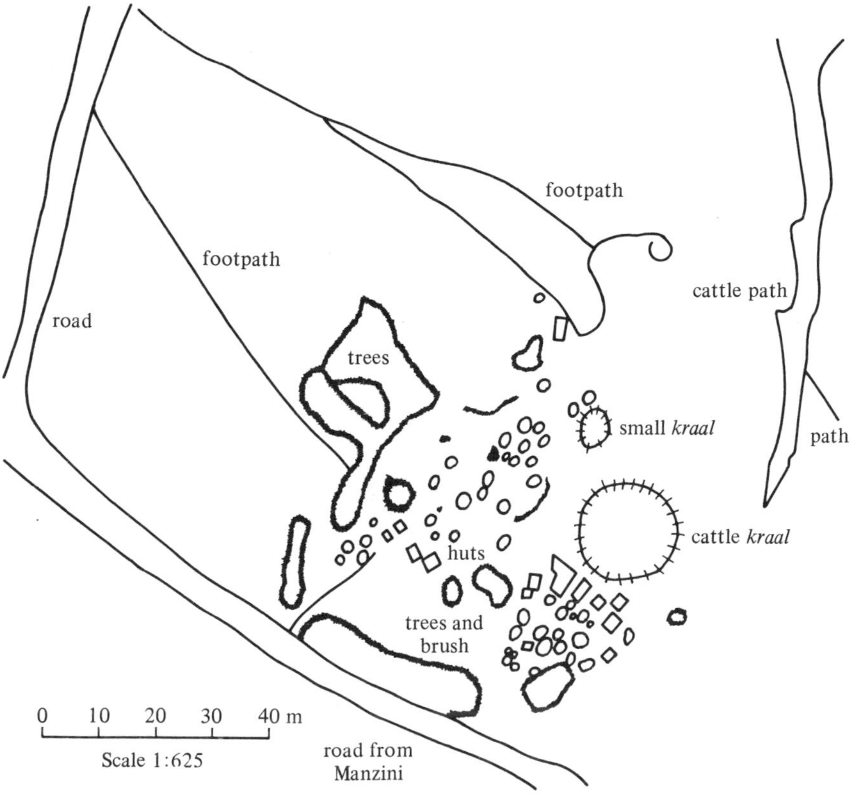

Map 10 Zombodze royal village (1973)
Source: Map drawn from enlarged orthophoto map on file at Department of Works and Communications, Mbabane, Swaziland

chapter;[3] features of litigant relationships and case content are discussed in Part II.

As few as twenty and as many as 150 spectators attended the Zombodze Court at any one time during my research between January 1985 and July 1986. Attendance at the court on Saturdays was greater when a meeting had not been held for a long time because of summer rains or because of tribute labour in the King's fields, or when the meeting necessitated attendance because government or royal directives had to be announced. The majority of regular spectators resided in the village and its immediate environs, although spectators came from widely dispersed areas.[4]

A list of council members included about twenty men as official members of the chief's inner council (*bandlancane*). Council members were socially differentiated from one another according to both ascribed and achieved criteria: they were brothers of the acting chief (non-royals); royalty (princes);

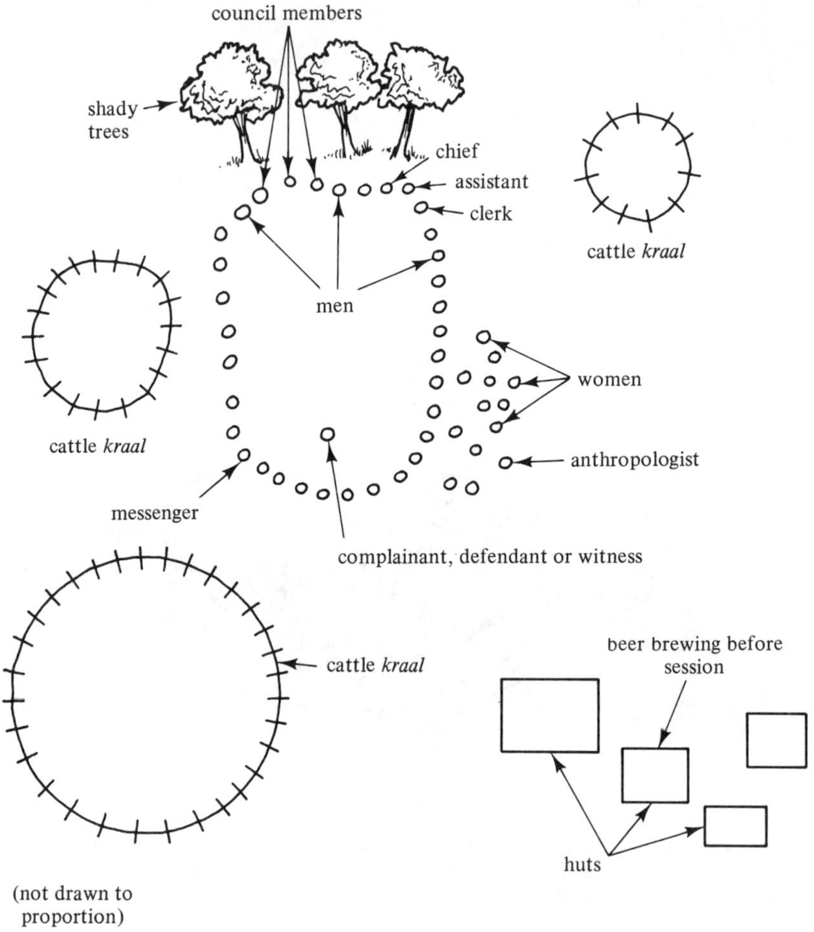

Map 11 Zombodze council session

men descended from families with historical ties to the royal family; or commoners of special ability and unusual interest in administrative activities. The youngest men were in their late forties, and the oldest were in their seventies and eighties. Several men had never been to school, while several others had completed formal schooling, including secondary school. The council members were not significantly differentiated from one another economically: most were 'wealthy' either in terms of the traditional criteria of cattle, wives and maize surplus, and others were 'wealthy' in terms of the modern criterion of money earned through urban or government employment. At least two men were employed as church ministers (see Map 11).

Kwaluseni

History

One older Zombodze resident told me that Kwaluseni did not exist when he made the three-hour walk to Manzini in the 1920s for the purpose of shopping. According to him, there were only open fields to see as he hiked through the area that has become the heavily populated Matsapha area. By the 1940s there were a few homesteads in the area, but settlement first blossomed after Independence in 1968 when the Matsapha Industrial Site was developed nearby and employment-hungry people flocked into the area on a permanent and temporary basis.

The Matsapha area, some of which came to be known as Kwaluseni, has not been granted much attention in historical accounts. The history of the Matsapha school has been covered more thoroughly (Kuper 1978: 104, 107, 159, 181) than the history of settlements. Residents who have lived in the area for some decades supplied me with oral histories, although no one was able to give precise dates for events that occurred before Independence.

Residents state that King Mbandzeni entrusted the Kwaluseni area to one of his wives, Queen Gwamile, who had a son, Bhunu, and a daughter, Tongotongo. After Mbandzeni's death, Bhunu was named King. Following Bhunu's death, Tongotongo was sent to look after Kwaluseni, which means '(place of the) King's cows'. Kwaluseni was given as a gift to 'a childless Queen'.[5] The history of Kwaluseni became closely linked with neighbouring Embikwakhe when two princes were brought from South Africa, where they had temporarily resided, and instructed to stay in Kwaluseni under the supervision of the childless Queen. Although the princes had asked the Queen Mother, Gwamile, if they might be given land for their own residence, she had refused, saying that they were needed in Kwaluseni. Consequently, they were assigned a *kraal* (livestock enclosure) called Embikwakhe, which means 'in front of' (the Queen in Kwaluseni). Early settlers in Kwaluseni obtained land from the princes at Embikwakhe.

As mentioned, the Kwaluseni area was extremely sparsely settled until the post-war years, the late 1940s and 1950s, during which time settlers began to pour into the area. Some new settlers were displaced from an area in South Africa, and other settlers came from various parts of Swaziland in search of new employment opportunities at the nearby Matsapha Industrial Site. The new settlers obtained customarily tenured land either from princes or from landholders who had received large tracts during early settlement. By the 1980s, the area had become densely settled, and agricultural and grazing sites were available primarily in the neighbouring Embikwakhe area.

The massive flow of settlers into the area created a serious rift between the 'originals', early settlers of the area, and the newcomers. Some of the newcomers were only interested in Kwaluseni as a temporary 'dormitory' for their workplace, but others intended to stay permanently. Relationships between originals and newcomers becıme increasingly strained as land and resource availability diminished, while settlers continued to arrive.

Community members commonly argue that the King wanted Kwaluseni to become a model township like Manzini; it was supposed to be unique as the only 'urban' area on customarily tenured Swazi Nation Land. The King, along with his urban planners in various ministries and government offices, hoped to develop Kwaluseni into a residential area with carefully measured and organized residential plots, garden sites and cattle-grazing areas.[6] The community was also to be provided with electricity, piped water and sewage facilities. If successful, Kwaluseni would be viewed as a development area which other customarily tenured Swazi areas might emulate.

The King realized that his plans, even though they were to be carried out within a Swazi rather than a British administrative structure, could not be easily fulfilled by a customary council consisting of privileged hereditary princes, a chief and long-time residents of the area. Apparently, he believed that the diverse new settler groups – comprising new residents, temporary residents and South African migrants – would complain about unfair land administration practices and would instigate land disputes, if traditional elites (princes and chiefs to whom new, temporary settlers did not owe allegiance) held power. Consequently, the King assumed direct control of the area. He tried to stave off political and economic competition between old and new settler groups by forming a special local council. This council, which originally consisted of about nine men, acted as his 'eyes' in the area. It operated in a traditional manner, according to customary law, but was 'modern' in that all members were equals.

The King's plan to implement a uniquely democratic council in the area was put into effect *c.* 1953. By the 1960s, the council had begun to experience serious factional disputes. Over the course of three decades, the disputes involved various issues, but the main problem concerned whether the council had originally been authorized by the King to handle land distribution or merely to implement development objectives. By the early 1980s, most of the original council members as well as the King had died, and no one could provide an authoritative answer. Another problem concerned how deceased council members were to be replaced (criteria and procedure for selection). After council members had died, replacements had been made, but power balances had become increasingly fragile. Disputes about council responsibilities and composition became so severe that the King's plan for creating a model township seemed doomed.

Although many current residents of Kwaluseni praise the township for its convenient location near Manzini and for its provision of services, such as electricity and piped water, they also uniformly condemn the township for giving rise to a host of problems barely known in the traditional rural homestead, such as crowded living conditions, high crime rate, litter and proliferation of *shebeens* (beer establishments). These people usually state that the revered King had the right idea in forming a local council to oversee the township, but that greed, an over-abundance of 'important' (traditional and new elite) settlers, and wilful misinterpretation of the King's original intentions, had destroyed the township's early potential. Some residents – mostly earlier rather than later or foreign settlers – also express doubt that a concentrated settlement is desirable, since, in their view, cattle husbandry and agricultural activities are better suited by traditional scattered homestead arrangements.

Many Swazis around the country are aware of the problems faced by Kwaluseni residents, and nearly everyone seems to agree that many changes must be made in the community. Unfortunately, few people agree either about the proposed changes or the political structure in which to achieve such changes. The King had been approached many times before his death with pleas to alleviate the political and economic crisis faced by Kwaluseni, and he had promised to provide a framework. His death in 1982 left the problem unsolved and created, in the words of one informant, a 'political vacuum'. Stated otherwise, no one was clearly authorized to take over control of Kwaluseni, but many people seemed willing to do so. Currently, princes, long-time residents and new residents are all vying for control.

Land disputes in Kwaluseni are strongly influenced by the political dispute for control of land and development administration. This dispute currently takes place on two levels: on the one hand, between a faction consisting of new elites and a faction consisting of hereditary princes, and on the other, between the Kwaluseni community and the Zombodze royal kraal, the area administrative centre. Kwaluseni residents, as participants in national ritual and as part of the national political framework, adhere to harmony ideologies: the problem is that local factions compete to interpret harmony ideologies according to their political interests (see Map 12).

Local court

At the time of my first visit to Kwaluseni village in 1984, the local council had split according to political factions. Residents commonly designated one council as the 'newcomers' council, which met in Kwaluseni village and was comprised largely of newcomers to the area, and designated the other as the 'originals' council, which met in Embikwakhe and was comprised largely of princes and early settlers.[7] The newcomers council claimed that the King had authorized them to handle both land distribution and development, whereas the originals council claimed that the newcomers were only authorized to handle development and that they (the originals) were supposed to distribute land. The newcomers council also claimed that the King had granted them autonomy from Zombodze, a claim which Zombodze dismissed.

Similar to Zombodze, land disputes frequently came before the newcomers and originals councils, although unlike in Zombodze, land disputes in Kwaluseni involved almost exclusively the litigant dyads of family member vs. family member and subject vs. subject. In some Kwaluseni land disputes,

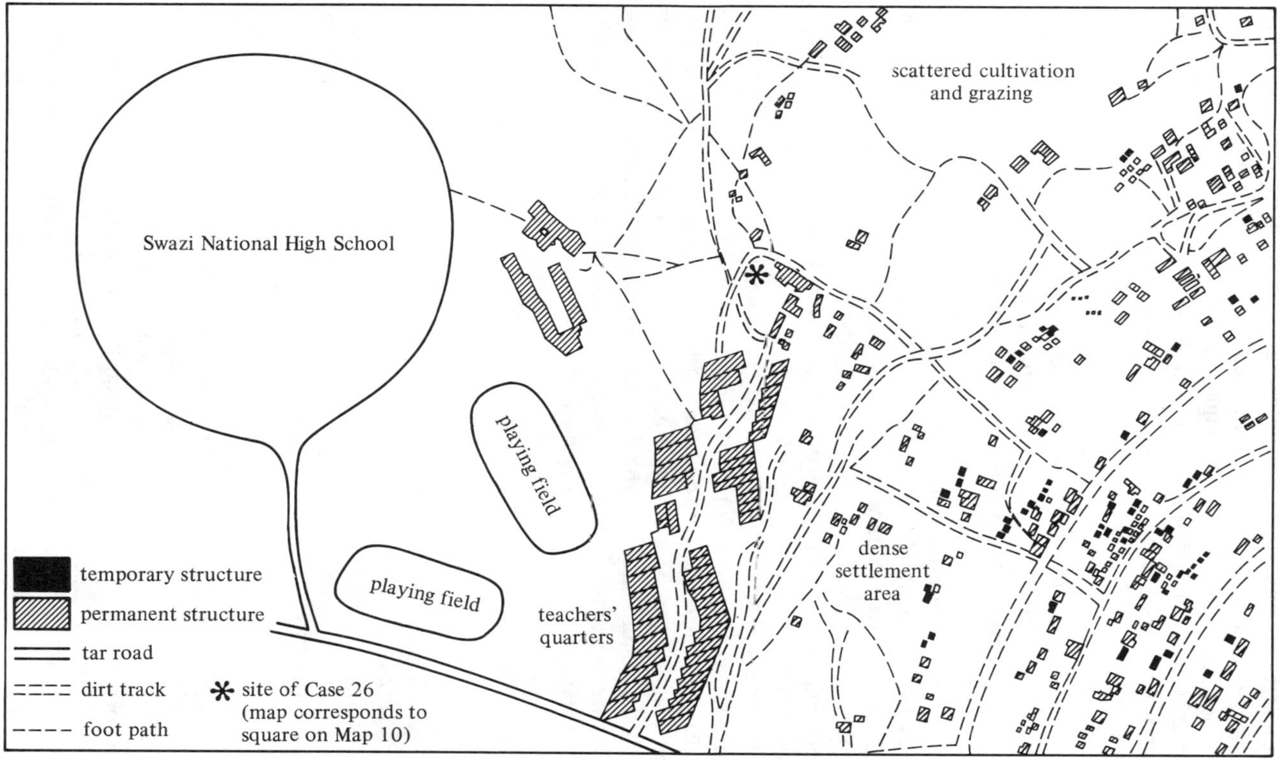

Map 12 Kwaluseni village

residents questioned the legitimacy of the newcomers council (subject vs. 'chief' dyad).

The Kwaluseni newcomers council, which tended to be more active than the originals council, can be described according to general and specific features. Regarding general features, it is unlike the usual Swazi chief's council in that all men are supposed to act as equals. There is no chief or deputy, but various men assume positions of council chairman, secretary, treasurer and messenger(s). The procedural format followed by the newcomers council (presentation of argument by litigants, discussion by public, decision-making by council and enforcement of decision) is similar to that followed by chiefs' councils.

The Kwaluseni 'Court' (i.e. meeting of newcomers council), like the Zombodze Court, can be described according to specific features of public attendance patterns and socio-economic characteristics of personnel. Although specific features are always defined by each particular court, such features were strikingly unique in the Kwaluseni Court. Between December 1985 and July 1986, an average of fifteen persons attended each meeting, although on one occasion 150 persons attended. Poor attendance was probably attributable to the political dispute in the area. Most spectators were local residents or outsiders who wanted to obtain land in the area. Unlike in Zombodze, seasonal changes, which demand variable agricultural responsibilities, did not prevent Kwaluseni town dwellers from attending.

Approximately eight to twelve men were members of the council, but it was difficult to establish an accurate number since members were constantly dropping out and new ones being added. The council members appeared to be socially equal in that all were commoners. Two men were in their thirties or forties, several in their fifties, and only one or two over sixty. The council members were minimally differentiated from one another economically; 'wealth' was primarily derived through paid employment. Most of the Kwaluseni council members had attended school and nearly all were employed: at least one council member was a church minister, two owned local shops, one built houses, one was employed by a meat corporation and one was employed as a civil service driver. In crowded, land-hungry Kwaluseni, men could not easily have the traditional form of wealth in cattle or maize surplus.

The patterns of social and economic status in Kwaluseni contrasted with those prevailing in Zombodze, where at least one-half of the council members were royalty or closely tied historically to royalty, where the mean age of council members hovered around sixty, and where some council members derived their sole or primary income from rural homestead production (see Map 13).

In summary, Zombodze and Kwaluseni are representative communities in Swaziland to the degree that most types of customary land disputes occur in one or both communities, but they are non-representative as far as frequencies of dispute types. I will argue in Part II that the rural base in Zombodze, with its

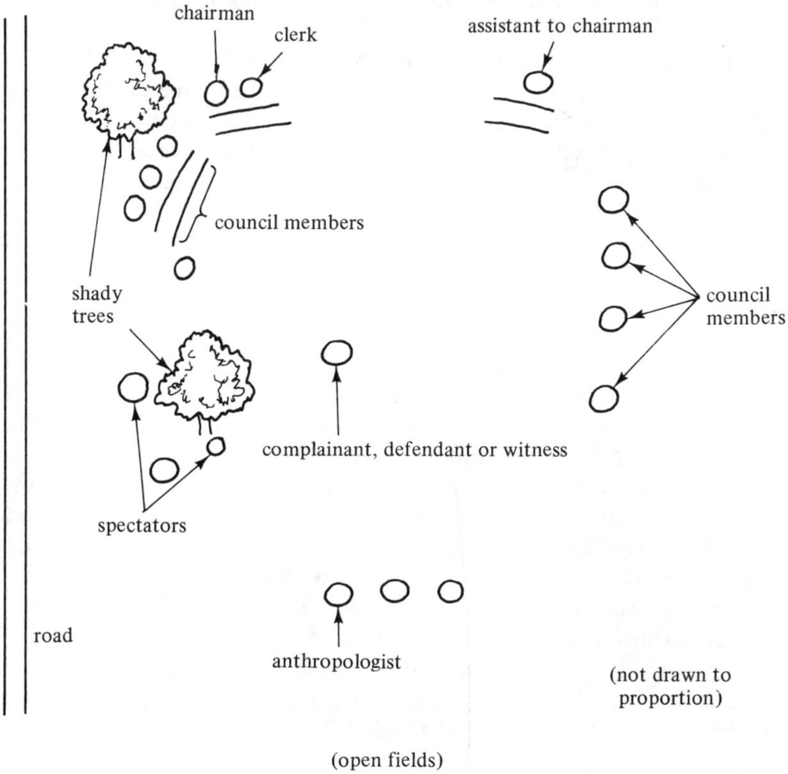

Map 13 Kwaluseni council session

more established population and council structure, gives rise to different interpretations of harmony than does the semi-urban base in Kwaluseni, with its new settler population and transitional council structure. In both Zombodze and Kwaluseni, disputants strategically produce and respond to harmony ideologies according to their interests in control, status or land rights.

Part II

Harmony and land

4

The politics of harmony: land dispute strategies

Law, ideologies and power

Law

Law has been defined as that which 'consists of general rules of external human action subject to enforcement by the coercive authority of the State or legal order' (Jacob 1986: 17; see also Rosenblum 1955: 2). In industrialized, complex states, 'the law' is recorded and widely understood as abstract, recorded ideas or values that derive legitimacy without obligatory reference to any individual. As a contrast, in developing countries such as Swaziland, subsystems of law, for example customary land law, may not be recorded and may be understood as ideas or values that derive legitimacy through reference to both cultural tradition and the stature of a particular individual or individuals. Customary law is instrumental to such individuals' interests and is enforced by them and their agents.

In Swaziland, customary law promulgated by chiefs receives legitimacy through reference to traditional values and practices and through reference to the right of the chief, as a hereditary ruler, to make and interpret law. The chief (assisted by his councillors and the local elite) serves as a legislator, executive and judge. As will be demonstrated in subsequent chapters, he imparts, particularly when charismatic, distinctive ideological colorations to due process and the rule of law, which may not prevail in another customary court. He has considerable discretion in deciding whether a grievance will be formally heard as a dispute, and in what type of customary legal forum this dispute will be heard. Thus, a disputant cannot appeal his case to the King or take it to a modern agency, such as *Ndabazabantu*, without the authorization of his chief. When law is so closely tied to individual powers in a customary legal system, such as that of the Swazis, primary political competitions occur within the immediate context of the local or national court, rather than outside the court, such as within a state legislature in a complex, industrialized society. Thus, general political and legal developments in Swaziland are strongly influenced by the specific operations of customary courts – i.e. interpretations of customary law by local Swazi authorities.

Ideologies

Political competitions occurring in the courts of all legal systems are characterized by the use of legal ideologies: law has been defined as 'ideological means of controlling social practice' (Sumner 1979: 267). Law is effective as an ideological force only insofar as it successfully constructs consensus outside itself in economic, political and cultural practices. Therefore, legal ideologies must be culturally constructed (see Werbner 1980), and they differ from ordinary ideology in that they are politically backed by the presence of a state/legal order which provides for sanctioning mechanisms. Legal ideologies legitimise the dual character of law, involving both coercion and consent (Hunt 1985).

Power

Legal ideology is closely related to power (Nader 1977; Nader and Serber 1976). Sumner has defined this relationship as follows: 'Law is not only ideology backed by instituted social power, it is also instituted social power articulated and reinforced by ideology' (1979: 265). In complex, stratified societies, law designates power relations in terms of general ideologies reflecting a social structure which divides people economically and politically (see Bendix 1953). As an instrument of power, law in such societies legitimizes the status quo and creates a structure of authority and property interest. Therefore, law is, among other things, an ideological instrument of the ruling class, imparting universal legitimacy to it and enabling political relations of domination to continue (Godelier 1982: 37; Sumner 1979: 275).

Legal discourse becomes instrumental to ruling class hegemony through its cultivated sacredness. Legal ideologies tell people what the world ought to be like, relying more on creating appearances than realities. The sacred, ideal nature of legal ideologies makes them meaningful to the general population, although they may serve the specific interest of the ruling class (see generally Ranger 1983). Thus, the paradox arises that law 'avoids the dirty images of politics and shares in its good side' (Sumner 1979: 276).

Godelier (1982: 38) comments that it is when ideologies 'do not appear to the exploited as illusions or as instruments of their exploitations that they contribute effectively in persuading these people to accept their exploitation'. This interpretation, like others (e.g. Hay 1975), implies that ideologies will be blindly accepted by those ruled when their exploitative nature is not understood, and will be ineffective when this nature is understood. In essence, it places the production and manipulation of ideologies in the hands of the rulers not the ruled.

In stratified Swazi society, ideology has been used until recently according to political rather than economic divisions. Ideologies have been used since the founding of the Swazi state in the eighteenth century, to support a hierarchy of political control associated with a largely egalitarian economy.

Therefore, the nature of stratification, as well as the state structure within which it occurs, are unlike European and American counterparts described by Bendix, Godelier, Sumner and others. Nonetheless, ideologies are used by a Swazi ruling elite (the royal Dlamini clan, closely affiliated clans and important territorial clans) to legitimate its power and create a structure of political authority.

If Swazi ideologies are viewed from the top-down (ruler–ruled) perspective as well as the bottom-up (ruled–ruler) perspective (see Nader 1984), interpretations and strategic manipulations of such ideologies by both Swazi elites and commoners become evident. Ideologies become transparent as a dual political strategy that is mediated through law and that is used by the rulers to cement their control and by the ruled to challenge this control (in the latter case through 'weapons of the weak'[1]). Despite Godelier's assumptions, the Swaziland data indicate that ideologies might be 'effective' – even when their 'exploitative' sides are understood by the ruled – because such ideologies serve some shared needs of rulers and ruled and because they can be manipulated by the ruled when their needs are not met.

Harmony ideology

Hay (1975: 55) argues that the effectiveness and endurance of an ideology is attributable to its elasticity and generality. It must be flexible enough to accommodate societal changes over time, and it must also be general enough to appeal to the populace while serving the specific goals of the rulers. Harmony ideology is one kind of ideology which is both elastic and general.

The meaning of harmony

Harmony was essentially a byword in early anthropological studies of law, although it was sometimes subsumed under different conceptual rubrics: for example, 'reciprocal obligations' (Malinowski 1926), 'balanced opposition' (Evans-Pritchard 1940) and 'making the balance' (Nader 1969). Reciprocity, according to Malinowski, meant achieving a mutual or cooperative interchange; balanced opposition, according to Evans-Pritchard, meant achieving equilibrium between opposed human forces; and making the balance, according to Nader, meant restoring relations to a former condition or to an ideal condition where conflict was absent. In all cases, the implication was that 'harmony' was present in relations characterized by reciprocity or balance.

Although the authors of early anthropological studies of law provided the framework for understanding harmony, they did not fully acknowledge, or even grasp, that notions of 'harmony' needed to be subjected to scrutiny and debate: from their perspectives, the presence or absence of harmony in observed proceedings was self-evident. Not until Starr and Yngvesson's paper on scarcity and disputing were questions raised about early models of harmony and interpretations of legal systems (1975; see also Greenhouse

1986; Nader 1990; Starr 1978a, 1978b). Starr and Yngvesson questioned whether the compromise model is inevitable if disputants are bound by multiplex ties, whether the compromise model is necessarily the main form of dispute management in face-to-face societies, and whether parties in face-to-face societies always accept balance and harmony. In fact, they argued that multiplex, ongoing relations are frequently not harmonious. They suggested that anthropologists would do better to ask about the nature of harmony and the relationship between disputing styles/outcomes and relative power. In subsequent writings, Nader (1990) noted that the idea of harmony must be broken into components in order to understand its origins, its uses and its consequences – its meaning and controlling power. In this regard, a question about harmony and controlling power, which has relevance both in the Swazi and the comparative context, may be posed: For whom is harmony achieved? The answer is investigated in this study with reference to analytic and informant perspectives of harmony.

Perspectives of harmony

A fundamental problem with the common analytic perspective is that it implicitly holds harmony, in the Durkheimian tradition, to be indicative of cultural adherence among cultural elements – something normal (Nader 1990). In other words, harmony ideologies, as interpreted by many scholars, imply that conflict is bad and its opposite is good. In fact, as discussed in the introduction, harmony is not necessarily 'good' or civilized, and conflict is not necessarily 'bad' or dysfunctional (Coser 1956; Simmel 1955). Both harmony and conflict can have 'good' or 'bad' consequences, depending on one's perspective (disputant, third party, outside observer). Nor is it objectively true that consensus has a greater survival value or that conflict inevitably poses a direct threat to group unity.

One needs to account for different perspectives of indigenous informants who interpret harmony and conflict. Harmony can come to mean what informants tell anthropologists it is. For example, Chanock (1985: 6), commenting on Marwick's account of the Chewa, and Starr and Yngvesson (1975: 554–7), commenting on Gluckman's account of the Lozi, indicate that the harmony ideologies enunciated by informants during dispute proceedings sometimes conflicted with practice, as evidenced by short-term outcomes and long-range consequences. Nonetheless, since the Chewa and Lozi conveyed a pervasive sense of harmony, the anthropologists transposed harmony from the realm of ideation to that of behaviour. Harmony can also mean what dominant 'outsiders' (e.g. colonialists) tell 'insiders' (e.g. indigenous populations) it should mean, what 'insiders' want such 'outsiders' to think it means, or what ruler 'insiders' (e.g. hereditary elites) want the ruled 'insiders' (e.g. commoners) to believe it means.

Analysis of informant relationships indicates that perspectives of harmony can be classified as offensive or defensive. From the offensive perspective, harmony advances the interests of the stronger party in a dyadic relationship, whereas from the defensive perspective, harmony protects the interests of the weaker party in a dyadic relationship. As an example of the offensive perspective, Nader's (1987, 1990) Zapotec research shows how colonialists used harmony ideology to suppress peoples. This perspective is taken by developers or colonialists who, possessing unilateral control, use harmony to advance their interests in relation to a 'recipient' culture. From the perspective of those persons holding superior power, harmony 'is an ideology of pacification and a way to civilize populations, a tool to create different cultural forms' (Nader 1987: 39). As an example of the defensive perspective, Nader's research also shows how the indigenous populations used harmony to resist external control. This perspective, a politics of adjustment and survival, is taken by the 'recipient' culture, which, believing that forces of disorder lie beyond their group boundaries, uses harmony ideology to present an image of peace (absence of conflict or irresolvable conflict), cohesiveness and accommodation to outsiders in order to maintain autonomy.[2]

The defensive perspective also emerges in intra-group relations, such as in developing, stratified societies, when traditional elites defend their interests against the expanding interests of new elites, and when commoners defend their interests against the prerogatives of traditional and new elites. Traditional elites may use harmony ideology to expand their private power in the name of the general good. Their strategies of harmony ideology are designed to dispel internal discontent with social/political arrangements and to foster the illusion that the socio-political system is 'working' and needs no interference/reform. In effect, their use of harmony ideology justifies current social arrangements, and in the process secures their own ruling class hegemony. Commoners respond to elites' strategies of harmony ideology in defence of their situational interests. Sometimes they initiate their own interpretations of harmony ideology. Harmony ideology may thus be used in two ways: by the rulers to defend or validate a legal/political superstructure of control, and by the ruled to defend or advocate an infrastructure of social relations. Harmony ideologies conveyed by the rulers are encapsulated within shared economic, political and cultural practices, whereas harmony ideologies manipulated by the ruled may be publicly accepted but strategically resisted in private practice (see Scott 1985).

Offensive and defensive uses of harmony, such as I will describe for the Swaziland context, have not been fully accounted for in the literature, although calls have been made for interactional models of law which attend to the impact of legal ideologies upon real people and real relations (Hunt 1985). In the past, studies which assessed jural norms frequently neglected ideological and social strategizing in dispute processes (Llewellyn and Hoebel's Cheyenne study 1941; see also Hoebel 1954), while studies which described individual strategizing, thus correcting the previous over-emphasis on harmony in small groups, under-reported normative foundations (Gulliver's Ndendeuli study 1971). Consequently, ideologies, such as that of harmony, were not conceptualized in terms of strategy configurations within the larger normative context. More needs to be known about the nature of normative structures, as they evolve under processes of legal codification, and about how indigenous populations respond to such processes – for what purposes and to what effects. If this information is assembled, members of such populations can be properly viewed, not as passive recipients of customarily evolving or introduced legal rules, but rather as creators of new legal forms. This type of analysis will clarify the linkage between imposed law and local level law, and can potentially take into account offensive and defensive aspects of harmony.

In this study of land disputes in Swaziland, political harmony at a national level is viewed as both the producer and product of individual strategies in local disputing processes. Dispute participants' strategies are informed by individual interests (personal options, aims and values) as well as by class interests (relative statuses and ranks). Both types of interests determine what each participant hopes to achieve in the short- and long-range outcomes of the dispute, and thus how he/she will produce and respond to harmony ideologies. Within the context of each case, harmony takes on different colorations according to the nature of the dispute and the status/control interests of the participants. It continuously evolves within various phases of a dispute, as participants compete to define shades of meaning. In effect, this interactional, multi-dimensional model of individual strategizing, which I propose, blends class interests within its rubric, revealing meanings and patterns of harmony in particular disputes and in wider socio-political competitions.

The principle of dispute containment

Despite the fluidity of meaning which harmony receives in each dispute case, it retains a widely understood and accepted meaning among Swazis. This meaning, which cuts across all individual and class differences, making harmony a shared cultural possession, expresses itself in dispute containment. The 'principle of containment' provides that all individuals will sacrifice their individual good to the extent that they will defend against incursions upon national integrity by foreigners or against destabilization of the hierarchy by ambitious Swazis. In abiding by the 'principle of containment', dispute participants seek to produce harmony through restricting cases to the lowest level of the hierarchy which has jurisdiction, thus averting intervention from higher levels and avoiding political competitions. A participant in the dispute process may attempt to advance private interests through assertive strategizing and dispute escalation, but this person may fail if the authorities successfully argue that individual interests have been promoted at the expense of hierarchical containment and thus political stability.

Organic and control harmony

In accordance with the assumption that harmony ideologies are derived from both normative and individual bases, I propose that Swazi authorities (elites) propagate two kinds of harmony. I designate these two kinds of harmony as organic and control (see Nader 1990).[3] Although some people might question the labelling of my interpretations with these terms, the terms convey subtle nuances I wish to contrast.

Statements about both organic and control harmony, as well as supportive case strategies, aim for dispute containment and stability in social/political relationships. However, organic and control harmony are not achieved in the same manner: differences arise in terms of how ideologies are internalized, the ends towards which ideologies are manipulated and the outcomes according to which ideologies are perpetuated.

Harmony that is organic, being rooted in social organization, is perceived as indigenously and fundamentally Swazi. Such harmony is the cultural backbone of social relationships. Organic harmony ideologies achieve consensus in social relationships through popular appeals to custom and shared values. Elite authorities perpetuate and propagate organic harmony ideologies by means of rhetoric in public arenas, particularly legal proceedings. These ideologies, being consensual, encourage a give and take in proceedings, with the consequence that all participants' strategies can be either initiative or responsive. The strategies thus interact on a horizontal plane of power. Elites' strategies of organic harmony focus as much on disputants' interests as on their own power interests; their strategies encourage dyadic dispute processing or dispute containment at the lowest possible level of the political hierarchy. Organic harmony strategies, which consider attitudes to be as important as behaviour in producing final outcomes, demand slow and careful deliberations. Such deliberations take into account long-range interests of all dispute participants as well as the society at large. The end results of a dispute in which organic harmony has been used achieve a considerable degree of consensus in attitudes as well as compliance in behaviour.

Harmony that is used as control has perhaps its strongest roots in the colonial, post-colonial and modern bureaucratic state. Such harmony is the behavioural backbone of political relationships. It is closely linked with both traditional and modern aspects of the hierarchical structure. Ideologies are used to control in the name of harmony when they derive their foundations from individual interests of elites, thereby seeking compliance in political relationships through power plays. Control harmony is thus constructed and contrived. Similar to organic harmony, elite authorities propagate and perpetuate harmony as control through rhetoric in legal processes. However, such harmony, being based upon power and force, tends to be one-sided (as opposed to balanced) in procedures. Since the elites' strategies initiate responses from commoners, interaction is on a vertical plane of power. Elites' strategies of control harmony focus primarily on their own power interests; such strategies encourage triadic dispute processing and dispute containment at that level which produces the greatest advantage to elites. Control harmony strategies, which consider behaviour to be more important than attitudes in producing final outcomes, rely upon indirect or manipulative argumentation. Deliberations primarily take into account short-term interests of elites, and outcomes, which are marked by winners and losers, are often produced rapidly in order to secure the status and control interests of elites. The end results of a dispute, in order to be characterized by control harmony, usually have achieved compliance in behaviour but little consensus in attitudes.

Internalization and manipulation of harmony

In this study, the harmony model is interpreted analytically as a belief system which is understood and generally accepted both by the Swazi rulers who produce it and by the Swazi commoners who consume it. In general, organic harmony ideologies are accepted by all Swazis as consensual tools for achieving larger social unity, whereas control harmony is accepted as a constructed, instrumental tool for achieving individual compliance in the interests of larger social and political unity. In specific cases, disputants quite probably believe that both organic or control harmony impede or contradict their interests, while the community accepts both kinds of harmony as means towards larger political interests. Statements about organic and control harmony use different means to legitimate the same outcome – appearances of 'harmony'. In particular, organic harmony ideologies use attitudinal persuasion to achieve agreement in feeling and action, while the exercise of control harmony relies upon physical coercion to achieve agreement in action only (unless, as some social psychologists argue, forced uniformity persuades people to think uniformly). The model thus adheres to a strict dictionary definition of harmony, allowing for both dimensions involving 'agreement in belief' as well as 'agreement in action', despite the tendencies of popular conceptions to emphasize the cultural and attitudinal aspect (organic) rather than the political and behavioural aspect (control).

As will be demonstrated in several case analyses, Swazi 'consumers' may buy harmony ideologies, particularly those supporting organic harmony, as interpreted by the rulers, but they manipulate such ideologies through strategies based upon situational variables. In this way, harmony ideologies underlie the ideal model of Swazi land administration (normative structure), while land dispute strategies serve as the nuts and bolts of actual land administration (expression of individual and group interests).

Gender and group interests determine, in part, specifically who is most likely to strategize, while immediate case circumstances, such as participants' status relationships, determine how they will strategize. Some disputant strategies pretend to approximate the ideal standards underlying harmony, whereas others contest and attempt to redefine such standards. Therefore, the elite rulers' and commoner subjects' interpretations of and responses to harmony ideologies interact and compete, infusing Swazi customary courts with a 'politics of harmony'.

The section which follows proposes five questions regarding the use of harmony ideology in Swaziland. These questions form the basis of data analysis in Part II.

1. What is harmony ideology(ies) and how does it serve the interests of Swazi hereditary elites?
2. Why is harmony ideology particularly important in the context of customary land disputes?
3. How do elites propagate harmony?
4. What kinds of strategies do Swazi elites use to propagate harmony and what kind of strategies do Swazi commoners use to manipulate harmony?
5. What classes of Swazi commoners are most likely to resist harmony ideology and under what conditions?

Swaziland as an example of harmony

1. The creation of a Swazi hierarchy: historical origins of harmony in Swaziland

The answer to the first question, 'What is harmony ideology(ies) and how does it serve the interests of the Swazi hereditary elite?', lies in analysis of the Swazi hereditary hierarchy of control. This hierarchy, which is supported by harmony ideologies regarding, for example, cultural/ethnic unity or common standards of morality, has served to consolidate and maintain powers of a Swazi ruling elite. The hierarchy provides the socio-political structure for interactions of 'political harmony'.

Dispute containment as a means to maintain hierarchical stability

As argued in Part I, the elites at the apex of the Swazi hierarchy have arguably used harmony ideology more effectively to preserve the integrity of the customary land tenure system than have elites of comparable socio-political structures in neighbouring African countries. A series of complex historical factors, including the charisma and longevity of former King Sobhuza, have contributed to the successful traditionalism of Swazi elites under colonialism. The Swazi hierarchy has succeeded in retaining and even expanding the powers of the King and chiefs (no Chieftaincy Act or Constitution) and in enlarging the customary land sector.[4]

One important way in which harmony has preserved the integrity of the Swazi customary land tenure system has been through dispute containment. Harmony, as conveyed by elites, incorporates a fundamental principle, referred to above as the principle of containment. This principle holds that disputes, particularly land disputes, should be contained at each level of the political hierarchy over which elites (family head, chief or King) ordinarily have jurisdiction. Dispute containment ensures the integrity of each level against outside interference, such as foreign developers, and discourages structural instability, thus class struggles. Individuals can usually be persuaded through ideologies backed up by sanctions to subordinate their perceived rights in deference to overall hierarchical stability and cultural continuity; however, they violate the containment principle when they choose to advance their causes through dispute escalation.

History of the Swazi hierarchy

A Swazi hierarchy of control was created during the seventeenth and eighteenth centuries by the dominant Dlamini clan. It did so through the amalgamation and ranking by conquest, treaty and peaceful incorporation of over seventy disparate, equal clans under a hereditary monarchy. The Swazi hierarchical ranking system came to consist of several units: the polygynous patriarchal family; the hierarchy of clans and lineages; the dual monarchy; the age grades; and the groups of specialists. According to anthropologist Hilda Kuper, rank became so pervasively intertwined within the Swazi social system that, for example, witches are organized in a hierarchical ranking of leaders and subjects, diviners are ranked in terms of abilities, and even the dead are buried according to complex rites recognizing rank (Kuper 1947a: 172, 166–72, 180; see also Gailey 1968; Hughes 1964c, 1972; Rosen-Prinz 1976).

In the early days of clan amalgamation, the Swazi hierarchy served to maintain centralized control over the structure of linked clans, while minimizing conflict among constituent clans. The stability of the ruling elite's control was achieved through a balance of power between the King, his mother, princes and commoners, as well as between the dual monarchy and the chiefs (Kuper 1947a: 46, 225; Hughes 1972: 250; Rosen-Prinz 1976: 55, 64, 71). The stability of the structure of linked clans was achieved through the creation of a system of age regiments and an administrative structure which included commoners as well as royal kin; age regiments and councils served as hierarchical 'leveling devices' (see Nader 1987: 12). Swazi hierarchy harmoniously blended authoritarian political privileges of birth with egalitarian participation in age classes and councils (Green 1984: 7; Davies et al. 1985: 37–44).

With the coming of Europeans in the late nineteenth century, a competition between two hierarchies developed: the traditional hierarchy, consisting of the ruling Dlamini clan and territorial chiefs, was forced to compete with a new, colonial administrative hierarchy. The new hierarchy, which was based upon colour discrimination and orientation towards the accumulation of wealth (Kuper 1947a: 229–30), presented an alternative basis of inequality and power. The result of competition between hierarchies was a dual political/legal system in which an individual might, in different contexts, be involved with either the traditional or introduced hierarchy. For example, if a

Swazi committed a crime such as murder, failed to pay his poll-tax or entered into a financial agreement with a non-Swazi, Roman-Dutch law, which was associated with the introduced hierarchy, operated. If he wanted land, or had a normal civil dispute with another Swazi, he was subject to traditional law and custom, which were administered by the traditional authorities. Nonetheless, the hierarchies were not kept distinct; there was always some overlapping of functions. In some situations, such as petty theft or minor assault, individuals could take complaints or cases either to the traditional or the territorial (colonial) authorities.

Resiliency of the Swazi hierarchy

Despite some overlap in functions, colonial authorities did not diminish the legitimacy of traditional authorities: the latter could not be identified as 'puppets of the colonial power' (Takirambudde 1983: 216). In the network of relationships brought about by the colonial presence, though the Swazi traditional leaders had lost their sovereignty, they were not directly associated with the colonial administrators. This fact placed national rulers of the Dlamini clan and territorial chiefs in a position of relative strength in their struggle for survival; they were not identified with the demands and evils of the colonial administrators. With the coming of Independence, the traditional authorities extended:

> the scope and power of tradition by virtue of the entrenchment and thus enhanced position of the Ngwenyama and the direct control of the state apparatus. The King was, as Vilakazi has correctly noted, at the top of both the traditional socio-legal order and the imported bureaucratic legal model. This configuration of power provides a clue as to the relative survival of the ideology of tradition and its influence in the legal sphere in post-colonial Swaziland. (Takirambudde 1983: 222)

The colonial authorities did not directly threaten the political control of the traditional ruling elite, and in fact supported the traditional hierarchy since it was perceived as friendly and well-ordered (Fransman 1978a: 28). Following Independence in 1968, a complex administrative system was fused together from parts of the dual hierarchy: on the one hand, traditional Swazi authorities, such as the King and chiefs, and on the other hand, colonial/post-Independence authorities, such as *Tinkhundla*, Parliament and government ministries (see Figure 3). Traditional authorities were not severely disabled by the new administrative/court system and the Swazi population was not resocialized to accept new institutions and foreign authorities (Doggett 1980: 41–2; Takirambudde 1983: 209–10).[5]

Threats to the Swazi hierarchy and protective responses

The more direct threat to traditional hierarchical arrangements came in the form of economic and social changes, ushered in alongside the Europeans' arrival. As discussed in Chapter 2, Europeans introduced Christian missions

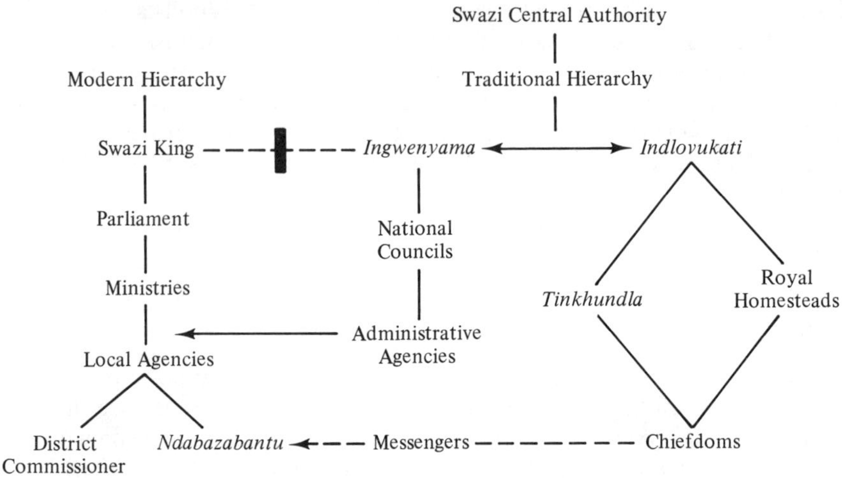

Figure 3 National administration

that taught values which sometimes conflicted with traditional values of kingship, such as those associated with rituals; they introduced a formal school system that provided new routes for attaining status; and they created skilled agricultural and civil service positions that gave rise to a new class of Swazi technocrats. These technocrats achieved status through wealth and attained positions in a modern bureaucracy. When Swazi commoners questioned customary values or obtained new wealth, and thereby status, the traditional patron–client system in which the traditional elites acted as patrons was destabilized (Sallinger-McBride and Picard 1984b: 33; see also Takirambudde 1983: 223). Russell (n.d.: 19) recognizes the threats incurred by recent changes when she asks, 'What are the implications of new stratification patterns for the older hierarchy?' Clearly, new categories of people were introducing new definitions of hierarchical harmony.

The current internal threat to the hierarchical structure of political relationships in Swaziland lies in several classes of people possessing inferior political power relative to their structural counterparts. One major class consists of women and another consists of new economic elites. Women's rights under customary law to positions of authority and land ownership are restricted, whereas new elites have all the modern advantages of wealth and education but cannot fully attain positions of authority in a system based on hereditary land control.

An interesting question concerns the measures taken by traditional Swazi elites to assert their control under changed economic and social conditions (see generally Levin 1985); such conditions challenge their ideological and instrumental control. For one, they have consciously and deliberately placed constraints and controls on processes of economic, social and legal change, particularly in the rural areas, in order to restrict the process of acculturation to foreign ways and thereby to minimize challenges to traditional values and their authority. As an example of such constraints and controls, they have attained political and economic power by permitting rural development programmes to progress, but only with the provision that committees be staffed by traditional elites. For another, they have attained economic power by assuming autonomous control without public accountability of the national corporation, Tibiyo. Most important, they have retained political power by controlling customary legal institutions, by banning political parties and by resisting legislation which would democratize the ruling national council and reduce the power of hereditary chiefs (Booth 1983a; Daniel 1983; Davies et al. 1985; Sallinger-McBride and Picard 1984b).

Sallinger-McBride and Picard explain what traditional political elites have done when faced with new threats to their control, particularly the possibility that individual land tenure would be introduced:

> There is little doubt that political elites see the idea of individual land tenure as threatening. The idea of permanent land tenure and the growing of cash crops are perceived as disturbing the right of avail on which Swazi society is based. Traditional elites see RDAs [Rural Development Areas], and the implicit assumption that changes in land tenure must accompany them, as threatening to the political fabric of society. In order to defend the patron–client system upon which political control in Swaziland is based, traditional elites have tried to manage the RDAs by ensuring centralized control over them and by trying to mitigate the social impact of the scheme at the grassroots level. As a result the developmental goals of an integrated rural development program came into direct conflict with the political concerns of Swaziland's ruling elite. (1984b: 35)

Despite the importance of concrete actions taken by traditional Swazi elites to overcome threats to their power, the most important actions have arguably been in the realm of ideology: elites have come to rely more manifestly on harmony ideologies, particularly those furthering control interests. Through harmony ideology they disseminate an image of order and efficiency. They also legitimize prevailing social relations. Harmony ideology therefore serves as a political strategy of survival which protects their hierarchical power-base from encroachments of 'superordinate powerholders and acts as a defence against organized subordinates' (Nader 1987: 25) – foreign developers and new elites. When Swazi elites successfully portray an image of harmony through rhetoric and dispute containment, they create the impression that they are in control and should not be interfered with. An image of harmony, which portrays decisions as balanced and fair, keeps ordinary Swazi citizens content with a system that is increasingly evolving in the direction of greater privilege for the Swazi royal family and hereditary elites: for example, the right to monetary tributes for land administration, economic advantage associated with large landholdings and greater access to government and civil positions. Citizens are persuaded through harmony ideologies that traditional elites must retain power if the viability of valued cultural traditions is to be preserved. Appearances of harmony keep development agents and technocrats content to accept minimal structural changes; they are led to believe that such changes are not desired by most Swazis and are not necessary. Nonetheless, harmony ideologies do not prevent people from strategizing behind the scenes to advance their interests. The elites do not hinder commoners' manoeuvres as long as everyone maintains an image of harmony and poses no direct threat to the elites' control.

2. *Harmony ideology and customary land law in Africa and Swaziland*

The answer to the second question, 'Why is harmony ideology particularly important in the context of customary land disputes?', must be investigated with reference to ideologies of land, the land hierarchy and the nature of land disputes. Harmony ideologies support a hierarchical political structure which, in turn, derives validity from land control. Harmony ideologies also diminish threats posed by land disputes to political control. Chanock notes that African political hierarchies derive authority from land:

> we must be clear that we are dealing not simply with a question of morals, kinship and family law, but with the control of labour, with rights to land and the transformation of a system of production . . . It was this that gave substance to the respect which we shall see was so jealously guarded by elders and chiefs (1985: 16).

Ideologies of land

In Swaziland, as elsewhere in Africa, land is deeply ingrained in the historical consciousness of people. In the past, it was overlaid with symbolic perceptions of protracted struggles against a colonial power. In modern times, it has become a measure of political power and citizenship in a young nation. Land lies at the heart of Swazi ideology, and customary land tenure is associated with a valued cultural system. As Hilda Kuper explains, Swaziland's customarily tenured land serves a variety of economic, social and ritual functions:

> They [the Swazis] won their subsistence from the soil, their major rituals were directed to increase its yield, the land was ritually identified with the King, with prosperity, health, and power, it was a focal point of national sentiment. To lose their land struck at the roots of their economic and political system (1947a: 74; see also Doggett 1980: 47; Russell 1983: 21–2).

Swazi ideologies of land, as expressed by persons occupying various positions in the traditional land hierarchy, support customary land tenure and discredit individual land tenure. The ideologies emphasize that customary land tenure is the source of desired national harmony and unity. They are largely propagated by the Swazi traditional elite in the context of, for example, customary court sessions or national meetings and rituals.

One ideology of land states that customary land tenure, as opposed to individual land tenure, ensures land access to everyone according to need (landlessness does not exist, except temporarily; Russell 1985). This ideology overlooks the fact that land is largely distributed according to considerations of hereditary rank or reputation. Another ideology states that development for everyone can be accomplished within the customary land tenure structure. This ideology belies the fact that the hierarchical structure of customary land tenure ensures that some individuals or groups will have access to better land, will have greater land security and will have at their disposal better material means for achieving development objectives. A third ideology states that continuation of the customary land tenure system is necessary for the preservation of national unity. This ideology overlooks the ordinary Swazi's occasional resentment of traditional authorities' demands for tribute offerings and labour. Tribute labour is sometimes viewed by Swazis as a compulsory service rendered for individual profit rather than a unified effort to promote national welfare.

The land hierarchy

In his study of customary land tenure, A. J. B. Hughes described how land is the ideological cement which cohesively organizes Swazi society into a 'hierarchy of land communities' (Hughes 1972: 67). Hughes explains that Swazis are bonded together in a homestead, the lowest level of the land community hierarchy, by kinship and territorial propinquity. He explains further that Swazis are bonded together by common political allegiances and territorial propinquity at higher levels in the land hierarchy. At each level of the land community hierarchy, different authorities who control land rights emerge: the homestead head at the homestead level, the headman-in-council at the ward level, the chief-in-council at the chiefdom level, and the Central Authority (King, Queen Mother and national council) at the national level. In effect, land bonds people together at various levels of the hierarchy. The Swazi 'traditional ideology' reflects that the King 'owns' and distributes land to constituent chiefs and that commoners have the right to receive land from the chief to whom they pledge allegiance.[6] Colonial legal imposition in the late nineteenth century impinged upon the autonomy of the Swazi King, but as Swazi Nation Land was left to traditional management, traditional rulers maintained effective land control.

As explained in Chapter 1, the Land Partition of 1907 created two land hierarchies: European freehold settlers controlled about two-thirds of the territory and the Swazi majority controlled only about one-third of the territory. The Swazi leaders and their subjects never accepted the Partition and over the years waged a struggle to regain land control. In this struggle to regain lost land, the Swazi traditional rulers played a dominant role – petitioning the colonial metropole, waging judicial battles, collecting funds for purchasing lost lands, placing the repurchased land under traditional control and ignoring land use recommendations of technocrats. The traditional leaders played a major role because of the 'centrality of the land issue in the Swaziland traditional ideology' (Takirambudde 1983: 219–20) and because 'the control of land was so critical to the traditional hierarchy and its supporting value system [that] nothing ought to be done lest it might erode such control' (Takirambudde 1983: 223–4).[7]

In modern-day Swaziland, traditional authorities continue to control the customary land hierarchy. Consequently, although customary land law has been affected by actions of the colonial administration, such as the introduction of freehold land tenure and a market-based economy, and although it is affected by modern-day government policy, such as the introduction of rural development programmes, customary Swazi authorities continue to maintain autonomous control over land. In effect, land law is one of the best preserved and distinct areas of customary law.

The nature of land disputes

Since land forms the common, shared idiom of Swazi ideology and the foundation of Swazi hierarchy, it stands to reason that land disputes are an important, although not the only, impediment to Swazi traditional elites' efforts to retain power.[8] Disputes, in general, are tied to political power; they are frequently used by individuals or groups to test status and to attain relative power.[9] Land disputes, in particular, are good indicators of power competitions, particularly when power over people is bound to land control. Land disputes are also good indicators of societal stress, particularly in situations of economic change.[10] Throughout Africa, land disputes have threatened, at worst, to splinter delicately forged national unity, or at best, to cause devolution of power from national leaders to regional leaders (chiefs or headmen). Moreover, land disputes in Africa have sometimes destabilized the position of chiefs: on the one hand, they have enabled chiefs to attain power and gain prestige when they were able successfully to wrest land control from other chiefs and when they were able to control effectively their subjects' land matters. But, on the other hand, when chiefs have lost land through inter-chieftaincy disputes or have failed to control their subjects' land disputes, their power has been jeopardized.[11]

Land disputes in Swaziland could in past times, as throughout Africa (West 1971), be resolved by chiefly acquisition of new lands or by commoners transferring allegiance to new chiefs. Following the arrival of European settlers, cash crops and a market economy were introduced, imbuing customarily tenured land with new value as a means for achieving status and material wealth. At the same time, Swazi population growth put increased pressure on customarily tenured land that had been significantly reduced in area by colonial land policy (Gina 1984: 3; Kuper 1947b: 3–8), thereby encouraging not only labour migration but also land disputes among Swazis and between Swazis and Europeans. Inter-chieftaincy disputes broke out when some chiefs lost more land than other chiefs and consequently were unable to satisfy the land hunger of current subjects or attract new followers. Disputes between chiefs and their subjects erupted because some families had to move into areas controlled by chiefs other than their own. Disputes between chiefs' subjects and European farm owners broke out when boundaries, or even legitimacy of land divisions, were contested. Disputes among a chief's subjects broke out because overcrowding in reserves increased competition for land (Kunene 1982a: 49–50; Russell n.d.: 7; Scott 1951: 438). A chief's subjects disputed about traditional problems concerning land transfers (loans and grants), land inheritance and boundaries; but they also disputed about new problems of self-allotment of land and women's land rights. In sum, leaders disputed with one another over land administrative rights, subjects disputed with their leaders over land access rights, and subjects disputed with one another over land use rights. Disputes under changed circumstances were blamed by Swazis, as they were blamed by other Africans, for reduced cooperation among kin, competition between neighbours, increased social differentiation, landlessness and corruption.[12]

In recent times, land disputes in Swaziland can no longer be alleviated by chiefly acquisition of new lands or by commoners transferring allegiance to new chiefs; land is in short supply and land rights are unclear.[13] Therefore, land disputes currently threaten traditional elites' efforts to portray a picture of harmonious land management activities in three ways: they are more socially disruptive than most other kinds of disputes; they have become more frequent and complex; and they cannot be quickly and satisfactorily resolved by customary legal institutions and customarily empowered authority figures.

If the proliferation and disruptiveness of land disputes threatens Swazi rulers' strategy of projecting an image of an efficient, harmonious land tenure system, then land disputes must be solved, denied or downplayed. The survival of the customary hierarchical structure of land administration depends upon this. Since the first option, solving land disputes, is the root of the problem, Swazi authorities at each hierarchical level (national, chiefdom, family) must deny or downplay land disputes. They rely on harmony ideologies to contain disputes at each hierarchical level, thus avoiding interference from non-Swazi administrators at the national level, from national authorities at the chiefdom level and from chiefdom authorities at the family level. Consequently, the paradox arose, as referred to in the Introduction, that Swazis, when questioned about land disputes, often denied the existence of those disputes which had been – or should have been (owing to disruptiveness) – contained.

3. Propagation of harmony ideology in Swaziland

The answer to the third question, 'How do elites propagate harmony?', lies in analysis of the methods used by the hereditary elite to convey their conceptions of harmony – how they render ideological conceptions concrete (see Hunt 1985: 33). The work of Comaroff (1975, 1978a) in Botswana and Perry (1981) in Lesotho provide an important clue: the role of political oratory. Comaroff demonstrates how political oratory among the Tswana is used, on the one hand, to legitimate and reinforce ideologies and, on the other, to evaluate the political performance of particular actors. In the context of customary land law, Perry illustrates how oratory can be used by chiefs in Lesotho to manipulate beliefs about legitimate authority for land matters and to gain control over land. Oratory is thus strategically used in Botswana and Lesotho by those competing for power as a tool of political manipulation, whereas it is used by spectators of the political process as an evaluative code. In other words, oratory, or rhetoric, serves as 'the vehicle by which the message [of elites] is rendered into a social construction upon reality [of the masses]...' (Schieffelin in Nader 1990). From the perspective of the social scientist, the ideological content of oratory serves as 'an index of the state of power relations at any time' (Comaroff 1975: 160), but oratory ('speech acts') must be analysed in context to reveal the constituent ideological elements (Hunt 1985: 33).

Laura Nader (1987) specifically links rhetoric in disputing processes with the production of harmony when she writes about 'the language of disputing' in Zapotec courts:

> the harmony model reflects less attention to the facts of specific cases than to the language of disputing in the village court as opposed to that used in state courts. Through their ideology of harmony villagers create an image of their society as cohesive and independent and thus fend off the outside world (Nader 1987: 23).

Harmony ideology supports norms of local equity and national unity. Therefore, Swazi authorities state, in the context of speeches made at customary legal proceedings and at national meetings and rituals, that customary legal and political institutions ensure equal participation, fair hearings and negotiated outcomes. They also state in church services that respect of authority and peaceful social relations ensure continuation of the Swazi way of life.

When Swazi elites propagate organic harmony ideology, they produce consensus through support of shared customs and values, and when they propagate harmony as control, they produce compliance through reliance upon external, and sometimes forceful, power plays. Organic harmony ideology is supported by specific statements about traditional status, sacred kingship, ethnic identity, custom and morality – all of which define inherent structural controls upon Swazi social relations. Control harmony is supported by statements about absolute power, threat of sanctions, reliance on modern authorities and intervention of a Christian God – all of which define external political controls upon Swazi social relationships.

4. *Strategic responses to harmony in Swaziland*

The answer to the fourth question, 'What kinds of strategies do Swazi elites use to propagate harmony and what kind of strategies do Swazi commoners use to manipulate harmony?', lies in systematic categorization of strategies. Most Swazis, including elites and commoners, recognize the validity of harmony ideologies in maintaining cultural cohesion and continuity, particularly in the land tenure system, under real or potential threats from local and foreign development interests. Therefore, when pursuing individual status and case interests, elites and commoners use strategies which downplay the structural strains inherent in the traditional hierarchical system of land control. In this way, they convey the appearance of a working system.

Strategizing about land rights

Elites and commoners use strategies to manipulate harmony ideologies and associated land rights. Their strategies compete either to protect elites' land administration rights or to maintain commoners' land use rights. Elites and commoners may invoke harmony in land dispute procedures through the rhetoric of their strategies, but in practice, they transform such procedures into competitive and interactive political processes. Elites' strategies ordinarily seek containment of land dispute either at a lower level or at the same level of the political hierarchy within which they exercise jurisdiction over causes and persons. Commoners' strategies, particularly those of persons in structurally weak positions relative to their opponents – such as women or new elites – seek hearings of land disputes by alternative forums which are presided over by members of other levels of the political hierarchy; commoners expect to get more impartial or favourable judgements in such forums. The conflict between elites' concerns with dispute containment and disputants' (occasional) concern with case transference to another forum creates stress in the dispute-processing system. Harmony ideology – again, the ideology of reconciliation and balance – serves to smooth over this stress, although sometimes through merely rendering the appearance of harmony. Therefore, when used effectively by elites, harmony ideology persuades commoners to accept dispute processing and outcomes in the elites' chosen forums, or alternatively, when manipulated effectively by commoners, it improves their outcomes in the forums chosen by elites or even permits them to select disputing methods and forums.

Elites' strategies

As explained above, elites conceptualize harmony as a tool to maintain internal coherence and avert outside intervention, thus ensuring their power. In their roles as authorities acting before customary legal forums, they perpetuate harmony ideologies through public ritual, religious practices and political rhetoric. They manipulate such ideologies through organic and control strategies which assert perceived land administration rights.

Elites produce or perpetuate harmony ideology for the purpose of legitimating and strengthening their perceived rights of land administration. In the context of disputes, elites, acting as authorities with the power of the

Swazi state behind them, use strategies which emphasize the cultural importance of harmony and their success in achieving it. If they can render the appearance of harmonious dispute processes and outcomes, they have demonstrated their effective administration and thereby validated their performances.

Elites' strategies thus involve definition and interpretation of harmony ideologies. As explained above, organic harmony strategies make statements about the elites' customary rights of land administration, including the moral basis for commoners' respect of their authority and the historical basis of their authority. Elites usually rely upon such strategies when they wish to encourage consensus through disputant negotiation and reconciliation, rather than produce compliance through third-party intervention. When third-party intervention cannot be avoided, elites procure testimony and evidence as fairly as possible and delay decision-making, in order to achieve equitable outcomes which protect the long-term interests of all parties to a dispute.

Control harmony strategies also refer to the elites' customary rights of land administration. However, elites rely upon such strategies when they feel compelled to produce compliance through forceful intervention of third parties (including police and urban bureaucrats,) or denial of forums, rather than produce consensus through negotiation and reconciliation. Elites tend to make rapid decisions in order to protect their immediate status and control interests.

Commoners' strategies

Commoners, on the other hand, conceptualize harmony as a tool to maintain cultural/social continuity, thus ensuring continuation of a valued life-style. They usually perpetuate harmony ideologies in informal, private practices. They manipulate such ideologies through assertion, avoidance and deception strategies which assert perceived land use rights.

Commoners respond to harmony ideology in several ways. In public, they espouse the intrinsic value of harmony; in this way, they convey the image that they are 'good' Swazis, thus peaceful and law-abiding. In the context of disputes, they usually support the authorities' interpretations of harmony, but they also use strategies to manipulate (maintain or acquire) land use rights. Ideally, they try to achieve the appearance of a harmonious life-style and dispute-processing style in order to gain widespread support for their immediate causes, but sometimes they may even use strategies to protest dominant or pervasive harmony ideologies, initiating their own interpretations. In any case, their strategies demonstrate that the reportedly conservative and powerful structure of administration by elites in Swaziland merely constitutes a normative structure which can be manipulated in many ways for many purposes.

Commoners' strategies thus involve either active interpretation and even production of harmony ideologies, or passive response and resistance to harmony ideologies. Active strategies involve *assertion* of perceived land rights before authorities/legal forums responsible for customary land administration. Passive strategies involve either *avoidance* of authorities/legal forums in which perceived land rights might be contested or *deception* of authorities/legal forums about the validity of land rights.

Commoners use assertion strategies when they choose to take private action against their opponents or to argue their customary land use rights before customary institutions. They try to control a situation by recruiting allies or by assuming individual control on the basis of personal attributes.

Commoners use avoidance strategies when they choose to avoid individuals or customary institutions which normatively decide upon customary land use rights. Such individuals and institutions are suspected of being unsympathetic and likely to deny their perceived land rights. Sometimes commoners seek alternative individuals or institutions to handle their disputes, thus violating harmony ideologies which promote containment or dispute resolution within responsible hierarchical levels.

Commoners use deception strategies when they choose to make false claims about land rights or lie about their personal status (e.g. marital status). They exaggerate or falsify land claims in order to win their case or invalidate their opponent's claims, thus protecting current claims or securing new claims.

In effect, elite authorities' harmony strategies are closely linked to their status/control interests. At the same time, disputants' assertion strategies make open, public statements about their perceived land rights – thus involving either compromise with or challenge of the authorities' harmony strategies or general control, whereas their avoidance and deception strategies usually make indirect manoeuvres to secure their perceived land rights – thus involving evasion of the authorities' harmony strategies and control (see Table 1).

5. *Harmony ideology and strategies in Swazi land dispute processes*

The answer to the fifth question, 'What classes of Swazi commoners are most likely to resist harmony ideology and under what conditions?', lies in examination of strategies used by Swazi subjects in land dispute contexts. Subjects who appear particularly likely to resist harmony ideology, as interpreted by the elites, are some women and new elites who occupy positions of powerlessness relative to traditional elites or men. Their strategies are important 'weapons' against power differentials (Scott 1985), but all the more so, given the pervasiveness and penetration of harmony ideology. As their disputes challenge status considerations associated with land administration and usufructuary rights, they are particularly threatening to maintenance of hierarchical stability. In effect, their disputes both reflect power struggles between individuals and social classes (see Starr and Yngvesson 1975: 563) as well as baldly illuminate the structural stresses emerging from such struggles.

Table 1. *Swazi elites' and commoners' strategies*

Actor	Swazi elites	Actor	Swazi commoners
Manipulation		Manipulation	
organic harmony strategies	1. *rules* – make statements about customary rights of land administration, including moral basis of commoners' respect for authority and historical basis of authority 2. *procedures* – avoid third-party intervention, but if necessary, procure testimony and evidence fairly and seek reconciliation 3. *outcomes* – delay decision-making to encourage reconciliation, but when necessary, recommend negotiation	assertion disputing strategies	1. *rules* – argue or seek clarification of customary rights of land use 2. *procedures* – acknowledge or accuse opponent privately of wrongdoing; take private action against opponent; approach third party or public forum with complaints (e.g. family head, chief's council, Magistrates' Court)
		avoidance disputing strategies	1. *rules* – avoid public confrontation about rights 2. *procedures* – take independent, evasive action; avoid people or institutions unfavourable to cause; seek assistance of 'alternative' people or institutions (distant kin, chief other than one's own, diviner, etc.)
control harmony strategies	1. *rules* – make statements about perceived rights of land administration, enforcing such statements with power plays 2. *procedures* – deny litigants access to forum of full hearing and prevent intervention of 'outside' authorities – except for enforcement or confirmation of own power 3. *outcomes* – avoid negotiation and support land rights of privileged persons through implied or actual threats (police and urban bureaucrats)	deception disputing strategies	1. *rules* – make false statements about land rights in order to protect current claims or lie about personal status (e.g. marital) in order to secure new claims 2. *procedures* – use deceitful tactics (e.g. deny true charges or falsify evidence) in order to win case or invalidate opponent's claims

When women or new elites have land-related grievances, they are usually not granted free and easy access to standard customary legal forums (e.g. family or chiefs' councils); rather, they must process their grievances by avoidance (of unsympathetic people and institutions) and 'lumping' behaviour. For example, they may resort to modern legal and administrative agencies. Such disputing activity renders their complaints 'invisible' (i.e. non-existent in customary framework) and thus non-threatening to hierarchical arrangements. On the other hand, disputes between persons bonded by equal positions of power are ordinarily not threatening. Consequently, classes of people, such as brothers or male neighbours, are granted more open access to customary legal forums and public processing of their grievances by adjudication or negotiation.

Both women and other classes of dissatisfied subjects who are not granted easy access to customary forums for processing their land grievances, can manipulate harmony ideology to make their disputing activities seem less threatening to customary hierarchical stability. They speak about harmony to create the image that reconciliation between conflicting interests has occurred and that the Swazi hereditary elite have not relinquished control. When they choose to challenge the elites' specific case strategies or general control, they use strategies to cloak their arguments in customary land tenure norms (see Comaroff and Roberts 1977, 1981; Perry 1981) and thereby strengthen their disputing legitimacy (e.g. gain access to disputing forums) and produce favourable outcomes.[14] In effect, persons occupying positions of weakness (status and power) relative to either authorities or their opponents manipulate harmony ideology and associated strategies to overcome customary structural rigidities and to promote new practices, just as the traditional elite use it to contain disputes and thus maintain hierarchical continuity and stability.[15]

Summary

Most Swazis subscribe to harmony ideology. Harmony ideology is the cement which promotes unusual social solidarity and ethnic identity in a situation of change.

Traditional hereditary elite (royal family and chiefs) propagate harmony ideology, primarily through political oratory and ceremony, for the purpose of legitimating their administrative roles and validating their performances. They do so to maintain internal cohesion and to ward off threats of external interference (e.g. from land development agents.) They propagate two kinds of harmony: organic harmony which achieves consensus through reference to customary values, and control harmony which achieves compliance through power plays. In the context of customary land disputes, harmony ideology is particularly useful to the elites in that it serves to downplay disruptions which could threaten their power-base centred on land control.

Swazi commoners accept harmony ideology because it originally served to unify disparate, warring clans in the eighteenth century and later to challenge and overcome the threats imposed by European culture contact and land deprivation in the nineteenth and twentieth centuries. However, they use strategies to manipulate organic harmony and to resist control harmony in specific cases. Both kinds of harmony influence who strategizes and the form which their strategies take.

Swazi land disputants who occupy weaker positions relative to their opponents, such as women and new elites (weakness defined by sex and birthright), rely on assertion, avoidance and deception strategies according to the control interests of the authorities and their own status relative to their opponents. In this way, they gain power to dispute and consequently achieve their aim of reaffirming or enhancing their land rights. Women use all types of strategies in disputing about usufructuary rights, whereas new elites primarily use assertion strategies in disputing about administrative rights. Women's and new elites' strategies are essential to their causes, since their disputes, more than those involving equals, challenge status differentials inherent in customary hierarchical political arrangements.

Traditional elites' propagation of harmony ideology and commoners' strategic responses to harmony ideology produce a 'politics of harmony' in Swazi land dispute processes.

5

Land dispute cases in the Swazi hierarchy

Background

This chapter deals with the widest range of power and status relationships in Swaziland's customary land control hierarchy. By means of observed and elicited land dispute cases, it illustrates how procedure and outcome are linked to position in hierarchy.[1] Moreover, it argues that harmony ideologies are used by authorities to justify procedures and outcomes. In effect, while authorities strategically use harmony ideologies to legitimate dispute-processing methods, thus reinforcing their control, case litigants strategically respond to harmony ideologies according to their immediate case needs. The power plays underlying the officials' and disputants' strategizing behaviour in each case produce a 'politics of harmony' in which all participants in a dispute struggle for validation of their interests – enhanced status and favourable dispute outcomes.

Swazi disputants' hierarchical status relationships are defined in this chapter according to a dyadic model of social and political relationships which are forged at different levels of the land community: family members with one another in a homestead; subjects with one another in a chiefdom; subjects with their chiefs to whom they pledge allegiance; and chiefs with the Central Authority (ruling Dlamini clan) to whom they pledge allegiance.[2] My interpretation of the dyadic model, which delineates six Swazi disputant dyads, well suits my main analytic goal of correlating disputants' relative statuses with their disputing styles, which involve strategy use.

Disputing styles are primarily characterized by disputants' strategic use of procedures and forums (Nader 1969). Swazi disputants rely on several kinds of disputing procedures: 'lumping it', avoidance, negotiation, mediation, arbitration and adjudication (Nader and Todd 1978: 8–9). They also rely on several forums for processing their disputes: on the customary side, the family council, chief's council, *Ndabazabantu*, Swazi (Nation) Court, Swazi Court of Appeal, Higher Swazi Court of Appeal, Judicial Commissioner's Court and King's Council; on the European-influenced side (Roman-Dutch law), the Magistrates' (Subordinate) Courts, High Court and Court of Appeal.

As indicated, disputing styles, i.e. disputants' choices of procedures and forums, are primarily influenced by disputants' relative personal and structural statuses in hierarchical Swazi society. These statuses consist of ascribed and achieved aspects. Ascribed aspects of status concern hereditary structural inequalities in the Swazi hierarchy. Therefore, some dyadic relationships in the hierarchy, such as that of subject with chief, define political relationships between structural unequals. Achieved aspects of status concern individual inequalities. Some dyadic relationships, such as that of subject with subject, define political relationships between equals who may or may not be social unequals depending on individual achievements.

In the section which follows, causes and outcomes of disputes as well as characteristics of disputants are described for the purpose of demonstrating the full range of disputant status relationships and customary disputing styles. In the subsequent section, eighteen land dispute cases are presented according to six disputant dyads. The strategies used by different parties in each dispute are delineated and compared, thus demonstrating the processes by which participants' status relationships produce disputing styles.

Total case sample analysis

The total case sample consists of over 200 cases collected through interviews[3] and attendance at Chiefs' Courts in twenty areas throughout Swaziland. Because the case data obtained through interviews vary greatly in quality, only 139 cases from the two courts of Zombodze (92 cases) and Kwaluseni (47 cases), which were visited on a regular basis between 1985–6, are analysed in Tables 2–4. Table 2 handles the causes of grievances, Table 3 the outcomes of grievance and Table 4 litigant characteristics. I personally witnessed about 80 to 90 per cent of the 139 cases. The tables answer three questions: What are the major causes and outcomes of disputes? What are the status relationships between disputants? and What are the differences in dispute configurations (disputant relationships and disputing styles) between the two research communities of Zombodze and Kwaluseni? The answers to these questions have implications for the 'politics of harmony'.

Causes of grievance

In Table 2, cases collected from the Zombodze and Kwaluseni courts are divided into eight categories which define subject matter: land administration; land dispute; routine administration; dispute administration; family; livestock; criminal and civil; and unknown[4] (some cases involved multiple causes).

The Zombodze court heard 23 land administration cases and 35 land disputes. The land disputes between subjects were varied and involved customary land rights (8 boundary, 2 land loan, 2 ploughing, 3 tree, 1 cattle path and 3 fencing); land disputes raised by chiefs against subjects largely

Table 2. *Causes of grievance*[a]

	Zombodze	Kwaluseni
Land (administration) 28 (total)		
land request	17	5
building request	3	
land gift request	2	
land addition request	1	
Land (dispute) 48 (total)		
boundary	8	
land loan	2	
land inheritance	2	
ploughing fields	2	
land encroachment	1	
use of private resources (e.g. trees)	3	
use of public resources (e.g. water)		1
cattle path	1	
cattle trespass		3
fencing	3	
illegitimate housing of immigrants		1
illegimate building activities		5
illegimate land allocation	1	
banishment	5	1
land ownership (inter-chieftaincy)	1	
authority for land administration (chief)	2	2
authority for land administration (*tindvuna*)	8	
Administration (routine) 18 (total)		
passport request		2
immigration request	2	
firearm request	1	1
merchant licence request	1	2
attendance and tribute to authorities	1	3
marriage and birth registration		2
request to take case to Regional Administration		1
school committee	1	
succession	1	
Administration (dispute) 9 (total)		
market		2
development project proposed	3	2
development objectives challenged		1
resettlement complaint	1	
disrespect of authority		2
cattle dip	1	
Family 11 (total)		
wife chases husband from home	1	
wife demands deregistration of children from stepfather		1
father demands son return from wife's home		1
mother registers under chief in daughter's husband's area	1	
husband deserts wife		1

Table 2 (*cont.*)

	Zombodze	Kwaluseni
wife runs away	1	
marital (general)		1
wedding custom violation	1	
imvimba collection	2	
insulamnyembeti cow	1	
Livestock (dispute) 7 (total)		
violation of *sisa* contract	3	
cattle ownership	2	
goat ownership	1	
sexual abuse of goat		1
Criminal and civil 12 (total)		
theft	1	1
assault		2
rape	1	
disorderly conduct (at shops)		1
improper operation of beer place		1
poisoning		1
witchcraft		1
false imprisonment	1	
insult		1
tenant complaint against landlord		1
Unknown 1		1
Total cases	92	47
	139	

[a]Some cases have multiple causes.

involved banishment (5 cases); and land disputes between chiefs involved jurisdiction over *emahambate* (sub-areas) (10 cases). The 12 routine and dispute administration cases were fairly evenly distributed over causes. Six livestock disputes and 3 criminal cases occurred.

The Kwaluseni court, as a contrast, heard 5 land administration cases and 13 land dispute cases. The land disputes between subjects largely involved cattle trespass (3 cases); land disputes raised by the council against residents primarily involved illegal building activities (7 cases); and land disputes raised by residents against the council involved challenges to the council's administrative rights (2 cases). The 15 routine and dispute administration cases were, as in Zombodze, fairly evenly distributed over causes. Unlike in Zombodze, only one livestock dispute but 9 criminal cases occurred.

Table 3. *Outcomes of grievance*

	Zombodze	Kwaluseni
Land (administration and dispute)		
land received through *kukhonta*	2	
land request denied	1	
partial land retraction by authorities	1	
land divided	2	
boundaries adjusted	1	
eviction from land	1	1
libandla looks for land	?	1
Administration		
libandla handles administration	?	8
development project accepted	5	?
Sanction (fine)		
cow	6	
money	1	2
Sanction (reprimand)		
defendant admonished	11	5
defendant favoured	2	1
plaintiff admonished	4	2
plaintiff favoured	11	4
group admonished	1	
Remand to another court		
case returned to family council	3	1
case referred to Swazi Court	2	3
case referred to King	3	
case referred to Magistrates' Court	1	
case referred to High Court	1	
No resolution		
parties told to reach agreement about compensation		1
parties admonished to be peaceful	4	6
name of King evoked to cease fighting	1	1
Case delayed	37	10
Unknown	6	5
Total cases	92	47

Outcomes of grievance

In Zombodze, 13 cases resulted in performance of administrative functions: cows were assessed as fines in 6 cases and a monetary fine in one case (see Table 3). A very high number of cases (37) were delayed. My informants attribute the delays to several factors: among them, cases coming on appeal to Zombodze are difficult to resolve, and Zombodze is distant from some areas under its jurisdiction, thus discouraging witnesses/litigants from attending.

Six cases were referred back to the family council or directed to the King, and 4 cases were directed to modern forums (Swazi Nation Court, Magistrates' Court and High Court).

In Kwaluseni, 10 cases resulted in the performance of administrative functions: cows were never observed to be assessed as a fine, but money was fined in 2 cases. Three out of 4 cases were referred to the Swazi Nation Court.

Litigant characteristics

The following disputant characteristics (plaintiff relative to defendant) have been tabulated for each case: sex; status; dyadic relationship; and location of residences (see Table 4).[5]

In Zombodze, 73 cases (out of 92) involved men as both complainant and defendant; only 20 cases involved women and no cases involved women as both defendant and complainant. More women (14) brought cases against men, than men against women (6). Most cases (41) were between people in the same chiefdom who were not neighbours, but 21 were between neighbours. Most cases (28 out of 92) involved the high–low status configuration in which the authorities brought a case against or before their subjects, or in which a family head brought a case against someone under his jurisdiction. In such cases, chiefdom authorities usually complained about tribute collection, ordered collection of national fees and proposed development projects. Occasionally, they raised a complaint against a subject for improper land use. Twenty-one cases involved the low–high status configuration in which subjects complained against the authorities – usually about land allocation or development projects. Only 5 cases involved the high–high status configuration in which chiefs (or *tindvuna* under jurisdiction of Zombodze) brought cases against one another.[6]

In Kwaluseni, 34 cases (out of 47) involved men as both complainant and defendant; again, this means that only 13 cases involved women. Two women brought cases against other women. Thirty-two cases were between people in the same chiefdom who were not neighbours, and only 4 were between neighbours. A significant 19 out of 47 cases involved the low–high status configuration in which subjects brought a case to their authorities – primarily a request to *khonta* and obtain land. In some cases they brought a complaint about land resettlement or reallocation. The high–high status configuration in which people of high hereditary rank dispute did not occur as Kwaluseni does not have jurisdiction to hear such cases.

Summary

Comparative analysis of the *characteristics* of disputants, the *causes* of disputes and the *outcomes* of disputes demonstrates a relation between relative personal and structural statuses of disputants and their disputing styles (choice of procedures and forums). Comparisons are made in the context of

Table 4. *Litigants' characteristics*

plaintiff–defendant	Zombodze	Kwaluseni
Litigants' sex		
male–male	73	34
male–female	6	5
female–male	14	6
female–female	0	2
Litigants' relative status		
high–high	5	0
high–low	28	14
low–high	21	19
low–low	4	0
unknown	19	10
Litigants' dyadic relation		
family member–family member	15	6
subject–subject	18	11
subject–chief	25	14
chief–subject	12	13
chief–chief	5	0
chief–Central Authority	3	0
Central Authority–chief	1	0
subject–Central Authority	1	0
Central Authority–subject	0	0
unknown	2	0
Litigants' residences		
neighbours	21	4
same chiefdom	41	32
different chiefdom	18	6
unknown	4	2
Total cases	92	47

differences and similarities between the Zombodze and Kwaluseni communities.

Interview and court data indicate that disputant characteristics of birthright and gender are the most important determinants of disputing style; royals and men have access to and the capacity to exploit a wider range of procedures and forums. In Zombodze, disputants occupy a wide range of structural (ascribed) statuses (from commoners to royals) and are in many dyadic relationships. As a contrast, in Kwaluseni disputants occupy fewer structural statuses (mainly commoners) and are in fewer dyadic relationships (mainly family member–family member, subject–subject or subject–chief). Residents of both communities are greatly differentiated in terms of personal (achieved) status, but more residents of Kwaluseni have achieved status through cash income.

Disputants of both high and low structural status approach the Zombodze officials for resolution of disputes involving both land use and administration. Court and interview data indicate that they rely on numerous disputing procedures such as adjudication, mediation or arbitration. As a contrast, disputants of low structural status usually approach the Kwaluseni officials for adjudication of disputes only involving land use. Many disputants do not approach the Kwaluseni officials because they question their legitimacy.

In Zombodze, royal disputants are given special consideration by the authorities. If they appeal, they have strong ties with the traditional authorities at the national capital. As a contrast, in Kwaluseni disputants are arguably granted more equitable consideration. If they appeal, they have stronger ties with the modern court officials in the nearby town of Manzini.

Rural–urban differences between Zombodze and Kwaluseni produce dissimilar causes and outcomes of dispute as well as characteristics of disputants. Thus, rural land tenure in Zombodze gives rise to more disputes about agricultural field boundaries and livestock, whereas semi-urban land tenure in Kwaluseni gives rise to more disputes about residential boundaries, resource use, community development and crime (Table 2). In Zombodze more outcomes involve assessment of livestock fines and remands to local or national customary courts, whereas in Kwaluseni outcomes involve monetary fines and remands to urban courts (Table 3). In Zombodze, litigants are more likely to be neighbours disputing about personal land use rights, whereas in Kwaluseni litigants are more likely not to be neighbours, but rather community residents, who are disputing about community development plans and administration (Table 4).

Selected case analysis

In this section, 16 actual Swazi land disputes are organized in each of 6 disputant dyads as follows: family member vs. family member dyad (Cases 1–3); subject vs. subject dyad (Cases 4–7); subject vs. chief dyad (Cases 8–9); chief vs. subject dyad (Cases 10–12); chief vs. chief dyad (Cases 13 and 14); and Central Authority vs. chief dyad (Cases 15 and 16) (refer to Case List, p. xi).[7] As explained in Chapter 2, organization of cases in dyads depicts disputant relationships within the Swazi political hierarchy.

The cases are organized primarily according to dyads and secondarily according to causes (e.g. boundary dispute). This approach was selected because informants describe disputes in terms of disputant relationships rather than causes, which are often multiple. It was also selected because it clarifies disputing in terms of status relationships within the Swazi hierarchy.

The cases were selected to represent a wide range of land disputes as experienced by people occupying various structural and individual statuses; to represent evenly the hierarchical political relationships defined in all dyads; and to demonstrate several kinds of disputing procedures and remedy agents.[8] In addition, the case studies were selected to represent land disputes in all regions of the country; 10 of the 16 cases occurred in the central middleveld in my two primary research areas, while the other 6 cases occurred in the highveld and lowveld. Finally, they were selected to demonstrate several kinds of harmony ideology and several kinds of strategic responses to harmony ideology.

The sequence of dispute events is presented chronologically in a case summary. After each case summary, the harmony strategies (organic or control) of the authorities and the disputing strategies (assertion, avoidance or deception) of the litigants are analysed. Following presentation of all case summaries and strategy analyses, a composite analysis of dispute causes and strategies is made.

Place names have been omitted from case descriptions (except for region), and Swazi clan names that are not the real names of the most important disputants have been provided (secondary characters are designated by an X, Y or Z). Details are missing in case descriptions when an informant was unclear or unsure about facts, when an informant provided details which seemed inaccurate, and when the case was in progress at the time of my departure from the field.

Land dispute dyads[9]

Family member vs. family member dyad

Background

Disputes between family members involve several dyadic configurations: for example, brother vs. brother; son vs. mother (e.g. the son restricts his widowed mother's land control, sometimes even attempting to evict her); son of homestead head vs. family elder(s); married woman vs. husband or affinal kin; married woman vs. co-wife; woman vs. consanguineal kin (usually brothers). The most frequent causes of dispute between family members, as the tables discussed above indicate, are: land inheritance (i.e. size or location of land allotment), boundaries of fields or residential sites, right to oversee land management on homestead, or right to exploit commonly held resources on land.

The containment principle underlying political harmony in the family member vs. family member dyad provides that grievances should be handled privately by the family council. Occasionally grievances between brothers or between a nephew and his father's brother over land divisions or succession becomes so heated that the chief's council is asked to intervene. Grievances involving a woman who has married into a homestead unit are usually not referred to the chief's council; in fact, a woman's husband's family council often will not deal with such a grievance since it claims that married women have no right to dispute about land. Women who wish to dispute about land rights on their natal homesteads find themselves in poorly defined positions; some resort to their own family council or chief's council about their grievances, whereas others resort to modern institutions like *Ndabazabantu*. As will be argued in Chapter 6, women are particularly likely to use resistance disputing strategies to violate the containment prerogatives of male homestead heads, and thus gain empowerment to escalate their grievances to disputing forums.

Land dispute cases

Disputes over inheritance rights. Several cases in the total sample involved one family member trying to evict another family member in assertion of inheritance rights, although the cases were usually publicly defined by the disputants as problems of rights to ploughing fields or resources (Cases 1–3). In disputant dyads involving men, a son of the deceased homestead head would try to evict another brother and thereby assume sole control over the land, or he would try to evict his father's brother (Case 1). Sometimes the son would try to assume control over larger land areas.

In disputant dyads involving women, a son of a deceased homestead head would try to evict his mother. Often such an action was instigated by the son's wife who wanted sole control over land and other matters within a nuclear family unit. Alternatively, the affinal kin of a woman would try to oust her from the homestead after the death of her husband or would otherwise limit her land allotment so severely that she would be forced to seek land elsewhere (Case 17 in Chapter 6). Finally, the consanguinal kin of a woman, usually her brothers, would try to oust her from her natal homestead following the death of the parents (Case 2). In one unusual case, a woman's husband tried to evict her from land he had obtained through *kukhonta* after she legally severed ties of their Western civil marriage; however, she succeeded in persuading members of the Chief's Court to evict him from the land.

Case 1 describes the unsuccessful attempted eviction of a deceased homestead head's brother by the head's son, and Case 2 describes the successful eviction of a deceased homestead head's daughter by his sons (i.e. the woman's brothers).

Case 1: The nephew who attempts to evict his father's brother

(data from case before Chief's Court, middleveld)

(Msibi is Gama's father's brother. Both men are married and fairly equal in status, except that Msibi is older. No information is available on their education or employment. Different clan names are used to differentiate the men.)

Case summary

A man (Msibi) claims during a hearing before the Chief's Court that his brother's son (Gama) has been ordering him to leave the land of his deceased brother. Msibi says that after the death of his brother, the heir to the land, his nephew (Gama), had been too young to keep the homestead running so he (Msibi) had assumed that responsibility.

Gama, in his own defence, argues before the Court that the problem lies not with disputed residential rights but rather with disputed ploughing fields. According to him, he had ploughed a particular field for five years until the present year when his uncle suddenly announced that he was going to plough it. Msibi proceeded to do so and told Gama that if he (Gama) tried to plough the field in the future, he (Msibi) would let his cattle trample the crops. After this threat, Gama ordered Msibi off the homestead; he justified his action on the grounds that he was heir to his father's land. In opposition to this action, Msibi argued before the Court that as 'father' he should be accorded due respect and deference.

The Chief's Court decides in favour of Msibi and reprimands Gama for disrespect of his elders, including members of the Chief's Court and Msibi, his 'father'. They fine the younger man a cow and warn him that he will be asked to leave the land if he fails to treat his father's brother respectfully. They also cite examples of the younger man's general aggressiveness towards members of the community in justification of their harsh sentence. One member of the chief's councils says: 'I am far older than this boy, but I would never tell my "father" to leave. One can't order his elders to do things. One is supposed to respect his parents. Was it showing respect to tell your "father" to leave?'

Strategy analysis

The chiefdom authorities used an organic harmony strategy to legitimate their land administration rights in terms of customary hierarchical arrangements: they reprimanded the defendant for not respecting his elders (social superiors according to both age and ascribed status). They used a control harmony strategy in response to Gama's assertion disputing strategy to enforce respect: they imposed a fine which was to be retained by the chiefdom treasury, rather than offered as compensation to the complainant. Thus, they backed up their initial organic harmony strategy with a control harmony strategy which ensured compliance with their own status/control interests.

Gama used assertion disputing strategies to retain his perceived land rights: when he believed that Msibi violated his hereditary land use rights, he ordered him off the family homestead, and when Msibi brought charges against him before the Chief's Court, he (Gama) openly argued that he had inherited land administration rights following the death of his father.

Msibi also used assertion disputing strategies to retain his perceived land rights: when he presented his opening arguments before the Chief's Court, he stated that his current land administration rights derived from his contribution as administrator during the minority of Gama. He argued both land use and administration rights in terms of hereditary respect: this disputing strategy had the desired effect (from Msibi's perspective) of encouraging the chiefdom authorities to respond with both organic and control harmony strategies – the former seeking social consensus and the latter ensuring wider political compliance through reference to notions of respect.

Case 2: The unwed mother who obtains land from distant kin after her brothers evict her

(data from informant X, middleveld)

(Shabalala is an unmarried woman with little formal education.)

Case summary

A woman, Shabalala, had borne children by a man who deserted her. She stayed at her parents' house, supporting herself and her children through making and selling handicrafts. She bought some cattle with her savings. She needed land only for a residence but not for cultivation – other than a garden.

After Shabalala's parents died, her brothers inherited control over the land. They informed her that since bridewealth had never been paid for her as she had never married, she would have to relinquish her own cattle to them or leave the homestead. She refused to accept their ultimatum. Instead, she sought out a sympathetic distant clan 'brother' who lived in another area and begged him and his wife (X) to take her and her young children into their homestead. They agreed, letting her build a temporary dwelling and giving her garden space. She borrowed land elsewhere to plough and used her earnings to buy other food products. Shabalala is currently waiting for her oldest son to reach adulthood, at which time he can *khonta* for her.

Strategy analysis

The brothers, acting both as authorities in a homestead family unit and as disputants, ensured compliance with their financial interests by using control strategies. They made their sister's, Shabalala's, land use rights contingent upon payment of *lobolo* cattle. When she objected, they denied her a disputing forum (control harmony strategy). By not recognizing her grievance within formal proceedings, they effectively contained the matter within the family, avoiding the attention of the chiefdom authorities. This secured their administrative control at the lowest level of the political hierarchy and averted interference from a higher level.

Shabalala, as an unmarried woman, had to receive land use rights on the basis of her brothers' goodwill; she had little support in customary land law to argue land use rights. She had neither guaranteed redress to the family council nor the right to lodge a complaint with the Chief's Court which usually orders that families settle domestic disputes on their own. As she was never married by customary or Western rites, she could not approach the District Commissioner or the magistrate for child support from her former husband. When she chose not to accept her brothers' restrictions on her land use rights, she used an avoidance grievance strategy. After avoiding her brothers, she used the assertion disputing strategy of actively seeking alternate authorities (mobilizing her broader kinship network at the family level) from whom she could obtain land use rights.

Disputes over scarce resources on common land

Case 3: The brothers who argue about wattle trees

(data from case before Chief's Court, middleveld)

(Masiya and Hlophe are brothers. No data is available on their ascribed and achieved (education and employment) statuses. Different fictional clan names are used to differentiate the men.)

Case summary

A man, Masiya, chops down a wattle tree which his brother, Hlophe, claims belongs to him since he planted it. Masiya claims that the tree is located on community property and cannot legitimately be claimed by Hlophe. Hlophe becomes furious and says that Masiya chopped down the tree because he is jealous of his children and resents the fact that he has no children himself. Hlophe accuses Masiya of witchcraft. The brothers are (and have been) on such hostile terms that they attempt no reconciliation. Hlophe reports the case to the chief's deputy.

Masiya presents his case before the chief's *bandlakhulu*. He claims that he thought no one owned the tree. No witness can verify who planted the tree or when. Masiya then utters a counter-witchcraft accusation against his brother. The chief becomes furious about this implied threat and comments angrily that Masiya will be fined a cow if he ever makes a threatening witchcraft accusation again. A *bandlancane* member notes that Masiya will also be held responsible if sickness or death should befall Hlophe.

Masiya is asked if he has any questions to pose to Hlophe. Masiya then asks Hlophe why he is denying that he threatened him. Hlophe refuses to answer but comments that it is embarrassing for them that their family matter is being publicly heard before the chief's council. The chief then announces that the case will be abandoned for the moment in the hope that the brothers will settle at home. People gossip that after many years of bitter disputes between the brothers, no solution can be easily reached. The chief makes the following closing comments:

> It is true that Hlophe did plant trees on his father's land which Masiya cut down. Masiya is convicted of cutting down Hlophe's trees – knowing that they were his. But because the council doesn't like people to quarrel, and because it wants the brothers to be friends again, it will warn Masiya not to use other people's property. If Masiya does this again, we will fine him heavily.

When I (the anthropologist) asked Hlophe if he was satisfied with the outcome which offered peace but no compensation, he replied, 'I am not satisfied, but will accept the decision because one has to respect the royal kraal.'

Strategy analysis

The chiefdom authorities recommended a negotiated outcome, admonishing the brothers to be peaceful and settle at home; they relied upon organic harmony strategies because their interests in land administration could better be served by seeking an ideological, consensual agreement rather than one based upon political force. They had no interest in involvement in this long-lasting domestic dispute, and thus, according to custom, encouraged containment at the family level.

Hlophe, the complainant, used the assertion grievance strategy of a witchcraft accusation to force Masiya, the defendant, to recognize the impropriety of cutting down trees on family land. Hlophe then used an assertion disputing strategy of escalating the grievance to the Chief's Court, where Masiya also used an assertion strategy of making a counter-witchcraft accusation. Masiya's strategy failed miserably before the public forum; the authorities decided against him but expressed only a warning. The two disputants acquiesced to the authorities' harmony strategies for the sake of public peace, but they indicated privately that they had not reached a consensus and would continue to simmer about grievances at home.

Subject vs. subject dyad

Background

Disputes between subjects involve neighbours or fellow members of the same 'land community'. The disputes are attributable to several land issues: land acquisition (land grant from chief/neighbour or land loan); field and residential site boundaries; individual land use (e.g. fencing); community land use (e.g. cattle paths, grazing areas, resources such as water); or redistribution of land (e.g. resettlement for development purposes or reclamation of unused land from the individual user).

The containment principle underlying political harmony in the subject vs. subject dyad provides that subjects should attempt to reach a private agreement about grievances; but when this fails, they should seek assistance from the chief's council. Unfortunately, private settlement is not promoted by customary land tenure: disputes between subjects are encouraged by the constant layering over and contradiction of land rights in the customary land tenure system. When an individual acquires rights over land, all requirements of his tenure are usually not specified. Moreover, circumstances (e.g. family's/neighbour's land needs or government resettlement initiatives) can crop up during the course of his own or his descendants' tenure. In essence, customary land use rights are not static; they are continually remoulded by individual and societal forces such as the actual occupation of land by the person possessing rights, the use of land by this person, the standing of this person in the community, and the land requirements of the larger political unit.

According to my informants, rising land shortages occurring over the last two or three decades in densely populated areas have resulted in a new kind of dispute: newcomers with insufficient land compel a long-term resident to relinquish excess land. This occurs through peaceful local negotiations of chiefs' councils as well as through compulsory government resettlement plans. In past days, vacant (unassigned) land could be found for newcomers or residents with insufficient land, but now, in many areas, claimed but unused land is reassigned.

Modern developments such as urban employment opportunities and labour migration have an impact upon rural land rights. A man may possess use rights to a field, and subsequently be absent for many years as a migrant labourer. His chief may place another man on the same land in the interval, without consulting his agnates. If the migrant returns and establishes the fact that he never relinquished his membership in the community, he is, according to Swazi customary land law, entitled to resume rights to the field he abandoned. However, the second user has also acquired rights to the field. The chief and his council discuss the rival claims and make a decision which they expect both parties to accept. Factors which influence their decisions are: a claimant's relationship to the previous cultivator; the previous history of the land; the present use to which the land is being put; and each claimant's status in the community. Ordinarily, when the decision favours the second user, the chief offers the returned migrant new land elsewhere in the chiefdom.

In one case reported to me, the chief sided with the former user who had been performing labour in South Africa for a short period. In another reported case, the same chief sided with the newcomer since distant agnates of the former user, who had never resided on the land, were trying to lay claim to it. In one case I witnessed, a member of the chief's council allocated to a newcomer a portion of land which was currently being used. As the council member was influential, the complaints of the current occupant were suppressed. Case 21, which is discussed in Chapter 6, demonstrates how a woman fought to recover customary land rights when her mother's plot was reassigned by her chief's council after several years' abandonment. The woman, who had been working in South Africa for many years, had no access to land without a husband or brothers who could *khonta* for her.

Land dispute cases

Disputes about land loans. Disputes about loans normally arise when the borrower refuses to return land upon the request of the loaner. Sometimes the borrower or his descendants deny that the land was merely loaned to them, insisting that they have acquired permanent use rights to the land through *kukhonta* or a grant. In cases in which the land has been loaned for many years and the original witnesses to the transaction are dead, such contentions are difficult to prove or disprove.

Several disputes about land loans reported to me had resulted in violence, including a killing and destruction of crops.[10] The following case demonstrates an interesting principle of customary law (respect and banishment) which was discovered in two cases in different chiefs' areas.

Case 4: The disrespectful subject who loses land he loaned

(data from informant who is member of chief's council, lowveld)

(Mbaso, as a long-term resident who has excess land to loan, has higher status than Dladla, a relative newcomer with insufficient land. No data is available regarding their education and employment.)

Case summary

A man, Mbaso, who has loaned a field to a neighbour, Dladla, informs him directly before ploughing at the opening of the summer season that he wants to resume use of his field. When Dladla seems reluctant to relinquish the land, Mbaso then informs the authorities that he wants to initiate proceedings before the chief's council to ensure that his land loan is returned. The authorities tell him that he has come to them at a busy season and they are not willing to handle the case until the winter season. They also inform Dladla that he might be ploughing the land for the last season.

Mbaso is angry that the council has given Dladla a year's grace. He states that the council members have taken this action since they favour Dladla (reasons unknown to anthropologist). In assertion of his perceived rights, Mbaso waits until Dladla's maize crop has nearly matured and then arrives with a span of oxen and ploughs it down.

At this point Dladla approaches the authorities for redress. Mbaso is fined five cows for disobeying the orders of the chief's council. Dladla is further instructed to plough the land next year. Once again, when the maize has grown almost to maturity, Mbaso ploughs it down. This time the chief's council is furious and informs Mbaso that because he has shown disrespect in violating their instructions regarding the land, he (and family)[11] must relinquish all rights to the land – he is banished from the area. He is also fined an additional five cows.

Strategy analysis

The authorities used two organic harmony strategies – one which denied Mbaso a disputing forum, and the other which encouraged peaceful relations between the disputants – because they wanted to pursue their own private agricultural interests; however, they also hoped that the grievance would cool until the time at which they could attend to it. When Mbaso disregarded their orders and forcefully ploughed down his adversary's crops, the authorities became angry that their instructions had been disrespectfully ignored. Thereafter, they relied upon control harmony strategies – one which fined Mbaso and the other which banished him – because they wanted to assert their interests in land control. They were no longer concerned with the legitimacy of Mbaso's land use rights but rather their own land administration rights.

Mbaso asserted his perceived land use rights by ploughing down Dladla's crops. In response, Dladla asserted his perceived land use rights (to standing crops on borrowed land) by appealing to the authorities. When the authorities fined Mbaso in order to sanction his disobedience and restore peace (control and organic harmony strategy), he responded with a disobedient reassertion of his perceived land rights.

Disputes about land boundaries. Disputes involving boundaries arise when a person accuses his/her neighbour of violating the boundary demarcations originally established by the chief and his council. Informants say that two neighbours should ideally confront one another; but failing to reach a private agreement, they should approach the chief's council for settlement.

Several members of chiefs' *bandlancane* explained how boundary disputes usually arise. A long-term resident in an area may extend his boundaries, even erecting a fence, when a newcomer is assigned land next to him. It would appear that he does this to protect himself from encroachment by his neighbour as well as to lay claim to additional land in case of future needs. He knows that as long as the land was empty before the arrival of the newcomer, he could request additional land from the chief; however, with the settlement of a neighbour, he fears he will have no opportunity to expand in the future. Or, a person may begin ploughing the unassigned strip of land which separates his field from that of his neighbour. This action, although not constituting an encroachment on the neighbour's fields, is viewed as the first stage of trespass. In addition, a person may begin ploughing part or all of a neighbour's field when he cannot meet his subsistence requirements or when he wants to expand cultivation, such as to plant cash crops. He hopes to get away with trespass. Finally, a person may plough land which his neighbour believes incorporates part of his own fields. In such cases, each disputant argues that members of the chief's council pointed out conflicting, overlapping boundaries.

Case 5 describes a dispute in which the boundaries of subjects as well as chiefs are in question. In such a case, one person ploughs part of his neighbour's fields, stating that Chief X assigned him that land. His neighbour, on the other hand, says that Chief Y assigned him a portion of the ploughed land. The subjects refer the matter to their respective chiefs. This kind of dispute is extremely difficult to solve since neither chief can claim authority to adjudicate a dispute involving the subject of another chief. In addition, the Central Authority may be unwilling to intervene.

Case 5: The subjects who pledge allegiance to different chiefs argue about the boundary

(data from case before Chief's Court, middleveld)

(Mtsetfwa, as a commoner, has lower ascribed status than his opponent's chief, Chief Matsebula. He believes he can get satisfaction from the central chief, C, at the royal kraal because Matsebula is not his own chief. No data is available regarding education and employment.)

Case summary

A man, Mtsetfwa, comes before the chief's council at a royal kraal[12] with the complaint that the chief, Matsebula, of the area neighbouring his own sent police to his homestead and had him unjustly jailed for two weeks.

When questioned by the chief, C, at the royal kraal about what he had done to provoke the imprisonment, Mtsetfwa says that he had done nothing. He says that he was taken from the jail to the Magistrates' Court on several occasions to hear the charges, but Matsebula, the complainant, failed to show up. According to him, he was in jail for two weeks until he was released. Then, Mtsetfwa, with the help of his family, secured the assistance of a lawyer. When he (Mtsetfwa) appeared in court, a statement was read that he had been imprisoned for beating up a chief.

After hearing this account, Chief C asks Mtsetfwa if he did, in fact, beat up Matsebula, and Mtsetfwa denies the charge. After some questioning, Mtsetfwa admits that the problem began with a dispute between himself and a neighbour, N. He says that N erected some fencing which cut off some of his fields. When he asked N why he did this, N said that it was no concern of his. Mtsetfwa became angry and cut the fence. Soon after, Chief Matsebula and some men came to Mtsetfwa's homestead and asked why he had damaged N's fence. According to Mtsetfwa, Matsebula told him that they had been informed about the dispute by N since Matsebula is N's chief. Mtsetfwa then told Matsebula to work out the problem with his own chief (Mtsetfwa's) (i.e. negotiate the problem with fellow chief with whom he was disputing about control over land). At this point, Matsebula allegedly became aggressive.

Upon hearing this testimony, Matsebula angrily stands up and says that Mtsetfwa is lying. According to him, Mtsetfwa told him to 'forsake' (get off his land) which is a highly unacceptable comment to make to a chief. He adds that Mtsetfwa also called his mother by her private parts (one of the worst insults) and threatened him with a knobkerry. He says that he fled in terror from Mtsetfwa. After hearing these charges, the large audience (100+ people) in attendance at Chief C's court gasps in astonishment that a chief (Matsebula) would be treated so disrespectfully.

Chief C asks Mtsetfwa to answer to these charges made by Matsebula. Mtsetfwa denies them and says that Matsebula is lying. When members of the chief's council admonish him for unacceptably referring to a chief as 'liar', Mtsetfwa tries to shift his approach by arguing that his complaint lies with false imprisonment and not the boundary dispute. He tries to build up public sympathy by describing his miserable experience in the 'flea-ridden, stinking' prison cell. Chief C admits that the case is about assault and false imprisonment but says that they have to consider the matter of boundaries since that is how the whole matter started.

Chief C takes the approach of inquiring into the character and actions of the disputants. He asks Mtsetfwa if he approached his own chief about the problem. Mtsetfwa says that he did when he was released from jail. Matsebula then asks Mtsetfwa if he knows that it is improper to tell a chief to 'forsake' and thus he (Matsebula) was right in approaching the police. Matsebula also asks Mtsetfwa if he performs duties in his regiment. Mtsetfwa says that he is a good citizen and reluctantly admits that he should not argue with a chief. Chief C interrupts Matsebula's interrogation of Mtsetfwa and reprimands Mtsetfwa for cutting the fence and for not going to his own chief sooner. At the same time, he acknowledges that Mtsetfwa was legitimately angry when he saw Matsebula acting in an area that was not his own.

After admonishing Mtsetfwa, Chief C turns to Matsebula and tells him that he should have answered the court summons (Matsebula says he did not receive it). He also comments that Matsebula's subject (and Mtsetfwa's neighbour), N, should have come to the meeting to explain his version of the dispute.

Chief C informs the group that the history of the area must be further investigated if disputes are to be prevented. He concludes the case by commenting, 'Would it be wrong for the two of you [Mtsetfwa and Matsebula] to meet privately so that Matsebula can tell Mtsetfwa why he had him imprisoned?'

In his case summary, Chief C tries to balance the differences between the disputants by criticizing both.

> Mtsetfwa's main complaint is that he was locked up, but the council feels that there is no complaint against Matsebula. The Magistrates' Court says that threats (like Mtsetfwa's) are the same as a real assault. You were wrong, Mtsetfwa, in that you threatened a chief with assault. What you did deserves more than being locked in a prison cell for two weeks. You, Matsebula, in your capacity as chief, shouldn't have gone to Mtsetfwa's homestead. You should have consulted your *libandla* and sent your *indvuna* [assistant], *umgijimi* [runner], or council members to Mtsetfwa's chief. You were lucky that Mtsetfwa didn't assault you.

Strategy analysis

The central chief and his council used organic harmony strategies which encouraged the disputants to adhere to customary roles and responsibilities (to authorities and neighbours). They also encouraged them to negotiate settlement privately and reside together peacefully. Their method of containing settlement aimed to prevent an inter-chieftaincy conflict which would disrupt at least two levels of the political hierarchy, i.e. two neighbouring areas and the royal administrative village.

Mtsetfwa initially responded to his neighbour's land transgressions with an avoidance disputing strategy which involved cutting his neighbour's fence. When the neighbouring chief intervened and had him imprisoned, he responded with assertion strategies (securing a lawyer) to protect his civil rights in a non-customary court. After the central chief became involved, he used a potpourri of disputing strategies before the customary Chief's Court: an assertion strategy to persuade others of the validity of his perceived land rights; a deception strategy to dismiss the charges of the neighbouring chief; and avoidance strategies (ignoring questions and emphasizing his suffering in jail) to deflect attention from his disrespect of the neighbouring chief's hierarchical superiority. In effect, Mtsetfwa responded to the central chief's organic harmony strategies with conciliatory disputing strategies.

Mtsetfwa's neighbour used an assertion disputing strategy which aimed to persuade his own chief, Matsebula, to intervene. Chief Matsebula used disputing strategies rather than harmony strategies in his capacity as a disputant acting against a man, Mtsetfwa, who was not his subject. He used only assertion disputing strategies, such as direct accusations and threats against Mtsetfwa and resort to modern and customary courts, for affirmation of his right to administer land and to receive respect. His high structural position necessitated direct declaration of his status and prerogatives.

Disputes about fencing. One of the most common disputes between community members over land use rights involves fencing. The problem lies not in obtaining permission of authorities to erect a fence but rather in defining boundaries where fences have been or will be placed. When fences are erected, latent boundary disputes often flare up and new ones arise because fenced land implies a more 'vested' right than does unfenced land. Fences demarcate residential/garden land and restrict grazing after the harvest. One chief explained that permanent fencing was not allowed traditionally but is now permissible if people can afford it.[13] He commented that people who want to fence must inform the authorities of their intentions, i.e. the kind of fence they plan to erect and the exact location. This chief believed that such action would prevent disputes.

Most fencing cases involve fields, although the following fencing case involved a cattle path.

Case 6: The subject who complains about fence at cattle path

(data from case before Chief's Court, middleveld)

(Mhlanga and Sibandze are neighbours of approximately equal achieved and ascribed statuses. Sibandze is employed; no information is available about education.)

Case summary

A man (Mhlanga) settles in an area, demarcating his field boundaries with a fence. One of his neighbours (Sibandze) comes to him and complains that the fence cuts off part of the cattle path. Mhlanga inquires about the legitimate boundaries from the man who had granted him part of his land, i.e. the court messenger, and is told that the fencing was properly placed.

When Sibandze continues to complain, Mhlanga takes the matter before the Chief's Court. He tells the Court that he placed the fence on his boundary and not on the cattle path. Sibandze, in offering his own testimony to the Court, complains that he had been at work when Mhlanga's boundaries were pointed out and thus had not been properly given the opportunity to confirm them. A witness for Sibandze says that several men pointed out to Mhlanga where he could properly erect the fence. The messenger informs the council that he went and investigated the land a second time. In his view, Mhlanga had moved the fence over the boundary even more than after his first investigation. Mhlanga denies the messenger's accusation. He claims that he had not finished erecting the fence when the messenger first investigated the spot. The chief notes that the main problem arises from the fact that Sibandze was not shown the boundary when Mhlanga was first granted the land. He tells the messenger to point out the boundaries and help the parties reach a settlement.

Strategy analysis

The chiefdom authorities used organic harmony strategies: they avoided reaching a zero-sum decision in order to permit the disputants to reach a private agreement about fence boundaries with the aid of the land grantor. It was in their best interest to encourage dyad containment (between disputants) and not to become involved since their status/control was not in question and since they could not easily reach an accurate evaluation about a private land loan.

Sibandze used assertion strategies in privately raising his grievance to his neighbour and publicly before the Chief's Court. He was concerned with confirming his perceived land use rights. Mhlanga, in turn, used assertion strategies in privately (with land grantor) and publicly (before chief's council) justifying his perceived land use rights.

He responded to the authorities' and his opponent's strategies in a conciliatory manner; he was a newcomer to the area and could be assertive about his actions but not combative about his land interests.

Disputes about trespass of livestock. A second common kind of dispute involving land use rights centres upon the movement of livestock over community paths to community grazing areas. Disputes arise when cattle stray into private fields adjacent to paths and damage crops.

Case 7: The subject who complains about crop damage from straying cattle
(data from case before Chief's Court and interview with Mdluli, middleveld)

(Sukati has achieved slightly higher status as a member of the local council. Mdluli and Sukati have both received several years of formal education and are employed.)

Case summary
A man's (Mdluli's) cattle stray into the fields of another man (Sukati) who resides about half a mile from him. Mdluli searches for the twenty missing cattle for two days. When he hears nothing about them, he decides to report the apparent cattle theft to the town police. At this point, Mdluli's children inform him that Sukati has impounded the cattle. Mdluli goes to Sukati and discovers that his cattle have not been fed or given water while missing. He asks Sukati to return the cattle to his custody, which Sukati does, but Sukati says that he will take the matter before the local council. Sukati, who is the brother to the council chairman, attempts no private settlement.

At the first hearing of the case before the council, Mdluli is fined 50 Rand. Some weeks later, the council chairman announces that Mdluli and Sukati must reach a private settlement about the damage caused by the cattle, including the fair compensation to be rendered.

Strategy analysis
The authorities initially attempted to impose a fine, which arguably constituted a control harmony strategy since it imposed a sanction without allowing confrontation between the disputants. Later, the authorities used an organic harmony strategy which encouraged the disputants to settle privately. They probably changed their harmony strategy since their land administration rights were under debate in the community: contrary to the usual situation, a control harmony strategy would force compliance and produce only a façade of consensus, thus exacerbating the simmering discontent in the community. As a contrast, an organic harmony strategy served to create the impression that the authorities were acting in both disputants', but particularly the defendant's, interests. In other words, it rendered appearances of legitimate, unbiased and just authority and thus desirably (from authorities' perspective) contained the matter in the local community.

Sukati used assertion disputing strategies (impounding stray cattle and reporting to the local council) to proclaim his perceived land rights. His position was strong in that he was a member of the local council and brother of the chairman. Mdluli used assertion strategies (reporting to the police and apologizing to the complainant) when he sought to recover his cattle; however, when he discovered that they had been impounded by Sukati, who was an important although controversial man, he attempted an avoidance strategy aimed at private reconciliation. The authorities responded to his strategies with organic harmony strategies; the defendant had not challenged their control, and further assertion of their own or Sukati's rights was not necessary.

Subject vs. chief dyad

Background

The containment rule underlying political harmony in the subject vs. chief dyad provides that a subject's grievances should be 'lumped' or reported privately to the chief: most of my informants stated that a subject is at the mercy of his chief and should not complain publicly about the chief's exercise of his hereditary powers over land. However, disgruntled subjects do have various means for condemning the actions of their chiefs: complain to the King (this can be difficult since a chief usually authorizes transference of a subject's case to the King); protest a perceived wrong before a public meeting of the chief's council; bring a case before a European-influenced court; inform the media about the problem, or otherwise discuss it in private meetings. The first two approaches are viewed by the traditional authorities as legitimate whereas the latter two are not.

The land-related complaints raised by a subject against his chief that were discovered in the course of this project involved land acquisition or maintenance rights: improper land allocation by authorities in connection with the Rural Development Board's plan to achieve optimum land utilization through resettlement (e.g. local authorities allegedly display favouritism in new land allocations); improper land allocation by chief in ordinary land settlement process (e.g. authorities allocate currently occupied land); unfounded eviction from land; or implementation of unpopular development initiatives. The research revealed several instances of ultimate sanction against a chief (occurring within the last decade): a significant number of subjects denied allegiance to unpopular or 'illegitimate' chiefs and threatened violence.[14]

Land dispute cases

Disputes about development. A chief and his council ordinarily try to ensure nearly unanimous approval from the *bandlakhulu* of a development project before implementing it. When a project involves resettlement of subjects or reduction/alteration of land allocations, affected subjects often object.

The next case demonstrates an unusual response to a development initiative by a man of local and national prominence. He resorted to a Magistrates' Court to protest the reduction and alteration of his customary land allocation. His son, who is a university-trained lawyer, defended his position.

Case 8: The subject who protests about land damage caused by road project

(data from interview with Mabuza's son and a member of the local council, middleveld)

(Mabuza is a long-term resident who has achieved considerable personal status in the traditional sector due to his long association with the King. His son received a university education and achieved prominence in the modern, bureaucratic sector.)

Case summary
One of the first settlers (Mabuza) in what has recently become a semi-urban area protests when the local council[15] informs him (in 1960s) that they are building a road which will cut through part of his property. The committee goes ahead with their plans, and in the process, cut his fence, damage his wattle trees and destroy part of his standing crops.

After the damage has been done, Mabuza takes the nearly unprecedented action of bringing a case before the Magistrates' Court. His son, a lawyer, handles his case. Mabuza (according to several interviews conducted by the present researcher) initially complains that the council is acting without the authority of the King. After the King appoints one of his influential advisers to represent the local council, it becomes evident that the King claims direct responsibility for ordering the development of the area. At this point Mabuza's son argues on behalf of Mabuza that he (Mabuza) may indeed be a 'tenant at will' on customarily tenured land, as his opponents argue, but a 'tenant at will' is nonetheless entitled to compensation (in this case for damage to fence, trees and crops) by a 'landlord at will'. The magistrate rejects the legal basis of Mabuza's son's arguments.

After the decision by the Magistrates' Court, the council informs the King that Mabuza is claiming to be an owner of the land which he occupies. The King calls Mabuza before him to answer to these charges. Mabuza denies that he believes he is an owner and states that he merely wants compensation for the investments he put in the land. The King takes no further action, and Mabuza's son advises Mabuza to abandon the case.

Strategy analysis
The local authorities used a control harmony strategy (land damage) which forced Mabuza to bear the consequences of their land administration prerogatives (land development) without a debate. When Mabuza responded with assertion disputing strategies before the Western-influenced Magistrates' Court, they persuaded the Court to abandon the case and thereafter resorted to organic harmony strategies before the customary King's council. Their organic harmony strategies legitimated their actions in terms of consensual national and local politics, i.e. the King's desire to promote community development. Mabuza's appeal to the Magistrates' Court had made containment at the local level impossible, and the local authorities thus had to undergo the risk of debate and designation of local control at a customary national forum.

Mabuza used an assertion disputing strategy (appeal to the Magistrates' Court) in response to the local authorities' control harmony strategy because he questioned their administrative right to alter existing land use rights (boundaries) and because he had no alternative if he hoped to protect his perceived rights. Ultimately, he resorted to an avoidance strategy which abandoned his public claims before the national authorities; he had no alternative route of appeal. The local authorities' organic harmony strategies had proved very convincing before the national authorities. Mabuza's avoidance strategy of abandoning the dispute in one forum but taking it up in another contrasts with an avoidance strategy in which disputing is abandoned because the situation is no-win.

Disputes about authority for land distribution. When someone discovers that a person has been allocated land improperly (e.g. by illegitimate authority figures or by legitimate authority figures under improper circumstances) and reports this fact, the latter is told to abandon the land. He/she may then attempt to lodge a complaint against the person who authorized the settlement, trying to recover the land or at least the '*kukhonta* fee' paid when the land was granted. Cases, such as the following one, indicate that a person who obtained land under false pretences of illegitimate 'authorities' may not be successful in receiving compensation for loss of land, constructions on land or the '*kukhonta* fee'.

Case 9: The man who receives land from illegitimate authority
(data from F, a friend of Maseko, middleveld)

(Maseko, as a youthful newcomer to an area, has low ascribed and achieved status. Lulane, as an older, long-term resident, has land and high ascribed status; he can allocate land falsely without suffering unfavourable consequences. Maseko has received some formal school education and is employed; no information is available on the education and employment of Lulane.)

Case summary
A man, Maseko, asks some people in a crowded area near a town how he can obtain land. He has come from a distant chiefdom and wants to reside in the new area because he is employed in the town. A man, Lulane, tells him that he has authority to allocate land. Lulane tells Maseko to give him some money, the *kukhonta* fee, which Maseko does, and Lulane then grants Maseko a plot of land for a residence. F, Maseko's friend, helps him construct his new homestead.

One day while Maseko and others are working on the new homestead, a man who claims authority in the area, Z, approaches them and asks who gave Maseko permission to build. Maseko tells him, that it was Lulane. When Z and his *liblandla* approach Lulane, they are told that this is untrue. F testifies on behalf of Maseko that he witnessed the land allocation and payment, but Z nonetheless orders Maseko off the land. Maseko is not given compensation for any of his expenditures, including the *kukhonta* fee. Nor can he bring a case against Lulane for his deception. Maseko's only option is to approach a chief in another area with a request for land, which he does with success.

Strategy analysis
Z acted independently when he questioned Maseko about building on land without proper authorization. However, he acted together with the local council when he questioned Lulane about making an improper land allocation. After he had begun inquiries, he resorted to control harmony strategies: he denied Maseko access to a disputing forum and ordered him off the land. It was not in his interest to engage Maseko in a public debate about Lulane's land administration rights. Ultimately, the matter could have expanded to a national forum as a debate about the extent of his own land administrative rights rather than Lulane's land use rights. He chose to evict Maseko and ignore Lulane's possible transgressions in order to maintain the status quo existing before Maseko's settlement.

Maseko's assertion disputing strategies first accused Lulane of making a false land allocation and then secured a witness on his own behalf. His avoidance strategy of obtaining land from another chief bent to Z's forceful control harmony strategies. Although Maseko's dispute was with Lulane, he ultimately had to counter the harmony strategies of Z who ignored his complaint against Lulane and thereafter focused upon his (Maseko's) illegitimate building activities. Z became his opponent against whom, as an authority, he was impotent.

Lulane's deception disputing strategy (lie about his illegitimate land allocation) deflected attention from his improprieties and avoided sanction.

Chief vs. subject dyad

Background

A chief may take a subject to task on several accounts: for example, improper acquisition of land; improper land use (building unauthorized dwellings, allocating part of land grant without official approval, or profiting excessively from land); or refusal to relinquish land upon demand. The ultimate sanction a chief may take against a subject is total withdrawal of land rights – banishment from the area.

The containment principle underlying political harmony in the chief vs. subject dyad provides that a chief can sanction his subject for any action which he considers in violation of the unwritten contract binding himself to the subject. He will do so in consultation with his council. Most commonly the reason given for banishment is disrespect of the authorities, but the underlying causes are complex and numerous (witchcraft, hoarding of wealth or criminal behaviour). The subject may appeal to the King, but frequently he will not be successful since a chief maintains considerable autonomy in the area under his jurisdiction.

Land dispute cases

Disputes about obtaining land under false pretences

Case 10: The couple who obtain land under pretence of being married
(data from two members of council, middleveld)

(Magagula (man) and Ndzimandze (woman) are both commoners. Magagula has higher ascribed status as a man, but Ndzimandze has higher achieved status as an 'original' resident of the area. No information is available on the education and employment of the disputants.)

Case summary

A man and woman (Magagula and Ndzimandze) come to a community from South Africa and approach the authorities with a request to *khonta* as a married couple. They are accepted in the area and granted land on the location where the woman's (i.e. Ndzimandze's) father's brother had formerly resided.

After some years, a dispute breaks out between the couple. They approach the council with a request for assistance in mediating their separation and property settlement. The main problem lies in determining who should retain land rights. Ndzimandze argues that Magagula had taken a girlfriend. She says that she should stay on the land allotment since it had formerly belonged to her father's brother. Magagula argues that Ndzimandze has another 'husband' in South Africa. He says that he should stay on the land allotment since the land is registered under his name, as a male (under customary law land must be registered in a man's name).

The council discovers that the couple are not legitimately married. In fact, they had apparently posed as a married couple so that they could receive and maintain land rights. The council decides that they have no right to the land and orders them both banished from the area. Magagula refuses to accept the decision of the council and disrupts the meeting with his counter-arguments at every opportunity.

Strategy analysis
The authorities used a control harmony strategy which ordered the eviction of disputants who had violated customary law by receiving land under false pretences. Such a strategy ensured compliance with their own control/status interests.

Magagula and Ndzimandze used an initial deception strategy (pretending to be married) in order to receive land from the local council (i.e. non-dispute situation). When they engaged in conflict with one another during separation, they used assertion disputing strategies (asserting land rights on the basis of gender, residency and outside sexual relationship of opponent) in arguing their case against their opponent before the council. Only after their initial deception was discovered did they respond to the authorities' accusations with assertion disputing strategies which argued their right to retain *any* land use rights in the area. The authorities took action against both of them in declaration of their land administration prerogatives; the dispute became a matter in which the authorities positioned themselves against the disputants. Magagula and Ndzimandze had no reasonable defence against the authorities' harmony strategies; restoration of balance in political relationships (authorities' reassertion of control) was achieved through their forced eviction.

Disputes about encroaching on neighbour's land

Case 11: The subject who encroaches upon neighbouring land
(data from member of chief's council, highveld)

(Zwane is a formally educated, wealthy man who has low ascribed status because he is a foreigner from South Africa.)

Case summary
A man (Zwane) came to Swaziland from the Republic of South Africa during the 1940s and *khontaed* under a chief. He was given a residential plot and fields. Adjoining his land allocation was land which had been granted to other people who were not using it. Over some years the people who were granted the adjoining land died. Gradually Zwane annexed the land by planting crops on more and more of the land each year. He also planted trees to render his claim permanent.

In the early 1980s (time of research) the chief's council begins searching the area for vacant land. There is little left since the population has grown rapidly. Some elders comment that Zwane is using land which he was not originally allocated. Subsequently, Zwane is told that he should discontinue use of the land since it will be reallocated. Zwane angrily refuses.

The chief's council brings a case against Zwane. There are no witnesses who can testify about the original land boundaries; the chief and council members who made the allocation are dead, as are the earlier occupants of the disputed land. Zwane argues that the present council cannot prove its contention that he has improperly encroached upon neighbouring land. The council argues, in rebuttal, that he is presumptuous to think that he, a newcomer from South Africa, could be given a much larger land allocation than the long-term residents of the area; in other words, he cannot logically maintain that the huge land area he now uses constitutes his original land allotment.

When the council informs Zwane that it will begin distributing the land to newcomers, Zwane states that he will appeal the case to the King. He then takes the case to the police at the national capital, where he is informed that he must return to his chief with his problem. His situation is difficult since a chief cannot reasonably adjudicate a complaint lodged against himself.

According to the researcher's informant, who is a member of the chief's *bandlancane*, Zwane will be banished from the area if he eventually loses the case before the King. In his view, Zwane cannot possibly win. The only way Zwane will be permitted to remain in the area is if he apologizes to the chief's council and pays a fine. The fine will be his formal acknowledgement that he was disrespectful of the chief's authority and greedy.

Strategy analysis
The authorities (chief's council), acting as both authorities and disputants, applied control harmony strategies (reallocation of Zwane's land, denial of forum and blocking of appeal to national authorities) in defence of their land administration prerogatives. Zwane's land encroachment and subsequent rejection of their directives constituted a direct attack upon their control. They only proposed using an organic harmony strategy, i.e. abandonment of eviction order, in the case that Zwane succumbed to their control harmony strategies and relinquished land.

Zwane used an assertion disputing strategy of appealing to the national authorities. He hoped that they would affirm his land use rights. Unfortunately, they denied his plea for relief because their interests could possibly have been hindered through involvement. Zwane then avoided his chief in the hope that the problem would subside. The chiefdom authorities had no difficulty in maintaining their local-level control through dispute containment.

Disputes about respect for authority

Case 12: The subject who is banished for witchcraft and disrespect
(data from chief's deputy, lowveld)

(Bhembe is a commoner. He is a wealthy farmer, but no information is available on his education.)

Case summary
A man (Bhembe) took out a bank loan so that he could buy seed, manure and equipment for planting maize and beans. After harvest, he sells most of his crop in order to repay his loan. He gives a small portion of the harvest as tribute to the chief but virtually nothing to his unsuccessful neighbours. People start gossiping that he is using 'spooks' to enrich his fields. They also tell the chief that he gave only a small portion of his crop to him since he thinks that the chief is lazy and merits nothing more. The chief does not summon Bhembe to answer in his own defence, but notes privately among his councillors that Bhembe has assumed increasingly arrogant and disrespectful ways. Apparently, a history of bad relations between Bhembe and his community has culminated in the current formal grievances. The chief's council banishes Bhembe on the grounds of witchcraft and disrespect.

Strategy analysis
The chiefdom authorities responded to the community residents' assertion disputing strategies (i.e. accusations against Bhembe of greed and insubordination) with control

harmony strategies (i.e. eviction). The authorities relied upon such strategies to maintain peace in the community and simultaneously to defend their land administration prerogatives (right to 'reasonable' tribute). Bhembe was not offered the opportunity to confront his opponents; his unpopularity was deemed sufficient to suppress his land rights.

Bhembe's strategies are unknown to the researcher; however, if he responded with disputing strategies, they failed since he was evicted.

Chief vs. chief

Background

A. J. B. Hughes, in his doctoral land tenure study of 1964, refers to land disputes which arise at higher levels of the socio-political hierarchy as: (1) disputes between one chief and another about jurisdiction over subjects and territory, and (2) disputes between the ruling Central Authority (i.e. King, Queen Mother, influential members of royal Dlamini clan) and a chief about allocated territorial rights. The former disputes are the subject of this section, and the latter disputes are the subject of the following section.

Probably the most basic explanation for the origin of inter-chieftaincy land disputes lies in the fact that chiefs gain power and prestige by exercising control over large tracts of land and over many subjects. Put simply, the more and better land a chief has, the more subjects he can attract and the more prestige he will attain. Although engaging in boundary disputes provides chiefs with one way of expanding or maintaining control over land, chiefs can also gradually expand their territorial claim by asserting jurisdiction over subjects in other chiefs' areas or by placing subjects on land that is not clearly under their jurisdiction. Sometimes a chief's subjects find themselves on land not under their own chief's jurisdiction because their ancestors had been placed there during early settlement of Swaziland when boundaries were vaguely established. Hughes (1972: 254) notes that one still encounters cases today of chiefs granting rights over land to homestead groups from neighbouring chiefdoms without insisting that they become their subjects. Such land tenants argue that they have a right to Swazi Nation Land under customary law, without regard to chiefs' separate claims, because they pledge allegiance to the King. Thus, inter-chieftaincy disputes can involve disputes about boundaries and about the legitimacy of Swazi citizens' settlement in a territory.

Disputes about the legitimacy of a group's or an individual's occupation of an area are extremely problematic. Sometimes a chief is not disturbed by, and even desires, the settlement in his area of another chief's subjects; but when he does not, he cannot easily evict them by his own edict since they are not under his jurisdiction. Nor can he appeal to the neighbouring chief to whom the group pledges allegiance since the chief would have little incentive to ask them to leave. In all probability, the neighbouring chief is suffering from a land shortage (perceived or actual) and welcomes the opportunity to drain off excess population. Moreover, the neighbouring chief may believe that residency of his followers in another area provides him with the opportunity to annex gradually that territory.

The containment principle underlying political harmony in the chief vs. chief dyad holds that an aggrieved chief should negotiate privately with his opponent. However, negotiations between high-status equals, both of whom have control interests at stake, are not likely to be successful. If one chief decides to encourage an outside agent to intervene, he has few options: he cannot easily appeal to the police or the Swazi Nation Court for eviction of unwanted settlers since these state organs do not have obvious jurisdiction in such matters. The only option open to such a chief is appeal to the Central Authority for permission to banish the trespassing individuals. Unfortunately for the chief, such an action requires years to be processed; national bureaucracy proceeds slowly because of a heavy case load and the necessity of carefully scrutinizing many extremely difficult cases. In any event, the Central Authority arguably has little incentive to resolve disputes about trespassing since it is more concerned with upholding its own authority than that of individual chiefs.

Inter-chieftaincy land disputes frequently fracture social relationships between neighbouring chiefs and their subjects. Such disputes rarely dissolve into amiable, lasting settlements. Moreover, they greatly hinder development interests: proposed projects cannot proceed in situations of jurisdictional dispute (territory and subjects) and when communities' energies are invested elsewhere.

Land dispute cases

Disputes between chiefs about boundaries. In the following case, a chief who wanted to test boundaries placed subjects in an area claimed by another chief.

Case 13: The chiefs who disagree about boundary

(data from interview with Chief Masina, highveld)

(Chiefs Masina and Sikhondze both have high achieved and ascribed statuses. Masina is younger and has received a higher formal education. He also has an important government position.)

Case summary

Chief Masina claims that the boundary to his chiefdom is a series of rocks which lie parallel to a road running through his chiefdom – that is what his father and the elders told him. Chief Sikhondze, on the other hand, insists that the boundary runs behind the rocks on Chief Masina's side of the road. In any case, Chief Masina controls most of the land on one side of the road and Chief Sikhondze controls most of the land on the other side.

According to Chief Masina, the problem began when the road was constructed. At that time the road symbolically replaced the traditional rock boundary. Chief Sikhondze instructed a couple of newcomers to build homesteads beneath the rocks on Chief Masina's side of the road. Now Chief Masina says that Chief Sikhondze is using uninformed newcomers as pawns in the 'cold war' between himself and Chief Masina. Chief Masina also comments that Chief Sikhondze has placed his subjects in the disputed area as a way to test his land claim – rather than directly confronting Chief Masina about the problem.

Chief Masina admits that the people of Chief Sikhondze's chiefdom would have had a right under the traditional boundary arrangement to settle beneath the rocks on his (Masina's) side of the road. However, modern circumstances create problems. First, the government established a 16 metre ban on building on each side of the road in order to account for future population growth and road expansion. This means that Chief Sikhondze's people cannot legitimately build at the base of the rocks on Chief Masina's side of the road. Secondly, the soil beneath the rocks is inadequate for advanced agriculture. Consequently, the newcomers under Chief Sikhondze's authority are forced by necessity to cultivate fields in the area which is clearly under the jurisdiction of Chief Masina.

Chief Masina has discussed the perceived trespass of Chief Sikhondze's people with his councillors and decided to overlook the situation for the present. He is concerned with implementing development objectives and does not want to engage in a tiresome land dispute.

Strategy analysis
Chief Sikhondze set the stage for dispute with Chief Masina by settling newcomers in a contested area. Chief Masina responded with organic harmony strategies which lumped his grievance and avoided confrontation with Chief Sikhondze; he believed that dispute containment would serve his own and his opponent's communities' interests in development. Neither chief could effectively produce either organic or control harmony because, even though they were authorities in their respective communities, they were disputants relative to one another. Thus, they could not produce consensus or compliance in their opponent's community, and they were unwilling to persuade the national authorities to attempt the same as a third party.

Disputes between chiefs about land development. According to most informants, land disputes between chiefs are frequently provoked by development projects. Such projects, by definition, require that area boundaries and chiefly jurisdictions be specified. Since development projects are desired by the community, chiefs will define boundaries in terms of their own interests – often relying on a land occupation pattern which existed generations in the past rather than a current land occupation pattern. Sometimes they fabricate or exaggerate land claims.

In the following ongoing case, two chiefs engaged in a dispute over a repurchased area adjoining a dam. Both chiefs were authorized by different government representatives to cultivate the land. When the first chief was instructed by a high-ranking official to leave the area, he raised a formal case against that official rather than the chief who opposed his land claim.

Case 14: The chiefs who quarrel about irrigated plots in a resettlement area
(data from interview with Chief Makhubu, lowveld)

(Chiefs Makhubu and Nsibande both have high achieved and ascribed statuses. Makhubu is young, has a university education and is employed in a government office; no information is available on the education and employment of Nsibande.)

Case summary
Several years ago Chief Makhubu (clan chief) was assigned land in a repurchased area after a dam was constructed. Officials at the Department of Agriculture gave him a map which designated the areas to be used for irrigated plots, grazing and residential sites. Soon after the subjects of Chief Makhubu began to move into the new area, Chief Nsibande, a neighbouring chief, began to allocate fields but no residential sites in an irrigated area adjoining the dam. Chief Makhubu had planned to assign fields in the area, but at that time it consisted of unused land.

When Chief Makhubu discovered the subjects of Chief Nsibande in his area, he approached the District Commissioner of the area asking for clarification. The District Commissioner issued a stop order which denied Chief Nsibande's subjects the right to farm in the area. He explained that if they were dissatisfied, they should obtain an official letter authorizing transference of the case to a ranking official responsible for the resettlement programme. The subjects of Chief Nsibande ignored the order and continued farming in the area. Chief Makhubu then approached a high official of the Central Rural Development Board (CRDB) and asked for assistance. The official confirmed that Chief Nsibande's subjects should not be in the area. He went to the area and ordered them to leave. He also declared that the crops which they had improperly planted in the disputed area did not belong to them and should therefore be sent to the King after harvesting. The subjects of Chief Nsibande were angry about the matter and returned to fight the subjects of Chief Makhubu. Blood was spilled and the police were called. The matter was then reported to the national authorities.

Chief Makhubu complains (during the interview with the researcher) that the major difficulty in the case, from his point of view, is that Chief Nsibande never brought an official complaint against him about the matter. Nor did Chief Nsibande go through lower channels – such as *Ndabazabantu* – in seeking an amiable settlement. Rather, he raised a case against the CRDB official with the national authorities.

In arguing their case before the national council, Chief Nsibande and his subjects maintain the following: first, ranking officials of a government agency authorized them to farm in the disputed area; secondly, their land has been taken from them by the authorities and their crops improperly seized; thirdly, their ancestors occupied the land before it became freehold land (after the Partition) and therefore they had the strongest claim to the land when it was repurchased.

Chief Makhubu, on the other hand, argues that he has documents and the support of top-ranking officials to justify his claims to the land. He also maintains that Chief Nsibande relies on outdated (pre-Partition) historical claims to the land and oral, rather than written, arguments of officials. Most important, he claims that he and his people suffer from poor soil and need the land more desperately than 'greedy' Chief Nsibande.

Chief Makhubu further argues that Chief Nsibande should have approached him about the matter. Differences in opinion could then have been discovered and negotiations encouraged. He also says that if both chiefs were supposed to occupy the area (same site or even adjoining sites), then government officials should have approached both him and Chief Nsibande and established a system whereby the two chiefs could cooperate.

Chief Makhubu is disconcerted by Chief Nsibande's claim to the land but primarily blames government officials for conducting confusing resettlement operations. He says that officials work at odds with one another. Most important, in his view, is that the government is experiencing considerable reorganization (in terms of personnel and objectives) within a short period of time. This results in a confusion on the part of current officials regarding the directives of previous officials. Moreover, contradictions in directives sometimes occur. Such confusion about and contradictions in directives could be alleviated, he says, if operations were conducted openly rather than secretively. For example, when he asked the current project manager to tell him who had previously ordered the settlement of both chiefs in the area, the manager refused to divulge the information, making clarification and confrontation nearly impossible.

Strategy analysis

The national authorities initially relied upon a control harmony strategy, forcing discontinuation of rivalries between disputing chiefs, but later relied upon two organic harmony strategies, postponing case hearing and eventually, decision-making. The latter strategies were organic because they aimed to encourage private settlement between disputing parties. Both the organic and control harmony strategies of the authorities served to produce peace (compliance) in the communities and avoided divisive entanglements by the authorities. Neither type of strategy produced true consensus.

Chief Nsibande, as a disputant of high rank, used at least four assertion disputing strategies: one strategy initiated a dyadic confrontation with Chief Makhubu and his subjects, one rejected the District Commissioner's orders, one encouraged combat between his subjects and Chief Makhubu's subjects, and one made direct appeal to the national council. Chief Nsibande initially attempted to assert his own and his subjects' perceived land administration and use rights through forceful private strategies which did not appeal to higher authority. He only formally asserted his land rights when called before higher authorities by Chief Makhubu. He may have used private force and avoided higher authorities because he felt his land claims would not be upheld. Nonetheless, when he came before the national council, he argued forcefully in assertion of his perceived land rights.

Chief Makhubu, who would have preferred to contain the dispute at a simmering inter-chieftaincy level, eventually responded to what he believed were land 'usurpations' and 'aggressions' on the part of Chief Nsibande and his subjects: he declared his position of administrative authority in the disputed area. He used four assertion disputing strategies: three strategies made appeals to government agencies (District Commissioner and Rural Development Board) or the national council and one involved direct combat between his subjects and Chief Nsibande's subjects. As a formally educated man, he believed his land claims were supported by clear, written government directives, and therefore, when these claims were contested by Chief Nsibande, they should have been done so through formal, legal channels.

Central Authority vs. chief dyad

Background

This section discusses land disputes between the Central Authority and a chief as well as land disputes between chiefs which involve the intervention of the Central Authority.

Land disputes which involve chiefs and the Central Authority should be analysed according to the different types of chieftaincies. As mentioned, there are three kinds of 'chiefs': (1) governors (*tindvuna*); (2) royals (*Bantfwabenkhosi*), and (3) clan (*sikhulu*). Each type of chief appears to have a different relationship with the Central Authority. Moreover, the nature of this relationship determines the rights which each type of chief exercises over land, including how land disputes are processed. Clan chiefs claim that they entered into a treaty relationship with the Dlamini rulers and may legitimately retain any powers which are not clearly vested in the Central Authority. Consequently, they are *theoretically* more likely to instigate land disputes and to resist unfavourable interference by the Central Authority. On the other hand, governor chiefs, who are placed on land through the good graces of the Central Authority, are at the latter's mercy. The situation of royal chiefs is less clearly defined since they are, in a sense, appendages of the Central Authority, and yet they tend to resist interference.[16] The Central Authority dispatches envoys (sometimes permanent officials such as a *Ndabazabantu* or Rural Development Officer) to investigate land disputes between chiefs or attempted banishments of subjects by their chiefs (in the latter case, when an individual threatened with banishment appeals to the King).

The containment principle underlying political harmony in the Central Authority vs. chief dyad holds that the Central Authority should not interfere in day-to-day land management activities within a chiefdom; however, the Central Authority may legitimately legislate on any matter which has significance to all Swazis. According to Hughes (1972: 253), the King thus ruled that any land which came under irrigation should automatically cease to be under the control of the chief of the area. Hughes further argues that most chiefs, especially clan chiefs, dispute the Central Authority's competence to make such a ruling, and consequently, huge areas of potentially irrigable land remain uncultivated because rights cannot be clearly established. Although the accuracy of Hughes' assertion that chiefs do not control irrigated areas may be questioned, my research does indicate that chiefs frequently and vigorously dispute rulings by the Central Authority about irrigated areas.

The containment principle also holds that the Central Authority may directly intervene in land affairs within a chiefdom if banishment is involved. Therefore, when a subject appeals to the Central Authority to overrule a chief's threatened banishment, the Central Authority must decide whether to assert its ultimate authority over land or to respect the autonomy of the chief in his area. In Cases 12 and 13 the Central Authority appeared to respect the rulings of the royal chief and the acting council chairman. According to Hughes (1972: 249), when banishment orders by chiefs have been overturned by the Central Authority, the chiefs have been unable to evict people forcibly without risking alienation of the Central Authority. Nor have such chiefs been able to rely upon the police; their main option has been to make life miserable for their unwanted tenants.

Although banishment cases usually involve evictions of subjects by chiefs, occasionally the Central Authority evicts a chief from his area. This situation occurs when a chief and/or subjects are forcibly removed from their area without land replacement. In a non-banishment situation, in which the Central Authority needs part or all of a chief's land holding for development, it tries to offer alternate land for resettlement. According to informants, forced evictions without land replacement have occurred with greater frequency since the death of King Sobhuza II in 1982.

In the context of land disputes or other land matters involving two or more chiefs, the Central Authority claims a clearly recognized right of intervention. However, according to several members of different chiefs' councils in the southern Shiselweni District, the Central Authority frequently postpones making a final ruling on a land dispute on appeal in the hopes that it will die a natural death. Such a dispute is ignored by the Central Authority for several reasons: to allow the heat of the dispute to cool down and the point of contention to be forgotten; to delay reaching a final decision until new local authorities (including a chief) are appointed; and to avoid making an unpopular decision. In essence, the authorities hope that the healing power of time and changes in personnel will help resolve disagreements and restore harmony. Regarding their own exercise of authority, they are caught in a bind about whether to preside over a land dispute: on the one hand, they demonstrate and validate their authority by adjudicating a land dispute, but on the other, they put their prestige and power on the line by undergoing the risk that they will make an unpopular decision which is disobeyed. By hearing a dispute but not reaching a decision, they validate their authority while avoiding heated entanglements.

Land dispute cases

Disputes in which the Central Authority intervenes on behalf of a chief's subject. A common situation in which the Central Authority interferes with a chief's local authority occurs when a chief's subject appeals against a resettlement or banishment order. In a resettlement situation, the chief is normally acting upon directives issued by the Central Authority, whereas in a banishment case, he is initiating the directive.

The following resettlement appeal demonstrates principles discovered in several similar cases.

Case 15: The woman who obtains the King's permission to retain land slated for development project

(data from informant who is uninvolved in the case, middleveld)

(Nxumalo is a commoner. She is old, has limited means of economic support and has had little formal education.)

Case summary

An old woman (Nxumalo) is informed by the chief that she will have to be resettled since the area in which her homestead is situated is slated for a construction project. She approaches the King and begs that she be permitted to remain in the area. She explains that she is too old to build a new homestead and has no children who can help her. The King gives her an official letter granting her permission to remain in the area. Nxumalo takes the letter to the chief's deputy. Consequently, when the builders come into the area, they are instructed to build around her homestead.

Strategy analysis
Nxumalo fought adverse development directives of chiefdom authorities in her area by using an assertion grievance strategy: she appealed directly to the national authorities. The national authorities intervened with an organic harmony strategy: they permitted her homestead to remain intact. They acted on behalf of a private citizen because their administrative control was not challenged, and further, because their intervention would not challenge the control of the chiefdom authorities who, in any case, had acted primarily upon national development directives. Although my informant did not specify, other informants indicated that the national authorities aided Nxumalo, who although poor and unaided by kin, had connections to royalty. Alternatively, they may have aided her because their actions would be generally interpreted as humanitarian, thus earning themselves respect and admiration.

Disputes in which the Central Authority challenges a chief's land rights. The following complex case involves the eviction of a chief and several relatives, who served on his council, from one of the chief's two land holdings. In the early part of this century, the ancestors of this chief had been instructed by the Central Authority to abandon a territory, but in compensation for their lost land, had been given a substitute area, B. In this recent case (1980s), the chief was ordered by a faction within the Central Authority (primarily several influential princes) to abandon Area B without being granted either a thorough hearing or a land replacement. Consequently, he had no alternative but to leave his subjects behind in Area B and retire to his other holding.

Case 16: The chief who is evicted by the Central Authority from his land
(data from member of Chief Dlamini's council, highveld)

(Dlamini is a high-ranking chief. Khumalo is an important high-ranking settler in his area. Both men have received a formal education and are wealthy.)

Case summary
Area A was allocated to X in the 1860s by King Mswati as a reward for military duties. X was also named chief of the area. Following the death of Chief X, Chief Y was installed. When Chief Y died, his successor, Chief Dlamini, was too young to take office, so Acting Chief Z took over in the interim.

During the chieftaincy of Chief Y (late nineteenth century), Europeans came into the area. In the 1930s, part of the land under his jurisdiction was subdivided as Title Deed Land and taken over by a European. Chief Y, along with other chiefs, complained about a land shortage, and consequently, King Sobhuza II appealed to the British authorities. In the 1940s, the British colonial government suggested to the Swazi King that land be bought back for the use of Swazis in agricultural schemes, known as the Native Land Settlement Programme. By this time, Chief Dlamini had been installed. Some of his subjects joined up with the new scheme.

In the early 1950s a foreign-owned company negotiated with Sobhuza II for exchange of some land occupied by Chief Dlamini's people with land at Area B. Area B was owned by another European. The above company bought the land from this European and turned it over to the King in trust for the Swazi Nation. Chief Dlamini received use of the land, while still maintaining control of several other areas. Problems arose in Area B because it was already occupied by farm dwellers who pledged allegiance to another chief. The subjects of the two chiefs disputed over land. In 1966 the agricultural scheme on Area B was renamed 'Swazi Settlement Scheme'.

The early phases of the present land dispute began, according to my informant, with a personal dispute between the *indvuna* of the area and an alleged subject of Chief Dlamini, Khumalo. Khumalo complained to the chief that the *indvuna* was having affairs with his wives. As a consequence, the *indvuna* was dismissed from the area. After the *indvuna* was dismissed, Khumalo approached Chief Dlamini and requested that he be appointed *indvuna*. Chief Dlamini denied the request, saying that a man cannot have someone removed from office and then try to assume the position himself.

According to my informant, Khumalo felt that historical developments had given him a right to act as *indvuna*. He had come to Area B from South Africa as a sheepherder under the employ of Afrikaaners. At some point he worked as a driver for the Native Land Settlement Scheme (now Swazi Settlement Scheme). He was registered under Acting Chief Z, but was an *indvuna* for the Boer's sheepherders. (Note: explanation about Khumalo's connection to farm dwellers is unclear in original interview.)

When the case at hand unfolds, Khumalo is angry about his rejection and tries to persuade residents of Area B (farm dwellers?) that land in a resettlement scheme should not be under a chief. His complaints are ignored by Chief Dlamini and his council, so he approaches the King who also denies his request to be named *indvuna* of the area. Failing in this manoeuvre, Khumalo persuades some residents of Area B to complain to the King that Chief Dlamini has erected his homestead and *kraal* in a grazing area. The matter continues for some years until 1982 at which time the King orders a committee of the local *Inkhundla* to look into the matter. Members of the committee investigate the disputed area and determine that the *kraal* had been properly placed. The King orders that Khumalo should be disciplined, but the former dies before his instructions can be carried out.

After the King's death, Khumalo again begins to plot. He approaches the Queen Regent who tells him to refer the matter back to the *Inkhundla*. Soon after, the Queen Regent is ousted in a palace coup. Khumalo approaches the 'Authorized Person' (person responsible for authorizing royal instructions during inter-regency), who orders that the *indvuna* be dismissed. Thereafter, Chief Dlamini and his council approach the *Liqoqo*, the country's ruling council, which assumed significant powers after the death of the King, with a complaint. When they are denied a full hearing, they resort to writing a letter of complaint.

According to the informant, extensive political manoeuvring begins at this point. The *Liqoqo* wants to oust Chief Dlamini from his area because the latter had been outspokenly opposed to the national power struggles which had resulted in the downfall of the Queen Regent. To this end, the *Liqoqo* calls about thirty men before the Regional Administrator's office (former District Commissioner) to inform them that they are to be evicted from the area.

The men threatened with eviction divide into two factions: one faction approaches several influential princes at the national capital for help, whereas the other faction approaches the High Court. Chief Dlamini feels that he can legitimately raise a complaint at the national capital because of the provisions of the Swazi Settlement Act; however, some princes at the capital refuse to help him, denying any knowledge of the matter. After some days, the same princes announce (via messengers) that they were aware of the situation after all and that Chief Dlamini is interfering with the intentions of the King (apparently some behind-the-scenes manoeuvring had occurred). They order Chief Dlamini to report again to the national capital. The hearing is tense and Chief Dlamini is not allowed to explain his position.

When Chief Dlamini and his associates are denied a full hearing before the customary tribunal, some of them decide to present a case to the High Court (Roman-Dutch law). They are told by some princes that no punitive action will be taken against them for recourse to the High Court. A couple of months later, several members of the *Liqoqo* report to Area B to inform Chief Dlamini and several important members of his council that they must leave the area since it 'belongs to the King'. Chief Dlamini's supporters then realize that they cannot report again to the High Court since the name of the deceased King has been invoked; legal action would be tantamount to sacrilege. Nonetheless, my informant believes that the King's name was exploited for selfish, political purposes.

At this time, one of the *Liqoqo* members who had opposed Chief Dlamini's appeal at the national capital comes to Area B and agitates residents (presumably subjects of the other chief) to press for Dlamini's eviction. Chief Dlamini and his council then report to the national headquarters and request, as is the privilege of a chief, to speak directly with the newly appointed Queen Regent. They want to lodge a protest about the 'interference in their area'. Unfortunately for their cause, several influential members of the former King's council, who customarily would have acted as messengers to the King or Queen, inform them that they cannot assist since *Liqoqo* members have denied them access.

Soon after, Chief Dlamini and four associates leave Area B after receiving threats by *Liqoqo* members that their property will be bulldozed down. They abandon without compensation modern homes, a butchery, shops, grinding mills and other establishments that had cost them over a million Emalangeni (*c.* \$500,000, 1985 exchange rate). Four of the men return to an area which is the main headquarters of Chief Dlamini (about 40 miles away); one man *khontaes* in a new area.

Chief Dlamini and his supporters decide not to take further action because of the cost and time involved. The abandoned area B is left with 3,000 people, 2,000 of whom are still under Chief Dlamini and 1,000 of whom are under the other chief who had also joined the Swazi Settlement Scheme. Tremendous administrative difficulties for Dlamini's subjects who are still resident in Area B have been created; they must report to Chief Dlamini in his distant area when they need assistance. No *indvuna* has been named in Area B to help alleviate administrative problems.

Strategy analysis

The royal faction primarily used control harmony strategies in an effort to suppress a powerful chief, Dlamini, who had challenged their control/legitimacy following the death of the King. Powerful faction members did not want to control Chief Dlamini's land themselves; they wanted to reduce the extent of his power and influence by reallocating part of his land area. They legitimated their actions in terms of complaints made by a discontented resident in Chief Dlamini's area, Khumalo. Many of the faction's strategies were actually control strategies disguised as organic strategies; such strategies were effective because they served to convince the (Western-influenced) High Court and the traditional national council that faction members were acting according to custom (i.e. by making land investigations and invoking the sacred name of the former King) and in the interests of national peace (i.e. by encouraging private settlement and non-use of courts). In practice, these strategies served to enforce compliance with their own control objectives and stifle protest among Chief Dlamini and his followers. After members of the royal faction had disengaged various legal bodies and stifled protest, they had no difficulty in using harsh control harmony strategies (i.e. threatening to evict residents forcibly from the disputed area and to destroy their property as well as actually using armed guards to ensure compliance).

Their clever use of manipulative strategies succeeded in defining and producing passive, obedient harmony according to their own land administration interests.

Chief Dlamini may have been an influential authority figure in his own chiefdom, but he was ineffective in his role as disputant against several powerful members of the royal family. He failed to gain access to the national council, where he hoped to condemn the power plays involved in the royal faction's disguised harmony strategies. Nor was he able to convince the Western High Court to hear and decide upon his case. All authority figures were afraid to jeopardize their positions by questioning the machinations of the royal faction. Chief Dlamini eventually used an avoidance strategy (abandoning land claim) in response to the potent control harmony strategies of the royal faction, thus succumbing to those authorities who had questioned and suppressed his land administration rights.

Land dispute causes according to dyad

The most common disputes in the family member vs. family member dyad involve brothers and succession rights (Case 3). Such disputes appear to have been exacerbated in recent years by land and resource shortages. Unlike in the past, a homestead head cannot easily divide up homestead land among his sons or otherwise seek land in the community. Disputes emerge in a variety of circumstances: when a son of a deceased homestead head is dissatisfied with his land allotment (Case 1); when the heir to a deceased homestead head refuses to share land and resources 'adequately' with his brothers, sisters or agnates, such as his father's brother (Cases 1, 2, 3); or when the oldest son of a deceased homestead head, who has migrated to an employment centre in a distant area, returns to reclaim his birthright. Disputes involving women are also common but remain largely invisible since most people deny that women can legitimately dispute over land; women themselves tend to enhance their opportunities by relying on informal disputing methods and non-customary legal institutions (see Chapter 6).

The most prevalent disputes in the subject vs. subject dyad involve land loans. Informants maintain that subjects are hesitant to loan land because they fear that it will not be returned upon request or that the authorities will not uphold their reclamation demands (Case 4). When they do loan land, disputes frequently arise (e.g. regarding use of land or duration of loan). Sometimes borrowers even insist that they were given land as a gift rather than a loan; this is particularly true when the original land transaction occurred between ancestors of disputants. A second increasingly common dispute between subjects involves boundaries (Case 5) and fencing (Case 6). A third common dispute between subjects involves access paths (Case 7). In crowded areas, paths for human transit are frequently cut off by fences, whereas paths for livestock transit are frequently not separated by fences from cultivated fields, resulting in damage to winter crops. A fourth common dispute between subjects involves rights to limited community resources.

The most common complaints in the subject vs. chief dyad involve perceived 'unfair' land allocations, land loss or resettlement for community development purposes (Case 8), and tribute-giving for land. Grievances which subjects have against their chiefs/other authorities often remain largely unstated since they are afraid to speak out against ranking persons to whom they owe allegiance. In the related chief vs. subject dyad, chiefs complain about subjects who erect buildings without authorization (see Case 25 in Chapter 7), who encroach upon land which they are not authorized to use (Case 11), and who disobey land directives of the authorities or are generally 'disrespectful' (Case 12).

All disputes in the chief vs. chief dyad are problematic, according to informants. Disputes in this dyad are least likely to result in lasting and amiable settlements. Most chiefs appear unwilling or unable to negotiate a settlement privately, and the Central Authority often fails to dictate and enforce a settlement. The main issue underlying inter-chieftaincy land disputes, according to informants, centres upon development projects and associated resettlement: chiefs are compelled by development interests and fears about land shortages to assert their perceived rights (Case 14). Few chiefs are content to overlook transgressions for an extended period as did the chief in Case 13.

Disputes in the Central Authority vs. chief dyad are not readily amenable to solution – unless the Central Authority intervenes to support a subject's reasonable request (Case 15). The Central Authority is the ultimate authority and may not be inclined to work with a chief in formulating a negotiated resolution (Case 16).

In summary, dispute containment and non-escalation of disputes, including the production of harmony, is not always achieved. Some types of disputes are more likely to arise and, of these, some are more likely to escalate to public forums. These disputes are characterized by disputant relationships which are particularly likely to impose political struggles upon the achievement of harmony.

Composite strategy analysis

General strategies and case interests are now analysed in order to demonstrate why participants occupying particular status relationships (relative to other participants) chose particular strategies. In this regard, two questions are: When do authorities use organic as opposed to control harmony strategies? and When do disputants use assertion, avoidance or deception disputing strategies? The answers, which refer to the relative personal and structural statuses (ascribed and achieved aspects) of authorities and disputants, depict the politics of Swazi harmony.

Authorities' harmony strategies

Swazi authorities tend to rely on organic harmony strategies when their personal and structural statuses are not threatened; however, they tend to rely on control harmony strategies when these statuses are threatened.

Data analysis indicates that authorities may use organic harmony strategies in cases involving litigants who are political unequals (structural status) relative to them but social equals (individual status) relative to each another. These litigants do not challenge their control. In such cases, the authorities exercise their dispute-processing functions with the aim of achieving compromise. For example, in Case 3 the chief ordered peaceful reconciliation between brothers disputing over rights to trees on the family homestead.

The authorities may also use organic harmony strategies in cases involving litigants who are social unequals relative to each other. Again, the authorities' interests in control are not at stake, and they can enhance their personal statuses through successful dispute processing. For example, in Case 7, the council chairman ordered a compromise between community residents disputing about cattle trespass – even though the complainant, as a member of the local council, had achieved higher personal status than his opponent.

The authorities may also use organic harmony strategies in cases involving political unequals (structural status) who challenge their control. In such cases, the authorities try to avoid local political unrest or dispute escalation with a neighbouring group. For example, in Cases 5 and 10, the authorities delayed the cases and ordered balanced settlement in order to secure long-term community consensus at the expense of short-term disputant compliance – even though both disputants in both cases had promoted their own land interests in violation of the authorities' land administrative orders. In Case 26 (Chapter 7), the authorities recommended compromise between disputants in order to suppress the dispute and thereby avoid long-range structural destabilization – even though one of the disputants had challenged their jurisdiction.

The authorities may also use organic harmony strategies – regardless of the social/political status of one disputant relative to another – when the evidence does not clearly favour one disputant over another. In such cases, the authorities' control is not challenged. For example, in Case 6 the evidence did not clearly favour one disputant over another, and the authorities thus recommended compromise or equal sanctioning.

The authorities may use control harmony strategies in cases involving litigants who are political unequals (structural status) relative to them. In such cases, the authorities reassert their control which the litigants have challenged. In several cases the authorities used control harmony strategies to suppress the challenges of a subject who ignored dispute-processing instructions (Case 4), who contested the authorities' land adjudication (Case 11) or who refused to offer 'adequate' land tributes (Case 12).

The authorities may also use control harmony strategies in cases involving litigants who are near political equals (structural status). In such cases, the authorities defend their control from direct challenges of high-ranking persons. For example, in Case 16, a faction within the Central Authority evicted a prominent chief from his land after the chief had questioned the faction's legitimacy.

Table 5. *Litigants' disputing strategies*

A. Litigants' disputing strategies, based upon authorities' harmony strategies and their own dispute interests
B. Litigants' disputing strategies, based upon opponents' relative status and their own dispute interests

A	disputant's response to authorities' harmony	accept authorities' harmony strategies and control	accept authorities' control but reject their harmony strategies in order to achieve better outcomes	reject authorities' control and harmony strategies in order to achieve better outcomes	accept authorities' harmony strategies and control but rely on alternative dispute-processing methods
disputant's strategies					
assertion		X	X	X	
avoidance					X
deception					X

B	disputant's status relative to opponent	low relative status	high relative status	high relative status and cost of avoidance high	high relative status and no disputing options	equal (low) relative status and few disputing options	equal (high) relative status and control threatened by dispute escalation	equal (high) relative status and control threatened or stakes high
disputant's strategies								
assertion		X		X	X	X		X
avoidance			X				X	
deception			X				X	

The authorities may also use control harmony strategies disguised as organic harmony strategies in cases involving high-status litigants who are political equals (structural status). In such cases, the litigants challenge their actions or even their political legitimacy. The organic rhetoric of the authorities' harmony strategies anchors their claims in custom, thus securing general ideological consensus. At the same time, the control actions of their strategies compels disputants to acquiesce and abide by their rulings. For example, in Case 8, community authorities used the organic strategy of achieving local consensus and support from the Central Authority by speaking about the King's desire to create a peaceful community; but they achieved disputant compliance through reliance on police force and court dictates. In Case 16, the national authorities (ruling faction) used the organic strategy of achieving support, if not complete ideological consensus, by speaking about their role in achieving the King's interests in national unity; but they also achieved disputant compliance through reliance on police force and court dictates. In both cases, control harmony strategies served to downplay the dispute before, or even after, 'outside' authorities (i.e. from courts influenced by Western law) could intervene. The strategies denied disputants access to a traditional dispute-processing forum, and at the same time persuaded the Western courts (High Court and Magistrates' Court) to relinquish jurisdiction.[17]

The authorities may rely on different harmony strategies in the same case when their control is threatened at one point in time but not another. Thus, the authorities in Case 4 initially relied on organic harmony strategies when the dispute began as a confrontation between two subjects over a land loan, but when it became a matter of one subject's disrespect for their authority, they switched to control harmony strategies. In Case 7, the authorities initially used control harmony strategies when the cattle of one subject destroyed the crops of a council member, but they switched to organic harmony strategies when the two disputing subjects reached a private compromise (see Table 5).

Litigants' disputing strategies

Swazi disputants rely on disputing strategies which involve assertion, avoidance or deception in response to the authorities' harmony strategies. Assertion disputing strategies usually make open, public statements about perceived land rights – thus involving either compromise with or challenge of the authorities' case strategies or general control, whereas avoidance/deception strategies usually make indirect manoeuvres to secure perceived land rights – thus involving evasion of their strategies and control. Disputants' assertion strategies are not only reactive to the authorities' harmony strategies; they may also initiate actions, persuading the authorities to respond with harmony strategies. Disputants' avoidance/deception strategies may also be initiating, but they tend to be reactive, avoiding confrontations about rights.

Disputants also rely on strategies which involve assertion, avoidance or deception in response to their opponents' strategies. In effect, disputants' strategies are not only produced as a response to the authorities' harmony strategies – they are also devised in response to other disputants' strategies. Therefore, disputants must first calculate how to reconcile authorities' harmony strategies, which further their (the authorities') control interests, with their own disputing strategies, which further their own case interests – relative to their opponents. Disputants consider their status relative to the authorities and their opponents when they select their strategies.

Data analysis indicates that disputants may use assertion disputing strategies in response to the authorities' harmony strategies in cases in which they accept the authorities' strategies and want to enhance their own outcomes without directly challenging the authorities' control. For example, in Case 6, a disputant accepted the authorities' efforts to encourage private settlement about boundaries, but he argued his case before the court in the hope that he might sway a compromise in his favour. In other cases, disputants may use assertion disputing strategies when they do not accept the authorities' harmony strategies but accept their control; they want to enhance their own outcomes. Thus, in Case 9, a man challenged the authorities' denial of his land rights, but he did not challenge their ultimate control. In still other cases, disputants may use assertion disputing strategies when they do not accept the authorities' harmony strategies and do not accept their control; they hope to achieve more favourable outcomes by directly challenging the authorities. Thus, in Case 9, a man challenged the authorities' strategies when they took over part of his land, and he also challenged their control (legitimacy) in the community.

Disputants may use avoidance/deception disputing strategies in response to the authorities' harmony strategies in cases in which they accept the authorities' harmony strategies and their control, but want to improve their own dispute outcomes through use of alternative procedures and forums. For example, in Case 3, a man who was disputing with his brother over trees accepted the authorities' efforts to negotiate a settlement between them, but he used the avoidance strategy of relying upon private witchcraft accusations to improve his outcome. In other cases, disputants use avoidance/deception disputing strategies when they do not accept the authorities' strategies but nonetheless want to achieve alternatives without challenging their control. Thus, in Case 4, a man challenged the authorities' organic harmony strategies, which denied him forum access and encouraged peaceful settlement, but he accepted their control. His avoidance (of authority) strategy of ploughing down his opponent's fields aimed to achieve an immediate outcome and ultimately, forum access. In still other cases, disputants use avoidance/deception disputing strategies when they do not accept the authorities' strategies and do not accept their control. Thus, in Case 11, a man challenged the authorities' strategies when they took over part of his land, and he also challenged their control – i.e. their administrative privilege to deny his land rights.

Data analysis indicates that disputants tend to use assertion disputing strategies in response to their opponents' disputing strategies when their opponents are of lower status relative to them. Moreover, they can rely on any procedures and forums, but they tend to use public forums if their case is strong and they want to make a point. For example, in Case 1, which involved unequal status based on age, a paternal uncle took his nephew before the Chief's Court because he knew that his age would give him a decisive advantage; he wanted to achieve public condemnation of his nephew. In Case 11, which involved unequal status based on hereditary (structural) rank, the chief's council used an open forum to condemn a disrespectful subject because they wanted to demonstrate their authority to other subjects. In the above cases, the disputants were confident that their higher status guaranteed them favourable outcomes.

Disputants tend to use avoidance/deception disputing strategies in response to their opponents' disputing strategies when their opponents are of higher status relative to them. Moreover, they tend to 'lump' their grievances or avoid their opponents, relying on no dispute-processing forum, when they are unable or unlikely to get a fair or favourable hearing. For example, in Case 2, which involved unequal status based on gender, an unwed mother avoided her brothers who evicted her; she obtained land from distant kin since no public forum would extend jurisdiction over her case. In Case 9, which involved unequal status based on hereditary rank, a man who received land from a false authority 'lumped' his grievance since no public forum would grant him a hearing.

On the other hand, disputants whose opponents are of higher status tend to use assertion disputing strategies when avoidance would incur high costs. In such cases they rely on public forums. For example, in Case 4, a man who was faced with land loss challenged his opponent, and later the chief. In Case 16, which involved unequal status based on hereditary rank, a chief challenged the land eviction orders of a ruling faction. Disputants whose opponents are of higher status also tend to use assertion strategies when they have no other options. For example, in Case 9, which involved unequal status based on individual accomplishments, a man challenged the eviction orders of the local authorities, who were also acting as disputants.

Disputants who are both of low status tend to use assertion disputing strategies to improve their dispute options and outcomes. They may rely on mediation, arbitration or adjudication procedures at any of a number of forums, depending on case circumstances (e.g. evidence). In Case 3, a man disputing with his brother took his case to the Chief's Court since he believed he could prove tree ownership. In Case 6, a subject who was disputing with another subject took his case before the chief's council for adjudication since he believed he could demonstrate improper fence erection. In Case 7, a subject

Table 6. *Authorities' harmony strategies, based upon disputants' status and their own control interests*

Disputant's status relative to authorities	Political unequal (social equal to opponent)	Political unequal (social unequal to opponent)	Political unequal	Political unequal	Political equal/unequal	Political equal or near equal
Authorities' control	not challenged	not challenged	challenged but stability essential	challenged	not challenged	challenged
Authorities' harmony strategies	organic	organic	organic	control	organic	control

who was disputing with another subject took his case to the local council since he was sure he could receive compensation for demonstrable crop destruction caused by his neighbour's cattle.

Disputants who are both high status (e.g. chiefs) tend to use avoidance/deception disputing strategies when dispute escalation would unnecessarily threaten their control. For example, in Case 13, a chief, who was disputing with another chief about vaguely defined land boundaries, 'lumped' his grievance rather than confront his opponent. On the other hand, either high-status disputant may use assertion strategies when the stakes are high (land loss or acquisition) or peaceful negotiation is unlikely. In Case 14, both disputing chiefs, who stood to gain or lose a sizeable tract of irrigated land, used the assertion strategies of forcefully asserting their presence in the disputed area and approaching government authorities.

Disputants who are of high status – but not quite as high as their opponents (e.g. chiefs vs. Central Authority) – tend to use disputing strategies according to status considerations in individual cases. In cases in which a high-status disputant's control is not challenged, he/she will be more likely to use avoidance strategies. For example, in Case 15, the chief whose resettlement order was challenged before the Central Authority by an old woman peacefully complied with the new orders. In cases in which a high-status disputant's control is challenged, he/she will be more likely to use assertion strategies. For example, in Case 16, the chief who was evicted by the Central Authority used every conceivable assertion strategy in protest (see Table 6).

Summary

Dispute participants' statuses have an impact upon strategy selection. Authorities consider their own status interests (control) when they formulate harmony strategies. Disputants consider the authorities' statuses when they select disputing strategies in response to their harmony strategies, but they also consider their own statuses relative to their opponents' statuses when they select their strategies. Dispute participants' strategic calculations about relative structural (political) and personal (social) statuses constitute a 'politics of harmony'. In effect, all dispute participants accept the value of ideological harmony for cultural survival, but they perpetuate and respond to organic and control harmony ideologies conveyed in specific cases according to their immediate interests.

6

'A woman is like a field': Swazi women's land dispute strategies

This chapter describes land cases involving women, in which harmony ideology was produced by male family heads and local authorities for the purpose of validating and producing consensus or compliance about male land control. I argue that male land control would be threatened if women could legally challenge male rights; therefore, women theoretically must not be permitted to dispute openly about perceived land access and use rights. The cases demonstrate that while women publicly express conformity to standards of male control, they manoeuvre behind the scenes to enhance their rights. A complex interplay between male elites' production of harmony ideologies and female disputants' strategic responses creates a 'politics of harmony' defined by gender.

As the following discussion indicates, Swazi women are described by the literature as occupying relatively powerless positions – in terms of land control – compared with Swazi men. Moreover, my male and female informants almost uniformly stated that, in theory, women have no right under Swazi customary land law to dispute about land. However, my case data, which I collected from two courts over the course of a year and from numerous interviews with women, indicate that female disputants enhance their disputing opportunities through application of assertion, avoidance and deception strategies. They devise their strategies based on the subject matter of the dispute, the political priorities of the male authorities overseeing their cases and their status relative to their opponents. Their status is determined by several interdependent personal characteristics: hereditary birthright (clan membership), marital status, individual personality (initiative and persistence), personal relationships and economic resources.

Women and land relations in Africa

Until recently most accounts of African land tenure systems placed men in the focus of analysis. Women's customary access and usage rights to land were either ignored or subsumed under male interests (see Brain 1976; Hay and Stichter 1984; Tadesse 1982). Upon the publication of Ester Boserup's book,

Women's Role in Economic Development (1970), and later a succession of articles and books on related topics (Mbilinyi 1972; Mullings 1976; Nelson 1981; Papanek 1977; Rogers 1980), gender imbalances in the treatment of people and subject matter, particularly in the context of land relations, were noted. Thereafter, women were increasingly the focus of interest. Writers thus interpreted the relation between African women and land during the late colonial and post-colonial periods as one in which women's customary corporate, allocative rights in land were undermined and suppressed, while a system of individual men's titles in land was promoted (Boserup 1970; Colson 1966: 2 and 1963: 151; Jacobs 1984; Okeyo 1980; Pala 1976; Rogers 1980). Other writers portrayed the relationship in more favourable terms, maintaining that changes, such as land adjudication, improved women's land rights (e.g. Njeru 1978: 30 and Brokensha and Njeru 1977: 12, 15 on Mbere). Still others observed that changes confused women's land rights, both improving and worsening their rights (Roberts n.d.: 12–13 on Kgatla).

While the literature on women and land tenure of the last two decades has been important in differentiating African men's and women's perspectives on land relations, it has tended to obscure local realities by emphasizing three ideal constructs. First, it generalizes about transformations in customary land tenure systems, thereby minimizing the significance of structural and historical peculiarities of each system for women's production and land use. Secondly, it emphasizes the experiences of the 'average' woman, e.g. the married women, while overlooking the experiences of women occupying other social and economic statuses – such as widows and women separated from their husbands. Thirdly, it emphasizes stereotypical responses of women to land relations – such as reliance upon male representation – thus denying women roles as actors who creatively deal with real life situations. In sum, arguments which typify 'average' women and ideal patterns of land relations fail to convey the dynamism of women's actual land-disputing behaviour; in practice, individual women use a variety of strategies to achieve their goals.

Although anthropologists have frequently commented on discrepancies between ideal formulations and actual manifestations of human behaviour, the literature on women and land tenure in Africa says little on the matter except to note that women's ideal land rights are highly variant in different cultures (Biebuyck 1964: 103–4; also 1963). Regarding land disputes, African women are usually described in 'ideal' terms of male control; in other words, they are supposed to occupy positions which are so structurally weak that they cannot reasonably dispute about land (see e.g. Moore 1986: 305; see contrary evidence in Njeru 1978).

In this study of Swazi women's relation to land, actual disputing behaviours of women, as revealed in case studies, are contrasted with ideal constructs. Case data are thus used to reveal local realities. Swazi male authorities' strategies of harmony ideology are analysed to demonstrate specific structural and historical circumstances influencing women's production and land use. Further, Swazi women's socio-economic characteristics are discussed to illustrate the range of women who dispute about land rights. Finally, Swazi women's land dispute strategies are analysed to demonstrate actual and creative, rather than stereotypical, responses to land matters.

Ideologies of gender: Swazi women

Male ideologies about the relation between women and customarily tenured land were often conveyed to me while I was doing research in Swaziland. On one occasion, a Swazi man summed up the prevalent male perception about women's involvement in land tenure, including land disputes, when he explained, 'A woman is like a field.' After being prodded to elaborate, he commented that Swazi men aim, first, to possess both women and fields, and secondly, to protect their rights over the products of both acquisitions, i.e. children and harvests, from the encroachments of other men. In his view, men are the inextricable link between women and land.

This man's view supports the interpretation of land relations in Swaziland which is usually stated in the literature: 'women have little control over the land distribution process' (Sachs and Roach 1983) and 'the customary land tenure system . . . has very little place for women' (Amoah 1978).

Scholarly interpretations of Swazi land relations similarly define women's roles in terms of male control: either in the private sector (family) or the public sector. When defining men's and women's roles in the private sector, the literature describes the normative situation in which a man receives a land grant from a chief in a new community or inherits land administrative responsibilities after the death of a homestead head (see Armstrong 1985; Hughes 1972; Kuper 1947a; Marwick 1940; Nkambule 1983). Men are assumed to have important roles in the land acquisition process, as an applicant's representative before a new chief or as a new chief's envoy to an applicant's present chief. The literature indicates that Swazi women are not permitted to represent themselves independently before the authorities when requesting a land allotment (Russell 1983: 13 and 1985: 21; Armstrong 1985: 53).

The literature also describes the normative (i.e. prescribed) situation in which Swazi men rather than women exercise significant land use rights as farmers (Riddell and Dickerman 1986: 21; Sibisi 1980: 12) and in which Swazi men rather than women make major decisions about land use on the homestead (Sibisi 1980: 11–12).

When defining men's and women's roles in the public sector, the literature describes the normative situation in which Swazi men assume primary roles as members of chiefs' councils entrusted with important decision-making responsibilities regarding land or as active participants in public debate. Women are only mentioned to the extent that they can expect to receive land from their husbands and be represented by their husbands in dispute situations.

My informants – both male and female – conveyed similar ideologies about male land control. In other words, nearly everyone stated in interviews that men have more significant roles in family decision-making processes regarding land use, in land access procedures within the homestead and chiefdom, and in land dispute procedures coming before the family or chief's council. They were in agreement that women, who cannot receive land in their own name, are theoretically not allowed to dispute about land. They stated that when women have a land-related grievance, they are 'supposed' to maintain harmony by quietly consulting with male family elders. Thus, when a married woman disagrees with a co-wife about land allocations, she should ask her husband for clarification. When she has a complaint against a member of her husband's extended family, she may resort to her husband's family council; however, members may not grant her a full hearing since the land is under their control. When a married or unmarried woman wishes to press a grievance about land rights on her natal homestead, she should try to influence her own family council.

Similar statements about male land control and the 'ideal' relationship between women and the land appeared in a questionnaire survey which was developed by University of Swaziland law lecturer Alice Armstrong. This questionnaire was primarily designed to elicit the beliefs of 67 male and female Swazi respondents regarding customary law provisions for women's roles in land matters. Survey results confirmed the ideal statements reported in the literature and interviews when respondents were asked to make ideal statements; however, when respondents were asked to report actual behaviours of women, numerous deviations from ideal statements appeared. Such deviations were particularly evident regarding women's actual involvement in land disputes. Twelve questions which cover issues of women's land acquisition, land possession rights and land disputes are discussed in this section (see Appendix).

Seventy per cent of the respondents confirmed that the normative pattern for gaining access to land – excluding inheritance – is through *kukhonta* by a married man. Seventy-five per cent also recognized the right of unmarried women/widows to obtain land through a son. At the same time, an equal percentage responded that unmarried men do not have the right to obtain land through *kukhonta*. In terms of land use, while men have the right to lend fields, 90 per cent of the respondents claimed that a woman cannot lend out her fields without the permission of her husband. Thirty-four per cent acknowledged the right of a woman's husband to take away her fields.

Noticeable diversions from ideal standards occurred in the responses to two items in the questionnaire, one concerning women's right to land and the other concerning women's possession of fields. Although observers of the Swazi situation claim that women have little place in the customary land tenure system (Amoah 1978), 72 per cent of respondents recognized general female rights in land and a significant 98 per cent replied that women 'own' fields. Moreover, respondents clearly deviated from the ideal that men exclusively inherit land. Ninety-three per cent stated that a woman can inherit land from her husband, and 63 per cent said that a woman can inherit land from her father.[1]

Respondents indicated contradictions in women's rights to land based upon marital status. Women are said to have essentially the same rights over their fields as man. Yet respondents said that a husband's control over land means that a woman risks the loss of her fields under certain circumstances. Nor can she freely loan her fields to another person without the consent of her husband. Another area of disparity concerned the rights of widows. Ideally, women whose husbands have died receive land from their in-laws, but many respondents reported that widows get land through sons who *khonta* for them. Access to land for widows and unmarried women seems largely to be determined by the presence of sympathetic male relatives who are willing to *khonta* for them or allot them land on the family homestead.

One question inquired into the involvement of women in land disputes. Slightly over half of respondents said that they had never heard of such disputes, and 20 per cent said that such disputes cannot exist because women do not control land. Of those who reported having heard about actual disputes, 21 per cent did not specify the exact nature of the disputes, but 8 per cent gave the following examples of situations in which disputes involve women: when no male is present on the homestead to defend land rights; when a woman returns to her natal homestead after a failed marriage and has no brothers who can defend her father's land rights; when a woman fights with co-wives over land allotments; when a half-brother rather than full-brother is chosen as heir to his father's land; and when a woman's neighbour claims her fields.

In summary, interview and questionnaire data indicate that when respondents are asked about *actual behaviours*, women appear to have greater involvement in land matters than ideal formulations would predict. Moreover, land dispute data point to a greater female involvement than might be expected. These findings confirm occasional comments in the literature to the effect that women's particular circumstances and personal initiative might influence their actual control over land (e.g. Armstrong 1985). Unfortunately, since little is known about women's roles in land matters, considerable confusion about their 'real land rights' (Russell 1985: 22), i.e. rights in practice, prevails. The important problem, according to Sibisi, is to recognize that women's powerlessness has been exaggerated (Sibisi cited in Russell 1983: 6) and that women's actual behaviour should be observed for the purpose of determining which kinds of women overcome traditional constraints and how they do this (Sibisi 1980: 14).

Strategies in Swazi land use cases

In this analysis of land disputes involving women, discrepancies between ideal and actual behaviour[2] are accounted for through analysis of strategizing behaviour.[3] The women's literature characterizes strategies as those used for recruiting aid and those for gaining influence in order to achieve certain ends (Collier 1974; Lamphere 1974, 1975; Stack 1974a, 1974b).

Harmony strategies of authorities

Ideologies are used by male homestead heads and chiefdom authorities towards two ends: to reinforce principles of male land control and to reinforce or establish principles of female land access and use rights. When men attempt to reinforce their control in homestead units, they emphasize the male prerogative to make major decisions regarding land use – for example, the crops grown, crops sold or land allotted. They also emphasize the male prerogative to exercise land production activities. When men, particularly community elders or members of the chief's council, attempt to reinforce their control at the chiefdom level, particularly in the context of land disputes heard before the Chief's Court, they emphasize that men control land and that women must rely on male relatives to grant and argue land rights. They also emphasize that men occupy superior social positions as compared to women and therefore must be accorded respect.

Actual male control over land in Swaziland is arguably threatened by such developments as male absenteeism due to migrant labour and female involvement in income-generating activities. Such developments encourage male homestead and chiefdom authorities to rely increasingly on ideologies to render the appearance of ideal, if not actual, male control. Harmony ideologies, in particular, make persuasive arguments about connections between cultural integrity, continuity, stability and male land control, associating harmonious social, economic and political relations with male land control. Strategies of organic harmony reinforce male land control by urging consensus about standards of relative status, custom and morality, whereas strategies of control harmony reinforce land control by forcing compliance about standards of absolute control and respect due to male authorities – both at chiefdom and modern bureaucratic levels. In effect, harmony strategies enable men to disguise gender interests as community interests.

One organic harmony strategy which promotes male land control involves reference to custom. For example, male authorities state that, according to custom, men must control land access and use if peaceful familial relations on homesteads are to continue. They urge settlement 'at home' by male family elders. Thus, in one case, the chief stated, 'It is Swazi custom that a woman's family first try to settle a matter involving her among themselves. Then if they fail, they can go before the chief's council.'

If settlement 'at home' fails and the case must be brought before the Chief's Court for settlement, the male chiefdom authorities argue that men must represent women. In a case in which a woman made an independent land request before the Chief's Court, the authorities admonished her for acting outside the realm of custom without male representation. One male court member argued that she should not be granted land because she had not gone through the legitimate, customary procedures of securing support from a male family member. He argued: 'There could be trouble for us if we granted her land. If she is legally married, her in-laws will make trouble. If no brother stands for her, there could be fighting among the men who try to enter her hut.' The chiefdom authorities also argue that men may not deal privately with women in negotiating settlement. Thus, in a dispute about boundaries, a man who approached a woman directly was admonished. A member of the chief's council asked him: 'Was it Swazi custom for you to talk to Mrs — without her in-laws being present?'

Another strategy of organic harmony which promotes male land control involves reference to relative status. For example, male authorities state that, according to standards of relative status, respect for male land control ensures harmonious community relations. Thus, in one case in which a woman forcefully and persuasively argued that a dairy project should be accepted in the chiefdom, the chief admonished her through a proverb which stated, 'Elders' meat is not supposed to be presented with a stick.' This proverb reminded her of her lower status in terms of age and gender relative to the male members of the chief's council.

A strategy which uses harmony as control may also involve reference to relative status (e.g. hereditary rank and gender). However, rather than aim at consensus through appeal to conventional wisdom, the authorities aim at compliance through threat of forceful intervention. For example, in a dispute about a land loan, the chief scolded the woman borrower who refused to relinquish land control. He said, 'This woman does not respect the council. We should call the police and have her put in jail for contempt of court . . . We should use this case to set an example as to what happens when people do not respect the rulings of the council.'

It should be noted that gender is an important criterion in male elites' production of harmony ideology, but birthright is even more important. Thus, in a case in which a woman complained to the chief's council that her parents had died and her brother was attempting to take away her fields, the chief admonished the brother stating: 'Do you remember when the council told people to stop fighting about fields? You must divide the fields, giving some to your sister.' He added, 'Who gave you the right to quarrel with your sister? Why didn't you ask for fields from your younger father?' In effect, the chief's harmony strategy was organic in that he referred to customary practice and relative status in order to urge consensus towards peaceful settlement. However, he placed birthright (respect for authorities) above gender in reaching a decision.

Disputing strategies of women litigants

Swazi women's disputing strategies not only respond to specific statements about and manifestations of harmony, as expressed in land disputes, they also respond to general male land control ideologies. Male land control ideologies indicate that land disputes should be initiated, argued and resolved by men: men should represent women before customary courts responsible for land disputes and they should control the decision-making processes of these bodies.

Swazi women's disputing strategies aim either to manipulate the rigid structural definitions of gender status (ascribed) and/or to enhance more fluid definitions of personal status (achieved). Their strategies fall into three categories: strategies of assertion, avoidance and deception. When using assertion strategies, women try to control a situation and assert perceived land rights by recruiting allies or by assuming individual control on the basis of personal attributes. Women who use assertion strategies either reject openly, minimize or manipulate the ideal standard of male land control. When using avoidance strategies, women avoid individuals – usually men – who might deny their perceived land rights or avoid institutions which are suspected of being unsympathetic. Sometimes avoidance means circumventing individuals who covet a woman's plot of land or avoiding legal measures. Women who use avoidance strategies evade the ideal standard of male land control. When using deception strategies, women exaggerate or falsify land rights. In essence, assertion strategies seek to manipulate the ideal of male control, whereas avoidance and deception strategies evade the ideal.

Disputing strategies of women's opponents

When men dispute with women about land, they tend to use strategies of assertion. They are usually in the position of being complainants who defend their perceived land rights against presumed transgressions of women. In only one case in my sample did a woman directly dispute at the Chief's Court with another woman over land. In this case, however, one of the women was representing her ailing husband (see Case 20).

Land dispute cases

Selected cases

As indicated above, inconsistencies between ideal prescriptions of behaviour and actual behaviour, which appeared in Armstrong's questionnaire survey data, found further expression in many of the approximately forty land disputes involving women in my case sample. Seven disputes are presented here as a means of assessing the types of harmony strategies devised by male authorities and the disputing strategies devised by women in each case. The disputes reflect four dyads in the Swazi social/political hierarchy: family member vs. family member (Cases 17–19); subject vs. subject (Cases 20 and 21); subject vs. chief (Case 22); and chief vs. subject (Case 23). All the cases, except Case 20, involved disputes about access rights; in Case 20 a woman was called as a defendant in a land loan case. All the cases, except Case 23, occurred in my research area. Five cases demonstrate women's successful use of strategies, and two cases, Cases 20 and 23, demonstrate unsuccessful use of strategies.

In each case summary, data regarding the woman's structural status relative to other participants as well as data regarding her personal socio-economic status are provided. Those aspects of each woman's socio-economic status which primarily determined how she strategized include marital status, individual personality (e.g. initiative and persistence), relationships with relatives, in-laws and neighbours, and economic resources.

After each case summary, the harmony strategies the authorities used (organic and control) as well as the disputing strategies the woman and her opponent used (assertion, avoidance or deception) are analysed. The Swazi clan names that identify the women are not their real names.

Family member vs. family member dyad

Case 17: The woman who argues with her in-laws about her land allotment after her husband's death

(data from interviews with Mamba and neighbours, middleveld)

(Mamba is widowed. She is educated and was employed until shortly before the interview.)

Case summary

Mamba was taken as the fourth wife of a former Swazi District Commissioner. She lived on his rural homestead, and his other wives resided on homesteads in distant locations.

The case opens when Mamba's husband dies, and his aged mother takes over control of the homestead. She manages her deceased son's bank account and indicates what the new land allotments should be. Mamba's mother-in-law refuses to give her money, locks her out of the house where she stayed with her husband, and allots her only a small plot of land. Mamba attributes her bad treatment to jealousy since she had been the youngest and favourite wife.

Mamba goes to the District Commissioner's office to bring a case against her in-laws for non-support. The District Commissioner orders her mother-in-law to give her money for the education of her children and to allow her access to the house.

When the oldest son of the main wife, i.e. the heir to the father's land, dies, Mamba is blamed for using witchcraft to cause his death. She is determined to remain at her husband's place, but as she senses a serious deterioration of relationships, she goes to the chief of her parents' area with her full-grown son and *khontaes* for land. She does this secretly since she wants to remain at her husband's place but also wants to hold on to the land in her father's area as security. She knows her in-laws are not likely to cast her out as long as they are unaware that she has land elsewhere.

Strategy analysis

In this case, no one was in a strong position to produce harmony. The District Commissioner, as a dispute-processing agent in the modern bureaucratic sector outside the chiefdom, intervened on Mamba's behalf, ordering her mother-in-law to provide her with financial support. However, he had no personal status/control interests in the chiefdom, thus neither the interest nor the ability to influence significantly social/political relationships.

Mamba's mother-in-law, acting as a temporary representative of her surviving sons following the death of her senior son, arguably produced control harmony; however, it is more likely that her actions against Mamba (restricting her land rights and accusing her of witchcraft) constituted assertion disputing strategies. She was not interested in producing a forced or consensual harmony in relationships and also had no permanent interest in personal status and control. Her primary concern was in suppressing Mamba's claims for the benefit of her sons.

Mamba used an assertion strategy when she took her grievance to the District Commissioner. He was only able to assist her with a child payment order – not with a guarantee of land rights, over which he had no control. Mamba, as a woman who had married into the homestead, did not have the status to protest her treatment to the chief's council; she had no guaranteed land rights. Her avoidance/deception strategy of secretly obtaining land in her area of birth served as an effective insurance policy against forced eviction by her in-laws.

Case 18: The woman who evicts her son in order to protect her land rights

(data from interview with Lukhele, middleveld)

(Lukhele is widowed. She is educated and employed.)

Case summary

When Lukhele's youngest son was still an infant, her latest lover was killed in an automobile accident. She decided to obtain land in a chief's area near her place of employment. At first she represented herself before the chief's council as a widow, but eventually she admitted that she had only intended to marry her lover. Thereafter, she was required to secure the assistance of a male relative who resided in another part of the country. She was also represented before the chief's council by her eighteen-year-old son. She was only granted a small plot in the crowded settlement around the royal kraal and therefore continued to plead for a larger land allotment where she could cultivate. Some men in the area protested that a single woman should not obtain land because her presence might provoke jealous competition among men. After two years, she was granted the desired land in her distantly located male relative's name. She paid taxes on her land from her salary and attended all meetings of the chief's council in order to be informed of local land policy.

As the case opens, Lukhele's oldest son has reached late adolescence and begun an active sexual career. After Lukhele disciplines him, he orders her off the homestead, basing his demands on his important role in her land acquisition and his future inheritance rights. Lukhele responds by forcefully ordering him off the land. He acquiesces. She refuses to communicate further with him. She relates that her youngest son should instead inherit the land because he has no father.

Strategy analysis

The chiefdom authorities' restrictions upon Lukhele's request for land, e.g. insisting that she obtain land in a male relative's name, constituted both organic and control harmony strategies: they were organic in that they derived from customary usufruct provisions and were control in that they protected current male land control prerogatives. When the authorities ignored Lukhele's dispute with her son, they were using an organic harmony strategy; they preferred not to get involved in a family matter in which they had no control interests. Moreover, they had no incentive to intervene since the community agreed that Lukhele's son deserved sanction (eviction from his homestead and denial of his land rights) for his promiscuous behaviour.

Lukhele's son, as a male, tried to assert forcefully his perceived land inheritance rights; but as a young man, he was ineffective at home against his large, domineering mother. He also did not approach the chiefdom authorities since he knew that they would be unlikely to support him.

Lukhele's assertion strategies (land requests before the chief's council) did not procure her land rights rapidly in the face of what she interpreted as arbitrary, self-seeking control harmony strategies of male leaders in the chiefdom. She believed that the leaders favoured men's land interests. However, once Lukhele had obtained the land, she successfully maintained her claim with minimal male intervention. When her oldest son challenged her land rights, she evicted him without protest from the chief's council and thereafter designated her youngest son as heir.

Case 19: The woman who disputes with her ex-lover about land rights and ultimately sparks an inter-clan struggle

(data from Chief's Court and interviews with several community residents, middleveld)

(Shongwe is single. She has limited education and is unemployed.)

Case summary

Shongwe wants to plough a field which she claims belongs to her family. She says that her father received the land as a gift for healing a princess. According to her and her mother, the field had been unused for some years because her brothers were away and she didn't need it. She claims her mother loaned the field to the powerful Y clan. According to her, the Y clan, in turn, had loaned the field to X, the estranged lover of Shongwe. X had then given the field to his third wife, who had ploughed it for seven years.

Shongwe goes out early in the planting season of the eighth year and ploughs the field. X is furious about this encroachment on his borrowed land. He claims Shongwe ploughed the land to spite him for taking another wife, but Shongwe and her mother claim that the land belongs to their family. X also argues that Shongwe ploughed the land in revenge since X had lost his job and was not supporting their children.

X tries to raise a case about the land dispute at the Chief's Court, but he fails. He blames his political disfavour with community elders for his failure, but members of the chief's council say that they are too busy with royal duties in the King's fields to attend to cases. After X's requests for a hearing of his case are rebuffed several times, he cuts down Shongwe's young crop.

Shongwe turns to the Swazi Nation Court in town with a destruction of property case, but the Court does not have jurisdiction over the customary land dispute. Shongwe seeks civil damages. The Court President hearing the case reprimands X for his strong-handed action against a woman and awards Shongwe several hundred Rand damages (*c.* $250). X considers appeal but abandons the idea. He begins making payments to Shongwe.

Some months later X persuades the chief's council to hear the land ownership dispute. Soon after the argument between Shongwe and X over usufructuary rights opens, a dispute over ownership rights begins between Shongwe's family and the Y clan. X no longer plays a role. The Y clan argue in rebuttal to Shongwe's claim that her family had loaned them the land that, in fact, they had received the land as a gift from royalty.

Strategy analysis
The chiefdom authorities used strategies which had both organic and control aspects. The strategies were organic in that they initially denied the complainant, X, access to a forum, and once a forum had been granted, they avoided rapid decision-making. Strategies used in this way aimed to promote either dissolution of the dispute, or, otherwise, private settlement for the benefit of disputant reconciliation and peace in the chiefdom. The strategies were control in that they protected the interests of the chief's council members; they aimed to avoid outside intervention by royalty on behalf of the important Y clan. The strategies were also control in that they condemned X for past insubordination by not providing him with a forum to air his land grievance.[4] Both organic and control strategies sought containment of the dispute at the chiefdom level, although the Y clan's prominence threatened royal intervention.

X, as a man, used assertion disputing strategies (protest to Chief's Court and private action against female opponent) to proclaim his perceived land rights. When he cut down Shongwe's standing crop, he avoided the chiefdom authorities – but only because the authorities had ignored his request for a hearing. X's role evaporated after the Y clan stepped in to protect their own land rights – upon which he based his own.

Shongwe was in a difficult position as a female litigant in a land dispute; few women represent their homestead's interests (her brothers were absent), and those who do usually cannot make the same forceful arguments before the male-dominated Chief's Court as do their male counterparts. At the outset, Shongwe asserted her land inheritance interest by ploughing the land she believed was her own – despite X's protests. When X destroyed her crops, she sought and received damages from the Swazi Nation Court which she believed was more sympathetic to women than the Chief's Court. When X challenged her before the Chief's Court, she argued her family's land claim forcefully.

Subject vs. subject dyad

Case 20: The woman who loses her land loan because she abuses use rights

(data from case before Chief's Court and interviews with X, Y, and several community residents, middleveld)

(Masuku is single. She is uneducated and unemployed.)

Case summary
When a sister of the nineteenth-century King, Mswati, was given to the grandfather of X, the King also gave the grandfather a plot of land in the area. X received a plot on the larger land area from his own father in the early 1950s. X moved his homestead up and down the hillside on which the extended family's land is located, until 1974 at which time he settled upon a location lower down the hill. Then, he built several permanent, well-constructed homes.

In about 1965, Masuku was brought by her own father to X's father with the request that she be loaned some land. The two men constructed a distant kinship tie in order to justify the land loan. The chief's council was aware of the agreement.

The arrangement worked well until Masuku moved her homestead across a small path, saying that the land in her present location was rocky. This posed no real problem until X moved his family's homestead to its present location. Then a confrontation over resource use and path access began. The most serious problems began in about 1983 when Masuku began to cut down wattle trees for her own building purposes and for sale. She also ploughed into fields which X claimed constituted his own land.

At the time when the simmering grievance reached a breaking point, members of X's extended family speak on an individual basis with Masuku about her transgressions on land which they had loaned. When she disregards their pleas, they call a family council meeting. Thereafter, they send a delegation to tell her to discontinue land misuse. X is given responsibility for handling the matter. When Masuku refuses to stop her offending actions, X's extended family decides to bring a case against her (1983) before the chief's council.

Masuku loses the case – possibly because X's family is large and well-connected to royalty. As a contrast, Masuku is isolated from her family, scorned for her promiscuity, and poor. The authorities order her to leave the area. She stops cultivating the land but takes no apparent action to vacate her residence. She appears to hope that she will be allowed to remain. When a son of X's brother returns to his family's land area and erects his own dwelling next to Masuku, she begins to dig trenches in the ground for the purpose of erecting a fence across a public accessway. She is warned by X and his brothers that she must not do this.

Masuku still seems uncooperative, so X sends his wife, Y, to represent his family's interests before the chief's council. Masuku does not come, so she is summoned the following week. Ordinarily Y would not represent her husband's family's land interests before the chief's council, but people say that X is ill and that Y can handle the matter well since she is a princess, is well-educated and speaks impressively. Masuku argues her case, indicating that she believes she has done nothing wrong. She makes a poor impression compared to Y. Although she is represented by her younger brother, her in-laws and other brothers will not support her. Apparently, they scorn her since she has had many lovers and did not properly observe the mourning rites after the death of her husband. When the council orders Masuku to get a land grant from her in-laws, she is silent; she knows they will not help her. At some point during the council members' interrogation, the court messenger intervenes, saying that he thinks she is being treated unfairly, but his statements have no impact. The council condemns Masuku publicly for violation of land loan provisions and for ignoring their own previous eviction order. She is told that she must vacate the land within two months, and failing that, the police will be summoned.

Strategy analysis

The chiefdom authorities used control harmony strategies (ordering eviction and threatening police intervention) to force Masuku to comply with their orders. They were not initially concerned with their own control interests but rather the control interests of X's family, a wealthy and royally connected local family which had settled early in the area. X's family exerted considerable political influence in the area. In any case, although the authorities relied predominantly upon control strategies, they judiciously heard testimony of witnesses in order to avoid appearances of heavy-handed dispute processing.

X, as a senior male member of his family, used assertion strategies with the backing of his brothers. He tried privately to persuade Masuku to abide by his family's wishes, but when she resisted, he approached the chief's council.

Masuku, as a poor, uneducated woman with few kinship connections, used assertion strategies (encroaching upon her neighbour's land) to lay claim to desired land rights. Unfortunately for her, these rights conflicted with those of X's family. She probably realized that her claims were not supported by customary land law (loan provisions), but she may have continued with her assertive actions in the belief that X would not take the trouble to challenge her. Moreover, she may have reasoned that even if challenged, at worst, she could only lose the land she had encroached upon; she probably did not reckon with eviction since she had resided on X's family land for twenty years. When her actions came under fire and thus her tenancy became dangerously threatened, she resorted to avoidance strategies, refusing to answer the summons of the Chief's Court. Masuku clearly hoped to protect her land claim by avoiding public hearing and sanction. Eventually she was compelled to assert her perceived land rights before the Chief's Court. When the authorities ordered her eviction, she disobeyed their order, digging poles for a fence to protect the integrity of her land claim. Thereafter, the chiefdom officials moved forcefully against her, and there was no possibility of her asking outside officials to intercede on her behalf; she had neither customary right to loaned land nor claim to civil or criminal damages.

Case 21: The woman who defends her family's land against counter-claims of a man

(data from interview with Kunene, middleveld)

(Kunene is separated. She is educated and employed.)

Case summary

Kunene, a middle-aged woman, has been separated from her husband for many years. About two decades ago, she went to a princess in her parents' area and asked her to persuade her (Kunene's) mother's brother to relinquish some of his inherited land allotment to his sister, Kunene's mother. Kunene also asked that her mother's brother be granted a substitute land plot. The princess agreed to assist her, and the requests were granted by the chief's council.

Some years later, when Kunene was in Johannesburg working, a man noticed that her family's land was unused. He approached the chief's council and asked that rights to the land be granted to him. The request was granted, and he gave the chief a cow.

As the case opens, Kunene is back visiting her home area and notices that someone has ploughed her family's land. As she has no brothers and her mother's brothers are uninterested in the matter, she approaches the chief's council on her own to raise a protest. She argues before the council that she wants to defend her mother's right to the land. In attendance at the meeting are a princess and a messenger who confirm that Kunene's grandfather had indeed received that land and given a gift of thanks. The man who had received the same land more recently also has a member of the royal family and a messenger confirm that he gave a gift of thanks. Kunene's representative, the princess, strongly supports her claim, asserting that many years ago, when the land was still being tilled by Kunene's grandfather, she (the princess) had regularly received groundnuts as tribute from the grandfather. Kunene explains that the land had come into disuse after her mother had separated from her husband and had no sons who could plough it. Kunene argues that her mother is now old and needs the land. (Privately, Kunene says that her mother cannot comfortably live with her brothers' wives and that her mother's children are all living in distant locations.)

After the chief's council deliberates carefully on the conflicting arguments, it decides in Kunene's favour. She then returns to the land and cuts poles to erect a traditional fence which proclaims use rights. Soon thereafter she erects a home for her mother. After some years, her mother dies, and she takes over the land.

Strategy analysis

The chiefdom authorities used organic harmony strategies because their control interests were not at stake. Moreover, as both disputants were represented by royal witnesses, they arguably felt compelled to balance fairly conflicting interests. They heard both sides of the dispute and decided in favour of Kunene whose family had occupied the land for many decades. They sought an alternative plot of land for Kunene's neighbour, in compensation for his loss.

Kunene's male neighbour assertively requested land from the chief's council, and when a dispute arose because of conflicts with Kunene's land claim, he used assertion disputing strategies to protect his claim. His rights, although legitimately obtained, were newer and more fragile than Kunene's.

Kunene used assertion disputing strategies to protect her claim: she argued her land dispute before the Chief's Court, she recruited aid from a princess and she erected a homestead immediately following a decision in her favour. She was not inhibited by her status as a woman because she knew that her land claims were strongly based upon customary rights derived through long-term family occupation and offering of tribute. Moreover, she was strengthened by the aid of a princess. Finally, she was encouraged (to act assertively) by the balanced and equitable organic harmony strategies of the authorities.

Subject vs. chief dyad

Case 22: The woman who challenges chief's council member when he threatens to evict her

(data from interview with Tfwala and neighbour, middleveld)

(Tfwala is separated. She is uneducated and unemployed.)

Case summary

Tfwala lived with her husband at her in-laws' homestead for some years. When she bore a son, her husband, for an undisclosed reason, officially repudiated her at the District Commissioner's Office (now Regional Administrator's Office). Thereafter, she lived at her parents' homestead until her children reached school age. At that time she moved to another area to take up employment; she needed cash to educate her children.

Eventually, Tfwala decided she needed her own home and land for cultivation. She approached the chief's council and requested land. When they asked about her husband, she explained that he had formally repudiated her at the District Commissioner's Office. Her thirteen-year-old son was present at the hearing, but she spoke for herself. She subsequently received the land she desired.

Some years after Tfwala settled on the land, a member of the chief's council comes to her privately and threatens to level her house and forcibly evict her from her land. Tfwala goes to the senior wife of the chief to investigate the threats. The chief's wife speaks with the chief who says that the threats are unfounded and that Tfwala can remain in her present location.

Strategy analysis

The chief's council member, acting as a private citizen with personal land interests, did not attempt to produce harmony at a public forum. Rather, he privately threatened Tfwala in the hope of intimidating her into abandoning her land claim.

Tfwala used the assertion/avoidance strategy of severing her marital obligations to her husband so that she could obtain land independently; thereafter, she made an independent land request before the chief's council. When her land claim was threatened by a council member, she counteracted his strategy with her own assertion strategy of relying upon an influential woman. It was in Tfwala's interest to settle the dispute without recourse to the Chief's Court, where men might side with the influential man challenging her.

Chief vs. subject dyad

Case 23: The woman who defends her land rights in deceased husband's area against threats of area residents

(data from interview with Fakude, middleveld)

(Fakude is widowed. She is educated and employed.)

Case summary

Fakude came to Swaziland from South Africa when she married her Swazi husband. She has been widowed for many years and desperately wants to receive a plot of land in her former husband's chief's area. Because her husband grew up with his grandparents in another part of Swaziland, he left behind no home on his parents' homestead.

For ten years Fakude has pleaded for land. Unfortunately, in the process, she has become embroiled in a dispute between two rival claimants to chieftaincy. As the immediate case opens, one chief assigns her land in an area claimed by another chief. A faction of men from the land-hungry location of the second chief come to her and threaten to kill her and her children through sorcery if she continues to build a house she has begun on the plot. They continue to harass her with rough telephone calls at work and unpleasant anonymous letters. In desperation, she approaches her brother-in-law, who is a District Commissioner in a nearby town. Unfortunately, he refuses to help Fakude out of fear that it would show bias on his part. Soon after, Fakude's laundry is stolen from her clothesline. When the laundry is found buried in a hole, Fakude becomes terrified that the incident represents a threat to her life. She goes to the first chief and tells him she will relinquish any claim to the land he has assigned her and that he should assign her land in an area he claims to control. The chief agrees and tells Fakude to go out with her sister-in-law and find a new plot. When Fakude looks for new land, she is told by everyone in the area that all the land is occupied. She finally gives up in despair, attributing her problems to people's dislike and suspicion of her as a foreign woman. Finally, the first chief assigns her a plot of very poor quality in a swampy area. Fakude believes he gave her this plot to relieve his sense of guilt in failing to help her with her problem. Fakude vows to clear the land and build on it. Neighbours laugh at her claim, but she perseveres. At the same time, Fakude learns that her first plot has been given to a widow. Upon learning this, she concludes that her own problems over the land have stemmed more from politics than from gender.

Shortly before the researcher's final interview with Fakude, her aged father-in-law dies and her brothers-in-law agree to represent her at the chief's council meetings. Up to that time, according to Fakude, her brothers-in-law were unable to help her because they did not want to ask their ailing father for permission. With the assistance of her brothers-in-law, Fakude hopes to maintain her second land claim.

Strategy analysis

Fakude's chief used her as a pawn to test his jurisdiction in an area under dispute with a neighbouring chief; he was not concerned with inter-chieftaincy harmony. As a foreign-born woman, Fakude had little claim to land (except that she was a widow with children), and therefore, she accepted the land he offered. Only when her situation became intolerable did her chief take an alternate route, offering her poor land in the undisputed area. He explained to her that he had no good land in that area to offer her.

Subjects of Fakude's chief's rival used potent assertion disputing strategies (sorcery and verbal threats) to persuade her to abandon her land claim in the disputed area. As Fakude was frightened by their actions and words, she privately approached her brother-in-law for help in an unofficial capacity (avoidance strategy). When he refused, she used another avoidance strategy which involved acquiescing to her enemies and relinquishing her land claim. Thereafter, she received poor land from her chief in the undisputed area, but she continued to hope for better land at that time when her brothers-in-law were finally willing and able to intervene on her behalf. Fakude repeatedly tried to bring her problems to the attention of her chief's council (assertion strategy), but her pleas were ignored; she needed the assistance of local-born men (i.e. her brothers-in-law) to add legitimacy to her claims. Fakude believed that her chief was unwilling to find her good land not merely because of a land shortage, but primarily because she was a powerless, foreign woman who could not add to his power and prestige as a chief (in return for giving her land).

Composite strategy analysis

Authorities' harmony strategies

As discussed in Chapter 5, authorities tend to rely on organic harmony strategies when their control is threatened, and they tend to rely on control harmony strategies when their control is not threatened; however, women, who occupy unequal positions relative to men (ascribed status), unless of royal birth, do not usually challenge the male authorities' general control. Rather, their strategies serve to challenge male opponents' strategies in specific cases or to enhance their personal (achieved) statuses.

Chiefdom authorities may use organic harmony strategies in cases which involve a woman/women in the family unit. They try to produce peace before the community becomes involved. Their control is not threatened. For example, in Cases 17, 18 and 19, the authorities' strategies prevented women from bringing their grievances before chiefdom authorities at a public forum. Women were denied the right to a public hearing since they possessed land under male guardianship.

The chiefdom authorities may also use organic harmony strategies in cases in which they are clearly in a position of superiority over disputants – one of whom is a woman – and their control is not threatened. For example, in Case 21, the chiefdom authorities granted Kunene a fair hearing because she and her male opponent were both equally connected to influential local families. They aimed to achieve consensus through restoring the customary land rights held by her family and through granting her opponent different land rights.

Both family and chiefdom authorities use control harmony strategies in cases in which women challenge their land control. For example, in Case 17, the family authorities, who acted simultaneously as disputants and dispute adjudicators, wanted to enhance their land control at a female in-law's expense. They restricted the youngest wife Mamba's inheritance and then denied her access to formal family grievance procedures. They believed her predicament would force her to abandon any inheritance claims. In Case 22, a chief's council member who wanted to acquire Tfwala's land also wanted to enhance his land control at a woman's expense. He resented the fact that a female neighbour had obtained land and believed that he could challenge her control.

Chiefdom authorities may use control harmony strategies in cases in which they wish to defend land rights of an important family against the challenges of women. In Cases 19 and 20, the land use rights of early settler families (*imisumphe*) were challenged by women. The authorities did not hesitate to threaten Masuku (Case 20), a poor, unconnected woman, with force if she did not comply with their eviction orders, but they proceeded cautiously against Shongwe who claimed royal connections. When Shongwe's claim was not fully substantiated, they switched from organic to control harmony strategies.

Chiefdom authorities may use control harmony strategies in cases in which political rivals acting on behalf of women challenge their control. For example, in Case 23, both rival claimants to chieftaincy used control harmony strategies in dealing with one another; their aim was to secure forcefully their threatened land administration rights. Fakude, as a foreign-born female, was a logical pawn in her chief's power struggles; the community accepted that she deserved only minimal chiefly assistance, while she was willing to accept any land that the community would offer.

Women's disputing strategies

Despite ideological formulations of male land control, many Swazi women achieve disputing power in actual cases through use of strategies. As demonstrated in the case sample, married women use strategies to dispute about land with their husbands (Shongwe), widows use strategies to avoid their in-laws (Mamba) or act independently of their in-laws (Fakude), and unmarried women use strategies to dispute about land with minimal help from a male relative (Lukhele and Kunene). Many women, such as Lukhele, Masuku and Tfwala, rely on influential, usually royal, women as envoys to defend their perceived land rights, and some even resort to 'paper men' (i.e. written documents from a regional administrative office or letters) to argue their cases at a distance (Lukhele).

Female disputants have the difficult task of reconciling male authorities' and disputants' strategies with their own assertion, avoidance and deception strategies. Women may use assertion disputing strategies in response to the male authorities' harmony strategies in cases in which they accept their strategies and their control. For example, in Case 21, Kunene used the assertion strategy of arguing her land dispute against a male commoner before the chiefdom authorities, she believed that her arguments were founded upon customary land use rights and that the authorities would decide in her favour. In Case 18, Lukhele used the assertion strategy of ousting her disobedient son from the homestead and announcing that her youngest son would inherit; she was confident that the authorities would accept her actions which enhanced peace in the community.

Women may use assertion strategies in response to authorities' harmony strategies in cases in which they do not accept the authorities' strategies but accept their control. They use assertion strategies because their cases are difficult and unlikely to be successful; they find such strategies to be worth the risk. For example, in Case 20, Masuku used the assertion strategy of declaring her land rights on the homestead (erecting a fence) – even after the chief had ordered her to vacate the land.

Women may use avoidance or deception strategies in response to male authorities' harmony strategies in cases in which they do not accept their strategies but accept their control. For example, in Case 20, Masuku used the avoidance strategy of evading the summons of the Chief's Court. She had learned from experience that she could not use assertion strategies advantageously before the Chief's Court, as it was predisposed to her structurally well-placed opponent who had royal connections. Moreover, she knew that assertion strategies would probably not achieve her ends; she was uneducated and unconnected in her family or community. In Case 17, Mamba also initially used an assertion strategy – in this case to challenge her in-laws (family authorities). When her assertion strategy failed to secure satisfaction, she used the avoidance strategy of appealing to the District Commissioner; she knew that she had little chance of success at the Chief's Court which would probably encourage private settlement within the family. Her avoidance strategy did not resolve the land dispute, but it did have the desired effect of achieving material assistance for her children's care.

Women may use avoidance or deception strategies in response to male authorities' harmony strategies in cases in which they do not accept their strategies or their control. For example, in Case 22, Tfwala rejected the assertion disputing strategies of a member of the chief's council who privately opposed her land claim. She rejected his right to exert private control in her land claim, but she did not challenge his general control as an influential member of the chief's council. Although she was not able to appeal to a family council, the chief's council or the Swazi Court for redress – none of which had jurisdiction – she resourcefully used the avoidance strategy of relying upon the assistance of a royal woman (high structural status). In Case 23, Fakude also rejected the harmony strategies and control of the male authorities in the chiefdom neighbouring her own. Again, no forum had jurisdiction over the matter. Her avoidance strategy of maintaining her land claim and ignoring the threats of her opponents bought her time but ultimately failed because their intimidation strategies were more potent.

Women also use assertion, avoidance and deception strategies in response to their opponents' disputing strategies. They act upon both their structural statuses, which are usually lower than those of male authorities and male disputants, and their personal statuses, which are sometimes high. Their personal statuses are more variable depending on good fortune and careful manipulation of factors such as male support, personality and economic circumstances. Women devise specific strategies according to opportunities presented by the customary and modern legal systems.

The customary system

Women have three possibilities for using assertion strategies within the context of the customary system. First, they may recruit assistance from male relatives or in-laws. Secondly, they may recruit assistance from other women. Thirdly, they may assume personal control. A woman who recruits aid from men tries to get a brother, half-brother or father to further her land interest in her home area (Lukhele and Tfwala), or she may seek the help of a son in her own area or in a new area (Mamba). In addition, a woman may try to persuade male members of a chief's council or members of the community to support her perceived land interests/rights (Lukhele and Kunene). A woman who recruits aid from other women will try to persuade an influential woman (usually of, or married to a member of, the royal Dlamini clan) to act as her public representative before a chief's council in land matters, to speak privately on her behalf to a community elder, or to speak to another influential woman on her behalf (Lukhele, Kunene and Tfwala). A woman who assumes personal control of a land matter tries to argue her perceived land use rights independently, or with minimum assistance from male relatives (Lukhele, Shongwe, Masuku, Kunene and Fakude). She defends her land claim or perceived inheritance right to land against counter-claims by men (Kunene).

Women who have strong male support prefer to persuade men to argue land matters on their behalf. In this way, they maintain the outward appearance of conformity to ideologies of male control. Those who rely on influential women may or may not have access to male support, but they prefer to use influential women on whom they can depend for assistance in land cases. Lukhele, Kunene and Tfwala depended upon the high esteem accorded women of rank in stratified Swazi society to add weight to their cases. They were able to strategize through influential women because they had strong ties with such women through marriage or friendship. Those who are not linked to influential women may persuade women of their communities to influence men on a chief's council by talking to their husbands or men they know in the community. Women who rely on other women for assistance have few male relatives or no male relatives.

In addition to family circumstances, personality plays a part in whether women choose to use assertion strategies. In general, enterprising, economically self-sufficient women, who are able to exert strong control over male relatives (Lukhele, Shongwe and Kunene) or have no male relatives available, are more apt to use assertion strategies than women who are more dependent upon husbands and male relatives.

Women have two ways in which they can use avoidance strategies within the customary system: they avoid people who are unsympathetic to their position, and they avoid unfavourable legal institutions. The latter strategy constitutes the widely reported practice of 'forum shopping'. A woman who avoids people unfavourable to her position puts distance between herself and members of the community unsympathetic to her land claims, such as selected members of the chief's council (Tfwala), in-laws who may deny her control over land (Mamba) or men who have the potential for making claims to her land (Kunene). In other cases, a woman may avoid unfriendly neighbours or co-wives who interfere with her land interests (Shongwe). A woman who avoids unfavourable legal institutions may try to avoid confrontation with an unsympathetic family council by taking a family land matter directly to the Chief's Court.

Women who use customary avoidance strategies often have male relatives, in-laws or lovers who are likely to oppose their independent land acquisition efforts. In addition, these women may be less sure of themselves and therefore more apt to use behind-the-scenes manoeuvring rather than public displays of power and influence, as aimed at by assertion strategies.

Women have two ways in which they can use deception strategies within the customary system: (1) they may lie about their personal circumstances; or (2) they may deceive legal institutions about their customary land rights. A woman who lies about her personal circumstances most often obfuscates her marital status in order to gain an advantage in a land matter. For example, a woman might falsely claim to be married (see Case 10 in Chapter 5) or a widow (Lukhele). Deception of the customary legal system involves relying upon male relatives, often distantly related, who are not recognized by the community or chief's council as a woman's official spokesperson in land matters (Lukehele).

Women who use customary deception strategies, as with customary avoidance strategies, often have male relatives, in-laws or lovers who are likely to oppose their independent land actions. Again, these women may be less sure of themselves and therefore more apt to use behind-the-scenes manoeuvring and deception.

The modern system

Women have two possibilities for using assertion strategies within the modern legal system: (1) they may recruit aid from government officials; or (2) they may assume personal control. As in the case of Fakude, a woman may approach a government official to gain his informal assistance on a land matter. Alternatively, a woman may personally assume control of a land matter and represent herself at regional administration offices. If she succeeds in obtaining the sympathy of a government official, he may intervene on her behalf, as in the case of Tfwala, who was able to make an independent land request from a chief.

Women use the same kinds of avoidance strategies in the modern system as they use in the customary system: they may avoid people with whom they lack favour, and/or they avoid legal institutions known to be unsympathetic to their needs – such as some regional administration officials and the police.

Avoiding unfavourable legal institutions involves opting to use a Swazi Court or a Subordinate Court, rather than a family council or a chief's council (Mamba and Shongwe).

Similar to the deception strategies used in the customary legal system, the modern legal system provides opportunities for women to distort their personal circumstances or to deceive legal institutions – such as some regional administration officials and the police – about their land rights. A woman may incorrectly inform officials of a Swazi Court or a Subordinate Court about her marital status or economic resources as a means of gaining support for a land request. As an alternative, she may withhold information about her actual intentions in bringing a land case before a modern legal institution (Shongwe). Instead of focusing on the land claim, she deals with issues of assault or destruction of property.

While virtually all women resort to strategies in the customary legal system, only some women are able to use strategies in the modern system. Women who are estranged from husbands or male relatives, regardless of economic circumstances, willingly seek the assistance of the Regional Administration. Those who have contracted a civil marriage may approach the Western Subordinate Courts for assistance in changing legally their marital status to single status for the purpose of advancing their land interests.

The extent to which a woman is able to use the modern legal system depends upon her economic status. Only those with the economic means to hire an attorney are able to take advantage of the Subordinate Court to pursue a legal divorce. A woman can collect damages for destroyed property in both the Swazi and Subordinate Courts. In sum, marital status and economic status are key factors in women's ability to use the modern system.

Summary

Swazi women cannot legitimately dispute about land since 'ideal', unwritten customary law formulations deny them independent land control. Their position in the customary system of hierarchical relationships, defined according to sexual status, is, in theory, weaker than that of men. This normative formulation is modified by elite women's high hereditary rank and ordinary women's strategic manipulations.

Nearly all women stated in interviews that their gender puts them at a disadvantage in initiating and publicly arguing land disputes; however, they usually concur with Swazi men regarding the value of dispute-inhibiting 'harmony' as a means to maintain cultural integrity in a situation of change. They state that the solution to their position of relative powerlessness is not to seek structural changes in the hierarchical customary land tenure system, but rather to manoeuvre strategically within the existing structure. Their disputing strategies manipulate organic harmony to their own specific case ends and sometimes resist control harmony.

Although the gap between ideal standards and actual behaviour enables women to manipulate the system towards their own ends, they suffer considerable costs, such as material losses and psychic frustrations. 'Modernizing' trends may have enhanced the opportunities of some women, particularly those who are wealthy and educated, but they have left most women unaffected. Should land reforms aim to reduce the costs of *all* women, both the customary and modern systems must adapt to the realities of women's need for land security.

In the land dispute cases presented in this chapter, Swazi women took leading roles. The cases demonstrate that women exert more actual power in creatively manipulating male ideologies, including ideologies about harmony, than might be predicted by idealized, patriarchal notions of male land control. In reality, women are not passive 'fields' that are controlled by men, but rather are actors who creatively strategize to defend perceived land rights.

7

'How could I take my land dispute to the person with the stick?': Swazi elites' land dispute strategies

This chapter describes land cases in which Swazi new elites struggle to assert land administration rights against competing claims of local and national traditional elites. New elites, comprising the new Swazi middle class, are educated and wealthy individuals. They are teachers, clerks, civil servants, traders, agricultural smallholders and artisans. Some are enterprising farmers or urban land holders who have attained some independence from chiefs (see Maasdorp 1976: 416; Picard 1983: 19; Sallinger-McBride and Picard 1984b: 18). As explained, traditional elites are ordinarily royals, members of important clans and territorial chiefs.

The dispute data presented in the following discussion demonstrate how traditional elites in Zombodze use harmony strategies to contain land administration challenges by Kwaluseni new elites. When Kwaluseni new elites are called before the Zombodze council to answer to charges of unauthorized land administration, they enhance their disputing opportunities through assertion, avoidance and deception disputing strategies. However, when new elites preside over internal land disputes in Kwaluseni, they use harmony strategies to enforce their perceived land administration rights against challenges of 'illegitimacy' made by some local residents.

New elites and land relations in Africa

The literature on African land tenure systems describes the many roles played by new elites. New elites, unlike women, are commonly credited with having assumed important roles in formulating national land policy and legislation (Silitshena 1979) or in brokering land law codes at the village level (Perry 1977). They are also credited with having achieved land control in both traditional and non-traditional ways: for example, through inheritance or purchase (Garbett 1967; Glazier 1976; Njeru 1978).

The literature on Swazi land relations, as a contrast, primarily describes the roles played by Swazi traditional (hereditary) elites. As explained in Chapter 1, traditional elites erected over decades various roadblocks which resisted democratization of the hierarchical ruling structure, thus enabling them to consolidate, maintain and augment both economic and political power, particularly over land, in the face of colonial and capitalist threats. They enhanced their power by suppressing the labour movement, by controlling mineral royalties and by securing independent control and tax-free status of the national corporation, Tibiyo. Most important, they secured their power by defining government structures in accordance with royal prerogatives. Therefore, Swaziland's present government merges traditional governmental structures with elements of the Westminster system. The King approves all candidates at the *Tinkhundla* level and nominates some members of the lower house and the entire upper house. He also selects the Prime Minister. According to Daniel (1982: 106), 'the Swazi cabinet and civil service are merely the administrative agents for decisions which originate with the King and Swazi National Council and reach them by way of a modern-type Parliament dominated by carefully chosen traditionalists'. In effect, Swazi traditional elites successfully contained changes or used them to their advantage.[1]

Therefore, unlike in many parts of Africa, Swazi traditional elites neither experienced significant changes in their base of power nor were they replaced by or significantly threatened by new elites. Traditional elites, namely territorial chiefs, remain truly 'traditional' rather than 'modernized', not having emerged from colonial bureaucracies. One does not find in Swaziland, for example, 'client chiefs', such as described by Joan Vincent, in Teso District, eastern Uganda, who were appointed within a colonial political environment (1896–1927), in which 'neither traditional rulers nor a principle of hereditary succession to political office were recognized' (1977: 140; see also 1971). Nor does one find the 'civil service chiefs' of Uganda (Fallers 1956), the 'warrant chiefs' of Nigeria (Meek 1937), or the awkward 'man-in-the-middle' chiefs of South Africa (Hammond-Tooke 1975) (see also Richards 1960).

The Swaziland literature infrequently mentions new elites; but when it does, it describes them as frustrated in their aspirations to upward mobility but not radicalized (Booth 1983a: 61). Takirambudde traces general Swazi acquiescence back to the colonial era:

> The Swazi populace conceded the leadership role to the traditional rulers which boosted their bargaining vis-à-vis the colonial administration. The traditional ruler's hand was further strengthened by the fact of the colonial power's inability to apply the divide and rule principle in the Swaziland context. The explanation for this was the ideological unity of the Swazi populace regarding the legitimacy of the traditional authority to spearhead the Swazi reaction. Moreover the absence of factionalism spared the Swazi Nation from the problems of internal fights which would have served to sap its energies (1983: 219).

Some observers state that new elites do challenge traditional elites in areas which the latter customarily controlled, such as land administration. Isobel Winter attributes the roots of this challenge to 'the spread of commodity production (marketed agricultural production) [which] created the conditions of the emergence of new elements within the rural social structure with an interest in challenging the hegemony of the "traditional" rulers' (1978: 29). However, most observers take the view that new elites' challenges have been more successful economically than politically, owing to lack of access to high-level private sector management positions and to highest levels of political decision-making (Booth 1983a; Sallinger-McBride and Picard 1984a: 19; 1984b). Moreover, this view holds that new elites' challenges, whether economic or political, will remain minimally successful in the near future. Picard comments on the inability of new elites to penetrate traditional structures:

> The inability of the Swazi aristocracy to integrate the civil service elements into traditional structures makes an expansion of administrative capacity and service delivery down to the grass roots unlikely in spite of Swaziland's relative prosperity and access to technical assistance. Economic development in Swaziland since independence has occurred in limited enclaves leaving the rest of the country relatively untouched . . . Swazi traditionalists are reluctant to allow the penetration of non-traditional elements to the sub-district level for fear of disturbing the traditional institutions which are perceived to have insulated Swaziland from the political and social instability which exists in much of the rest of Africa. Thus, significant changes in Swaziland's pattern of 'enclave' development and extreme dependence on South Africa are unlikely to change significantly in the future (1983: 22).

The Swaziland literature on new elites has been important in clarifying structural continuity in land tenure administration, but it has sometimes obscured local realities by relying upon ideal formulations. The most important of these formulations emphasizes that traditional elites are successful in reinforcing their hereditary rights of land control, while new elites are unsuccessful in their challenges of this control – when they even challenge. Unfortunately, as in the case of women, this formulation downplays or even overlooks the struggles, sometimes successful, of new elites for land control.

In response to calls by anthropologists and legal scholars, notably Chanock (1985), Van Velzen (1973) and Werbner (1977), for analyses of both individual strategies and group struggles at all levels of political processes, I look at the interactive behaviours of traditional elites, new elites and ordinary citizens in Swaziland's local and national customary court processes. My analysis has two aims: to convey the full political arena of Swazi customary land control struggles, and to demonstrate through case studies of strategizing behaviour the actual roles played by new elites in land administration. As will be demonstrated, both new elites and traditional elites strategically enunciate and interpret harmony ideologies, creating a 'politics of harmony' according to which privileges of ascribed status compete with privileges of achieved status.

Ideologies of birthright: Swazi elite

As in the case of women, 'traditional' ideologies provide the framework for widespread resistance against new elites' struggles to control land administration. One of the most important ideologies maintains that Swazi cultural integrity is closely linked with a land control pattern in which land distribution normatively proceeds through a hereditary King who oversees land administration functions of hereditary chiefs. Chiefs, in turn, normatively distribute land with the assistance of their councils to family heads. At the lowest level, family heads normatively handle important decision-making responsibilities regarding land, including resolution of land disputes (Hughes 1972; Kuper 1947a; Marwick 1940; Nkambule 1983).

My interview and questionnaire responses, in keeping with the dominant ideological formulations conveyed in the literature, almost uniformly state that the customary system of land administration is stable. Informants indicate that traditional elites have retained significant control over land administration. Moreover, they argue that new elites accept customary land tenure arrangements in the interest of 'cultural and social stability'. At the same time that informants describe a conservatism in customary land tenure relations, they also acknowledge that hereditary privileges of land control are threatened by the introduction of a cash economy, the education of commoners' children and the expansion of urban bureaucracies. According to informants, a group of new elites, which is dissatisfied with the traditional system of hereditary privileges, including land control, has attained a fragile power-base. My land dispute data provide even further evidence of new elites' power-base.

Emergence of Swazi new elite: Kwaluseni as a case study

As discussed in Chapter 3, Kwaluseni is the only semi-urban settlement on Swazi Nation Land (so-called 'communally' tenured land) (see Butler 1974: 170). Although the King established several guidelines regarding how community administration was to proceed, several developments over the last three decades have caused the guidelines to become increasingly distorted and unclear.

Land tenure practices in Kwaluseni remain conservative. Aspects of European land tenure which do not conflict with indigenous political and economic interests are accepted (e.g. measurement of plots and demarcation of development areas), whereas those aspects which do conflict are not accepted (e.g. sale of land and granting of title). Still other aspects, which do conflict, are sometimes practised, if not wholly accepted (e.g. rental of dwellings) (see Fransman 1978b: 319).

Kwaluseni has a land administration problem shared by many other African communities: it seeks to reconcile a traditional administrative structure and customary land use practices with demands for modern development (e.g. universal land registration and provision of services). In Kwaluseni, as in many other urbanizing communities in Africa, 'traditionalists' tend to argue that the customary structure and practices have been distorted, while 'modernists', who are frequently synonymous with new elites, argue that greater immersion in the 'modern way' has yet to be achieved. Traditionalists and modernists are not merely engaged in an academic struggle about the merits of opposing development objectives; they are importantly engaged in a political struggle for recognition to carry out these objectives. Their struggles take place at the national level in the context of government agencies and at the local level in the context of rural development agencies.

Struggles about development in Kwaluseni take place between local factions, which, contrary to Takirambudde's statement about Swaziland's colonial experience, currently play an important role in new elites' challenges of traditional elites' hegemony.[2] The struggle in Kwaluseni for administrative control, particularly over land, involves factional struggles on two levels of the Swazi political hierarchy. As explained in Chapter 3, one level involves the Kwaluseni 'originals' and 'newcomers' councils which are competing for control in Kwaluseni, while the other level involves the Kwaluseni newcomers council's struggles for greater independence from Zombodze, the regional administration centre. Again, the originals and newcomers councils disagree about community administration and development – who should set the standards of development and who should control this development: collecting national fees and tributes; summoning labour to perform royal duties; performing burials; planning development projects; and distributing land.

The originals faction takes a politically conservative route, allegedly arguing that standards of development should be established and controlled by a traditional council headed by hereditary elites, primarily the local princes. The newcomers faction, as a contrast, takes a politically innovative route, arguing that standards of development should be established and controlled by a 'modern' council headed by those persons, including new elites, who have attained economic power in the community through business and wage labour. The originals faction reportedly favours the interests of long-term residents, while the newcomers faction states that everyone's interests, regardless of date and circumstances of settlement, should be given equal consideration. The originals faction also maintains that Zombodze should continue to serve as the hierarchical linkage between Kwaluseni and the national authorities, whereas the newcomers faction minimizes Zombodze's role (see Figure 4).[3]

The newcomers faction meets as a council more regularly than the originals faction. The originals council resents the perceived 'interference' of the newcomers council but indicates that it is waiting for formal directives from

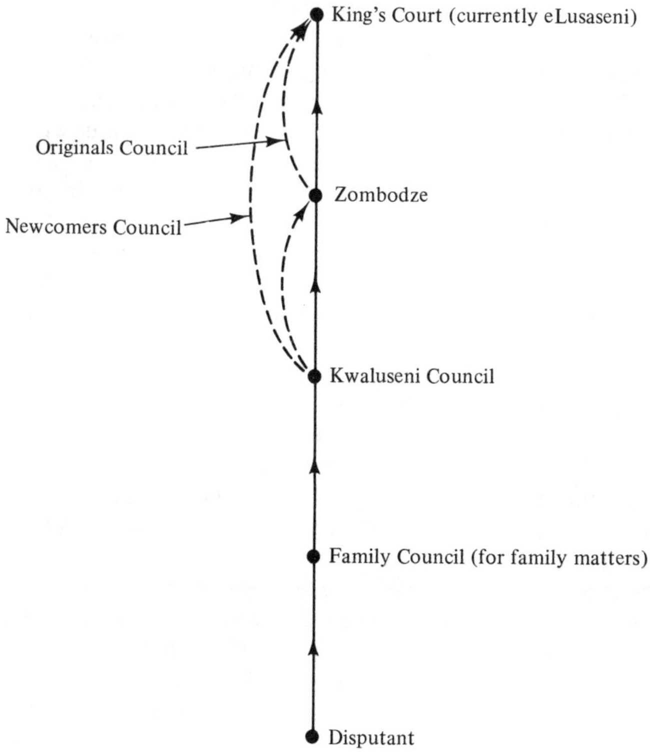

Figure 4 Hierarchy of forums for Kwaluseni residents

the national authorities before assuming full powers. On several occasions it has made forceful protests against the Kwaluseni newcomers council for allocating land and collecting special funds on behalf of national authorities.

The originals and newcomers factions are influenced by at least four unofficial plans for community development.[4] The first two plans are represented by the leaders of the two primary factions, whereas the second two plans are represented by influential leaders in the community who do not participate directly in the factional struggles.

The first plan is advocated by the informally recognized head of the originals faction, a hereditary prince, whom I shall call Nxumalo. Nxumalo, who has had wage employment, assumed acting headship of his family after the death of his father. His position of leadership in the community is uncertain since he was only appointed to act on behalf of his deceased father and father's brother, who, in turn, had only acted as regents for the minor son of the deceased *indvuna* (community leader). Nxumalo protests that the newcomers faction's authority is illegitimately derived from the political support of sympathetic royals and the police. He says he has no personal interest in heading the community council but that he will not stand by and allow the newcomers to usurp the rights of the princes and long-term residents. In his view, the best plan for development would be to elect council members who would be under the supervision of the hereditary *indvuna* (successor to be named) and the hereditary local princes.

A second plan is advocated by the head of the newcomers council, whom I shall call Motsa. Motsa owns a local business and rents out several local dwellings. He assumed leadership of the local council, which was created by the King in the 1950s, after the death of his father, a prominent and early settler. Motsa claims he rightfully inherited his position from his father who had been selected by the community and subsequently appointed by the King. He argues that the members of the newcomers council – most of whom he selected himself – can legitimately represent the community. He says he has no personal interest in acting as council chairman, but his enemies argue that he profits as chairman since he allegedly receives fees for land distribution and denies licences to businesses which compete with his own. In his view, the best plan for community development would be to elect council members who are equal and (presumably) under his chairmanship.

A third plan combines the interests of both the originals and newcomers factions. This plan states that the newcomers council no longer acts in the best interests of the community. It argues that community development will proceed best if council members are elected and act under an elected council chairman who assumes an advisory rather than a supervisory role. It recommends consideration of the originals' interests in that the council should consult with the princes about local matters.

A fourth plan rejects proposals of both the originals and newcomers factions. This plan states that community development will proceed best if a town council is elected and development tasks are assigned to formal sub-committees. It argues that only those originals or newcomers who have special bureaucratic or technical skills should assume roles on a newly elected council. It also argues that some development tasks should be undertaken by trained professionals in the Manzini government offices.

Each faction seeks acceptance of its own community plan, but it operates within constraints defined by the traditional land tenure structure. Therefore, neither faction advocates implementation of land tenure practices which would cause severe disruption of the traditional social/political structure, such as abandonment of the King's headship over the land community. In effect, faction members derive individual and group power by manoeuvring within rather than against the customary land tenure structure.

The manoeuvres of faction members are aided by strategies which, in general, aim to show that they, rather than their opponents, most closely approximate the ideals embodied in the customary land tenure structure. Specifically, their strategies manipulate cultural symbols of power and legal rules and forums, or in regard to land, the customary land administration structure and customary land tenure practice.[5]

The next section describes strategies of harmony ideology propagated by both traditional and new elites in the context of customary court meetings. Traditional elites assume leadership positions either on the Zombodze council or on the Kwaluseni originals council, whereas new elites primarily assume leadership roles on the Kwaluseni newcomers council. Traditional and new elites differently rely upon competing interpretations of harmony to legitimate their perceived administrative rights of land control.

Strategies in Swazi land administration cases

Harmony strategies of authorities

Swazi traditional elites use harmony to maintain and justify their land control prerogatives in the face of challenges posed by foreign development agents and an expanding class of local elites. When traditional elites present an image of harmonious social and political relationships underlying land tenure, they convey the impression that their administration of the customary land tenure system is efficient and adaptable. New elites also use harmony to demonstrate that they could or presently do administer the customary land tenure system efficiently and fairly, thereby building their sometimes weak legitimacy. Both traditional and new elites use harmony either organically or as control according to status interests and case circumstances, although political relationships in the Swazi hierarchy persuade traditional elites to rely more on organic harmony and new elites to rely more on control harmony.

The statements made in court sessions by authorities – both traditional and new – indicate interpretations of harmony. Harmony ideologies make persuasive arguments about the connection between cultural integrity, continuity, stability and the control of elites, including over land. But both traditional and new elites use strategies to render the appearance that they most legitimately and successfully accomplish the standards underlying harmony ideologies. In effect, harmony ideologies enable both traditional and new elites to disguise their special interests as community interests.

Organic harmony strategies further the land interests of both traditional and new elites by achieving widespread ideological consensus through reference to shared cultural and historical bonds. One organic harmony strategy achieves consensus through reference to custom. For example, in a land dispute, one chief stated: 'According to Swazi custom, a person may not allow another person to build on his land without consulting the council.' Another organic harmony strategy involves reference to the cultural bonds forged through sacred Kingship. In a land dispute, the chief admonished a disputant: 'The land belongs to the King. People may not fight over it.' Still another organic harmony strategy involves reference to traditional bonds inherent in relative status. In the fencing dispute described in Chapter 5 (Case 5), the chief admonished the plaintiff: 'Did you know that you were telling a chief to go away? Did you think you could say this to a chief? Did you think he was wrong in going to the police?'

Control harmony strategies further the land interests of both traditional and new elites by achieving disputant compliance, if not widespread ideological consensus, through forceful interventions in individual cases. One control harmony strategy achieves disputant compliance with orders through reference to the absolute power of the authorities. For example, a member of the Kwaluseni council once admonished a disputant: 'We will weed out people who are causing disputes.' Another control harmony strategy threatens the intervention of urban authorities. In a case in which the Kwaluseni council accused a resident of illegal (unreported) building activities, a council member admonished the accused: 'Bulldozers will be sent in to dismantle unauthorized homesteads and lawyers will be of no use to disobedient people [who built homesteads].' Still another control harmony strategy threatens intervention of supernatural powers such as the Christian God if the elites' dictates are not followed.

Disputing strategies of Kwaluseni new elites

When new elites in Kwaluseni do not wish to challenge the authority of the traditional elites in Zombodze, they lump their grievances and avoid confrontations. When they wish to challenge the authority of the traditional elites, they use assertion, avoidance or deception disputing strategies. When they wish to defend their authority against the challenges of other new elites or ordinary residents, they use control harmony strategies.

New elites' strategies enable them to accrue power which bespeaks their achieved rather than ascribed status. In particular, their strategies aid them in gaining access as disputants either to traditional or modern disputing forums, where they can advocate their interests. For example, some strategies aid them in appealing to national authorities, such as the King, to process their grievances and legitimate their claims in customary terms (Cases 11 and 15). Other strategies aid them in appealing to modern bureaucrats and court officials, such as the Regional Administrator, police or High Court judge, to put the force of the modern state behind their claims (Cases 8 and 16).

New elites' strategies may also aid them in creating or supporting new disputing forums. Control strategies – such as those which distribute favours, promise services or threaten sanctions for noncompliance – aid in building factions which support new forums. Organic strategies – such as those which adopt symbols of office and create a supportive genealogy – aid in legitimating claims in historical and cultural terms.

If some strategies of new elites aid them in creating new forums, other strategies aid them in legitimating their powers over these forums. The strategies can be so effective that disputants will protest their impotency against them, as did the disputant in Case 26. This disputant responded to the control harmony strategies of the newcomers council by commenting to the Zombodze council, 'How could I take my land dispute to the person with the stick?' Clearly, as this disputant's comment indicates, new elites have more impact upon customary land administration than the literature and common ideologies acknowledge.

Disputing strategies of Kwaluseni/Embikwakhe residents

Disputants, who are ordinary community residents, rely on strategies which involve assertion, avoidance or deception in response to the authorities' harmony strategies and to their opponents' disputing strategies. They consider relative status and case circumstances in selecting their strategies. In effect, ordinary community residents not only struggle to retain land use rights against challenges posed by other residents, they also struggle to retain land use rights against disruptive disputes between traditional and new elites about land administration rights.

Land dispute cases

As indicated, special historical and geographical conditions in Zombodze and Kwaluseni have produced land disputes which are qualitatively and quantitatively unlike those recorded in other research areas; at the same time, disputes in both communities involve struggles between high-status persons – some distinguished by birthright and some by personal achievement – over land use and administration rights.

The three land disputes discussed below demonstrate that normative formulations of land administration are not rigid. Land disputes provide an arena in which ambitious new elites can use harmony strategies to preserve or gain administrative powers and to justify dispute resolutions, thus challenging and redefining rules of customary land law. The disputes came before the Kwaluseni newcomers council, although the third, Case 26, went to Zombodze on appeal. They reflect three dyads in the Swazi social/political hierarchy: subject vs. subject (Case 24); chief vs. subject (Case 25); and subject vs. chief (Case 26). Following all case summaries, the harmony strategies that the presiding authorities used (organic and control) as well as the disputing strategies that the case litigants used (assertion, avoidance and deception) are discussed. The Swazi clan names do not represent the real names of the authorities and disputants.

Subject vs. subject

A chief's subjects dispute with one another about land usufructuary rights. The following case involved 'illegal' (according to customary law) sale of land rights, including renting of dwellings.

Case 24: The man who tries to sell building rights on his land allotment
(data from case before Kwaluseni council, middleveld)

(Nkambule is a newcomer who works at Matsapha, and Gwebu is an original with excess land. Motsa is the newcomers council chairman.)

Case summary
A man, Nkambule, comes before the local council and says that he was given a plot of land on a man's, Gwebu's, allotment. According to Nkambule, Gwebu told him that he could build a residence for his family; however, after Nkambule had begun construction of a four-bedroom house, Gwebu had reneged on the land grant and told Nkambule that he must abandon the house and occupy another one for which he would have to pay him 900 Rand ($450). Nkambule argued that the arrangement was unfair, whereupon Gwebu ordered him to leave the land entirely.

Gwebu then tried to sell the four-bedroom house which Nkambule had under construction. When Nkambule continually refused to leave the house, Gwebu's wife threatened him with a spear. She injured Nkambule's child on another occasion. Both Gwebu and his wife told Nkambule that they planned to harvest the maize crop which he (Nkambule) had planted.

Nkambule argues before the council that Gwebu had told him he could build a permanent residence. In other words, he interprets his land rights as having been permanently, not temporarily, granted. He says that if Gwebu really thought he had built illegally, as he (Gwebu) maintained, then he should have come to the committee with the complaint. Nkambule argues that he had been given permission by Gwebu to build.

The council chairman, Motsa, asks Nkambule if he had *khontaed* in Swaziland previously. Nkambule says that he did. Motsa then pointedly inquires of Gwebu whether he had demanded money for the house. Gwebu says nothing but looks surprised by the question. When the chairman further asks Gwebu if he had reported to the council that he had settlers on his land, Gwebu hesitates before answering that he did not report the presence of Nkambule and his family because he thought that they would only be short-term visitors. In response to this, Motsa comments that Gwebu must be lying since short-term visitors would never be allowed to construct a four-bedroom house. Motsa then asks Gwebu why Nkambule's child was injured with a digging pick. Gwebu responds that his wife had accidentally hurt the child while digging sweet potatoes. The audience motions disbelief at this explanation.

Motsa calls Gwebu's wife to testify. She says that Nkambule had been given permission to build a temporary mud and stick shelter, not a permanent concrete dwelling. According to her, when she and Gwebu had discovered Nkambule's apparent intentions to settle on the land permanently, they had told him to halt his building activities. When he refused, Gwebu had approached the area's runner with their complaint. She maintains that she had told the runner that it was best if Nkambule and his family leave since the two families did not have a healthy relationship.

When one of the council members tells Gwebu that he is not allowed to settle someone on his land without reporting to the council, Gwebu responds that the council should instead condemn Nkambule for 'acting like a chief in building where he pleases'. Gwebu explains that Nkambule had asked him to take him to the committee to *khonta* formally, but he had refused since he only wanted Nkambule to reside on his land temporarily.

At this point, one of the council members asks Gwebu what he plans to do with the house since he wants Nkambule to leave. Gwebu suddenly says that he really doesn't want Nkambule to leave, and he wonders what the problem is all about anyway. The council laughs with disbelief that Gwebu denies there is even a dispute.

Motsa then offers his opinion and a temporary decision:

> According to Gwebu, you [Nkambule] have not been thrown out. The committee has decided that Nkambule can return to his place. There is no reason that he should be chased away. Go back, Nkambule, peacefully with your wife.
>
> The King made a rule that if the first settler tries to chase the second settler away, and the first settler has not told the council that he has placed someone on his land, then the first settler must leave and the second may stay. This is the first settler's penalty for having illegally settled someone on his land.
>
> In this case we will keep the spear that Gwebu's wife used and forget the case. But if there should be trouble on that homestead again, we will bring out the spear. Also, we will try Gwebu [his wife] for attacking Nkambule's child with a pick. We will then reconsider that he settled someone illegally on his land.

'Chief' (i.e. authority) vs. subject

Members of the Kwaluseni newcomers council disputed with residents about land usufructuary rights: impermissible allocation of land by one subject to another subject, impermissible renting or construction of dwellings, and improper resource use. The following case demonstrates the council's attempts to sanction residents who constructed buildings without permits.

Case 25: The women who erect a kindergarten without permission of the authorities
(data from case before Kwaluseni council, middleveld)

(Motsa is the newcomers council chairman.)

Case summary

A woman allows several women to build a kindergarten on the land allocated to her husband. The kindergarten provides the working women of the neighbourhood with day care for their children. Each woman pays a nominal fee which covers only basic operating costs.

When Motsa and the council members learn about the kindergarten, they protest that it has been built without their knowledge or authorization. They also state that they alone can determine where people can build and how land is to be used. They order the women to dismantle the structure. They further inform the women that they will find an alternate location for the kindergarten. Although the women request repeatedly that they be granted permission to remain in their present location, the council refuses.

Subject vs. 'chief' (i.e. authority)

Sometimes a subject appeals a grievance about his chief's land administration to the Central Authority. According to my informants, cases which are appealed usually involve actions on the part of the chief which the subject believes severely infringe his rights – such as partial withdrawal of land rights, resettlement or eviction. In the following case, a subject protested before the higher authorities at Zombodze when the Kwaluseni authorities reallocated portions of his land.

Case 26: The man who protests when the authorities assign plots on his land allocation

(data from several sessions of Zombodze Chief's Court and several interviews, middleveld)

(Simelane is poor and has had primary school education. Motsa is the newcomers council chairman.)

Case summary

One of the first settlers to arrive in the Matsapha area was a man named Z, an important official of the former King. According to long-term local residents, Z received land in about the 1940s from the local *indvuna*, Mazibuko, as a reward for having 'carried the blankets' of King Bhunu (i.e. for serving as his personal attendant).

According to informants, Y came to Swaziland from South Africa in the 1950s. He approached Z and asked him to grant him a plot on his land where he could build a temporary residence. Z consented, and Y built a shelter. Some years after Y had settled, around 1957 or 1958, King Sobhuza announced that all unregistered residents in the Kwaluseni area were to leave. He had noticed that the area was heavily populated with newcomers who pledged allegiance to no chief and who only wanted to be near their place of employment at the Matsapha Industrial Site and the town of Manzini. King Sobhuza wanted to ensure ordered settlement and development of the area. As a result of King Sobhuza's order, Z told Y that he must leave.

Soon after, a princess happened to pass the area and noticed the shelter Y had built. She inquired as to why a temporary residence had been constructed there. She commented that it did not seem sturdy enough for the elderly father of Y to reside in. Therefore, she arranged to take Y before the authorities at Zombodze Royal Kraal, where he was formally introduced and granted the right of settling on Z's land.

In the 1950s, the King appointed a council of community elders to oversee local affairs. By the time the King died in 1982, most of the original council members had died. The son of the former council chairman assumed his father's position. The son, Motsa, indicated he was doing the community a service since development would not proceed unless someone took over the reigns of control.

Motsa was approached by numerous land-hungry people who asked permission to settle in the area. As the area had become extremely crowded, he granted them plots in one of the few open areas – which also happened to be the periphery of the land which a descendant of Y, Simelane, claimed was the family allotment (the * on Map 13 marks the area in dispute).

As the dispute formally opens, Simelane has just succeeded, after many requests, in persuading the Zombodze Royal Kraal to hear his complaint against Motsa's newcomers council. Both Simelane and Motsa's council raise numerous arguments in defence of their respective actions.

In defence of his perceived land use rights, Simelane argues (before the Zombodze council) that the Kwaluseni newcomers council has no right to reallocate his family's land which was obtained through *kukhonta*; it has no right since he (Simelane) committed no wrong to justify reduction of his land holdings. Moreover, in his view, it has no right since it was not legitimately (legally) constituted by community elections and consent of the King. Simelane argues that the council is acting in its own interests;

as an example, he notes that the council has settled its young secretary on his land claim. His arguments are strongly persuasive to the Zombodze council when he explains that the new settlers on his land impede his land use, particularly since his private access path has been cut off by their dwellings. Simelane relies upon testimonies of several originals who are resident in Embikwakhe (Nxumalo, head of the originals faction, privately supports him).

In defence of their perceived right to handle land administration in Kwaluseni, the newcomers council members argue (before the Zombodze council) that Motsa had inherited the office of council chairman from his father, that the national authorities had approved the appointment of all council members, and that the King had ordered Zombodze to cease playing a political role in the area. Privately, they point out that Zombodze is too far away to understand Kwaluseni's history and needs. Moreover, they indicate that the King had ordered the Zombodze authorities to stay out of the area in order to ensure that a local council could promote development in a modern, 'progressive' fashion (Western-style) and without the interference of royal interests.

In defence of their actions against Simelane, the newcomers council members argue that Simelane did not even reside on a regular basis in the community, that he was not the legitimate son of Y and therefore had no right to represent the family in a legal case, that Y's family had not legally registered with the area chiefs when they first came to the area, that Y's family had been told that they could only settle on their land temporarily since the nearby high school was going to expand, and that Y's family has misused the land – by renting dwellings against customary practice, by leaving debris in the area and by operating a beer-brewing establishment without a licence and to the detriment of children at the nearby school. Most important, they argue that reallocation of the complainant's land furthers local development interests, including organized settlement. Privately, they point out that Y's family consists of foreigners who should never have been granted a large tract of prime land in crowded Kwaluseni.

The Zombodze council puts Simelane in an awkward position when it asks him why he did not approach the Kwaluseni council with his complaints. Simelane responds memorably, 'How can I ask for help from people with the stick?' In other words, he believed that he could not achieve a fair settlement from the newcomers council which was acting simultaneously as an authority and a disputant. Moreover, he believed he was powerless against the council's control strategies.

The Zombodze authorities, fearing disruptive dispute escalation between disputants and supportive factions, repeatedly postpone the case over a period of two years. They hope that the problem will 'die' out. When Simelane refuses to relinquish his land peacefully, the Zombodze chief takes all possible measures to ensure that all disputing parties are present during hearings. He also orders numerous on-site investigations of the disputed area. He seemingly hopes that this strategy will give appearances of active involvement in the case without forcing resolution. When Simelane persistently requests that a decision be reached, the Zombodze chief finally consents to voice an opinion publicly.

The Zombodze chief's concluding speech is filled with utterances about harmony:

> What is done to the people at Kwaluseni is very bad. There is a council which was chosen by the King. But the bad thing is that there is no chief. So, the people there must have a chief. The area is a slum. People build houses wherever they want – particularly around the school boundaries; this makes it impossible to extend the school. For the Simelane people, it is painful since people built on their plot and closed the path. Since it is very expensive to buy building materials for homes, Simelane should have mercy on these people [who have been settled on disputed land], and they should be allowed to stay. No more houses should be built there. The Simelane family should live in peace with those people and treat them as good neighbours.

Composite strategy analysis

There are three important questions which one might raise regarding the authorities' manipulation of harmony and the disputants' responses to different forms of harmony: when do the Kwaluseni authorities rely on organic harmony and when on harmony as control? When do the higher authorities at Zombodze intervene in Kwaluseni cases, relying on which type of harmony? and When do disputants use assertion, avoidance or deception strategies in response to the authorities' version of harmony or to create their own sense of harmony?

A quick overview of the data indicates that in Case 24, the new elites of the Kwaluseni newcomers council primarily used strategies of organic harmony, and in Case 25, they primarily used strategies of control harmony. In Case 26, the new elites at Kwaluseni used strategies of control harmony, whereas the traditional authorities at Zombodze used strategies of organic harmony. Further analysis is needed to explain why these harmony strategies were used in these cases.

Authorities tend to rely on organic harmony strategies when their control is not threatened, and they tend to rely on control harmony strategies when their control is threatened. The authorities in Zombodze and Kwaluseni devise harmony strategies according to different control requirements posed by cases in each community. At the same time, disputants tend to rely on strategies which involve assertion, avoidance or deception in response either to the authorities' harmony strategies or to their opponents' disputing strategies. Kwaluseni residents' assertion, avoidance and deception disputing strategies have the difficult goal of achieving favourable outcomes in a situation in which traditional and new elites are disputing over land administration rights.

In Case 24, which involved a land grant, the authorities of the Kwaluseni newcomers council opened the hearing without clear direction. They judiciously explained points of customary law and allowed the disputants to tell their accounts before they offered any opinions (organic harmony strategies). Nkambule, as the complainant, opened his arguments with an assertion disputing strategy. He argued that Gwebu's intentions can be judged from his actions (i.e. he wanted to make money illegitimately from granting land without approaching the authorities). Nkambule argued that Gwebu had granted him permission to reside on the land permanently. Gwebu's avoidance/deception disputing strategies were: to indicate surprise about the suggestion that he had asked for money for the house (avoidance); to deny all charges about crop ownership and the cause of child's injury (deception); and to reinterpret all arguments when the case goes against him (deception). Gwebu argued that he had only granted Nkambule temporary building rights because it would be highly inappropriate, according to customary law, to receive payment for a dwelling.[6]

The authorities responded to the disputants' strategies by relying on organic harmony strategies to restore social relationships; their control had not been challenged. In turn, Gwebu responded to their strategies with feigned ignorance about his impropriety. He admitted to wrongdoing (albeit indirectly) and agreed to reconciliation with Nkambule. The authorities noted that they would only resort to control harmony strategies if the disputants did not resume peaceful relations. The Zombodze authorities and the originals council played no role in the case.

In Case 25, which involved illegal building activities, the authorities of the Kwaluseni newcomers council used control harmony strategies; they ordered the women who had built the kindergarten without their permission to dismantle the structure. They used these strategies because the women had challenged general male control and had specifically challenged the newcomers council's control by not acknowledging wrongdoing in building a kindergarten without authorization.

The women responded to the authorities' control harmony strategy with an assertion disputing strategy: they argued that they did not act improperly in building on private land because they were not seeking profit from their ventures. They therefore requested that they be granted building approval retroactively. When their request was denied by the Kwaluseni newcomers council (control harmony strategy), they did not appeal to the national authorities.

After the Kwaluseni authorities used harsh control harmony strategies to enforce compliance, they resorted to an organic harmony strategy: they offered to find the women alternative land on which to build the kindergarten. The authorities probably used this strategy since they needed to render the appearance of peaceful settlement in the face of opposition from Nxumalo's originals council and the Zombodze council. Their strategy prevented violent disputing between local factions and dispute escalation to Zombodze, but it did not produce consensus.

Comparison of Cases 24 and 25 raises several questions regarding how and why the authorities on the newcomers council selected particular harmony strategies. In Case 24 they did not punish illegal land use activities (sale of land rights), but in Case 25 they did punish similar illegal activities (unsanctioned building). Moreover, in Case 24, in which the defendant acted in his own self-interest, they did not impose severe sanctions, whereas in Case 25, in which the defendants acted in the community's interest by providing a public service, they did impose severe sanctions. This raises the questions: Why would the authorities apparently overlook disputant motivations, thus severely sanctioning (using control harmony strategies) those residents with altruistic motivations and not sanctioning (using organic harmony strategies) a resident with selfish motivations? Also, why would they risk further unpopularity and cause their legitimacy to be even more severely scrutinized – a situation that would arise if they harshly sanctioned the women in Case 25?

In answer to these questions, I argue that the authorities' perception of status relationships, as well as their control interests associated with such relationships, are central. Therefore, in Case 24, in which the authorities (newcomers council) served as a third party (adjudicator) in a dispute about land use rights between two community residents, their control of land administration was not challenged. Although Gwebu violated the perceived land allocation prerogatives of the authorities, he did so only out of self-interest (profit motivation). As a contrast, in Case 25, in which the authorities acted as disputants in a dyadic confrontation with community women who collectively violated their (authorities') land administration prerogatives, their control was challenged. Although the women's illegal building activities aimed to benefit the community, they seemed to undermine the authorities' development directives for the area. In effect, the authorities sanctioned the women severely – not because the women were threatening to the customary hierarchical structure of hereditary land control, but rather because they seemingly challenged the legitimacy and authority of particular individuals (newcomers council members).

In Case 26, which involved a dispute over land administration rights, the authorities of the Kwaluseni newcomers council initially relied on control harmony strategies when they decided to allocate Simelane's land to three new settlers. Their actions indicated that they did not acknowledge Simelane's land rights; otherwise, they would have sought his consent.

Simelane used assertion disputing strategies in response to the control harmony strategies of the Kwaluseni authorities. His strategies aimed to defend his land use rights before the Zombodze Chief's Court and to refute the Kwaluseni authorities' presumed administrative rights. His structural status was lower than the Zombodze traditional authorities, and his personal status was lower than the Kwaluseni new elite authorities. Therefore, his strategies could not aim to challenge relative statuses, but rather to defend his customary land rights against perceived transgressions of the newcomers council. He explained to the Zombodze council why he sought redress from it rather than the Kwaluseni council.

The Kwaluseni authorities, when called before the Zombodze authorities, were put in the awkward situation of occupying roles as both authorities and disputants. As authorities, they ignored Simelane's accusations that they were not legitimately selected and installed to represent the community; they did not want their political status to be debated by the Zombodze authorities. Initially, they used an avoidance strategy, refusing to answer the summons of the Zombodze chief's council (they deny its jurisdiction). When this failed, and they were called before Zombodze as disputants, they relied on assertion disputing strategies. Their strategies aimed to assert the autonomy of Kwaluseni from Zombodze, to demonstrate how Simelane misused his land allotment and to argue that Simelane's land was needed for development. In sum, their strategies refuted Simelane's right as an individual to the disputed land. They cast doubt that he was the true family heir and that he was using the land appropriately according to customary land law. They interpreted the matter as an individual's (Simelane's) grievance about land use rights rather than as the community's factional struggle about land administration.

The Zombodze authorities relied on organic harmony strategies from the beginning to the end of the dispute. Initially, they refused repeatedly to hear the case, encouraged private reconciliation, ordered inspections of the disputed area and postponed reaching a judgement. They hoped that the dispute would die or that the disputants would reach a private agreement. Eventually, when they were pressured by Simelane to reach a decision, the Zombodze chief, on behalf of the authorities, admonished him to be a 'generous', peaceful Swazi who shared his land with landless newcomers. The chief warned the newcomers council that it was acting improperly in allowing people to *khonta* since only the Zombodze council could grant land access; however, he ordered no actions against the council.

In this case, a major analytic problem concerned why the Zombodze authorities relied on organic rather than control harmony strategies. This was problematic because in private interviews, several Zombodze court officials told me that they believed Simelane's land claim was valid and that the Kwaluseni council had no right to interfere with this claim. Moreover, they stated that the Kwaluseni council must be falsely assuming powers since they were never informed by the King that it should handle land administration. From their perspective, the Kwaluseni council was only authorized by the King to direct development.

In response to this problem, I suggest that the Zombodze authorities strategically used organic rather than control harmony strategies to dispel the particular kind of political challenges posed in this case. Again, questions of status and control are important. First, they used organic strategies which served to downplay a dispute (by promoting consensus) between two levels of the hierarchy, thus containing the dispute at the upper level (royal kraal) and preventing intervention from an even higher level (national capital). This function was important to the Zombodze chief whose status as chief was unclear; he had not yet been formally appointed as chief, following the death of his father.[7] His individual control could be weakened if the newcomers council challenged his jurisdiction before the national authorities. Secondly, the Zombodze authorities used organic strategies which served to downplay a dispute between two factions at a local level. This function was important to both the Zombodze council and the Kwaluseni newcomers council, whose collective, administrative control could be weakened if repressive control measures were used or if a decision was publicly taken in Simelane's favour. Their control could be weakened because the dispute was likely to erupt into severe political unrest: an open and violent power struggle between local factions (involving all development plans) that would provoke the intervention of the police, the courts and national authorities.

The case demonstrates the difficult situation of an ordinary community resident (Simelane) who was caught between the efforts of authorities at two levels of the land hierarchy to define and produce harmony. Because the authorities' versions of harmony were incompatible – the Kwaluseni authorities using control harmony strategies to deny his land rights, thus enhancing their own power and control, and the Zombodze authorities using organic harmony strategies to deny him access to a forum and outcome, thus producing acquiescence – Simelane could not get case satisfaction. The conflicting harmony strategies of competing authorities cancelled each other out, failing to produce community consensus or lasting disputant compliance.

Simelane thus lost his case to the overriding interests of the rural Zombodze authorities in attaining consensual harmony. Their organic harmony strategies rendered the appearance that they were in control of the areas under their jurisdiction and that subjects and subordinate authorities were reasonably content. Simelane also lost his case to the tactics of the semi-urban Kwaluseni authorities in maintaining an imposed harmony which defended their fragile positions of power. Their control harmony strategies eventually suppressed Simelane's protest and discouraged the Zombodze authorities' intervention.

Summary

The cases discussed in this chapter indicate that harmony ideologies serve both traditional and new elites in rendering the *appearance* that tensions have been contained and social solidarity maintained under conditions of change. Traditional elites make statements about harmony to reinforce their hereditary land rights and placate new elites, whereas new elites make statements about harmony while manoeuvring behind the scenes to enhance their land administration interests – without producing undue instability. As in the case of women, new elites arguably prefer to manipulate customary land tenure rules and procedures to their own ends rather than promote individual freehold tenure.

Traditional and new elites in Kwaluseni are engaged in a struggle to implement opposing plans for community administration and development. They seek support of their plans through faction-building. Although the community is divided by several factions and plans, two dominant factions and plans have emerged. The two primary factions – the so-called originals and newcomers factions – use harmony ideologies to legitimate their competing plans. Ironically, the factions could, in theory, use harmony ideologies to reconcile differences and thus achieve a compromise between plans, but, in practice, they use such ideologies to disguise differences and sharpen conflicts, thus making reconciliation and compromise even less likely.

The factional dispute in Kwaluseni, although possessing unique features, has implications for many parts of Africa. It well exemplifies an issue which many African countries have faced: whether a country will continue as a largely traditional polity with a customary land tenure system, or whether there will be a shift of power to new elites with changes in the land tenure system. When this shift has occurred in some countries, many local areas have been pressed to resolve problems now faced by Kwaluseni: among them, reconciliation of competing local interests, determination of roles to be played by urban bureaucrats and technocrats in local affairs, and clear enunciation of development objectives. At this time, Kwaluseni, among Swaziland's customarily tenured areas, most strongly faces these problems; but in the future, other urbanizing Swazi communities will be confronted increasingly with similar dilemmas. As development problems are gradually resolved in such communities, it should be hoped that land disputes will diminish in frequency and severity, and harmony will take on more social, and perhaps less political, dimensions.

In the land dispute cases presented in this chapter, Swazi new elites played important roles. As with the cases involving women, these cases demonstrate that new elites exert more power in land administration processes than the Swaziland literature usually acknowledges. In reality, traditional elites are not totally effective in warding off threats of new elites. New elites have found ways to use harmony towards bringing the 'stick' of land control within their own grasp.

8

Conclusions

The political harmony of land disputes

Throughout Africa, development initiatives have granted renewed priority to land tenure research. Unfortunately, land disputes, as a focused area of study, have seldom been given deserved attention. This book has focused upon different kinds of customary land disputes involving people of varying social/political relationships in Swaziland. My argument has been that land disputes reflect significant, although subtle, changes in customary land tenure. These changes are revealed through analysis of dispute participants' case-by-case strategizing.

The model of political harmony presented in this book has considered important aspects of African land development and reform: the adaptability of customary land tenure; the compatibility of indigenous elite interests with development interests in land; and the processes of change in customary land law. The example of Swaziland demonstrates the resiliency of a system of customary land law, and its struggle to balance competing interests of traditional Swazi elites, new Swazi elites, Swazi commoners and foreign development agents/freehold landowners. This resiliency is ensured through the most important dimension of Swazi customary law and procedure – that of 'respect' (*inhlonipho*) for customary hierarchical status relationships. Swazi elites use customary procedures and ideologies to define the nature and borders of the hierarchical structure, and Swazi commoners find ways to manoeuvre within it. Land reforms emerge within the structure when status relationships and associated control are not threatened.

Customary law and land disputes: conceptual problems addressed by the harmony model

As indicated, the book has used, in the context of land disputes, different harmony concepts to examine several issues which have repeatedly been defined as problematic in scholarly texts about customary law: legal structure, context and change.

Legal structure

Chanock (1985) has argued that historians tend to look at conflict from the perspective of the larger legal and political structure, downplaying the minutiae of smaller transformations. Many anthropologists, too, were more concerned about structure than individual manipulations (Evans-Pritchard 1940). Although some anthropologists, such as Comaroff (1975), Gulliver (1971), Perry (1981) and Turner (1957), have vividly depicted small-scale legal or political processes at the local level, they have not always fully emphasized the larger structure. As a contrast, this Swaziland study has shown on a case-by-case basis how real people are manipulating customary land law to achieve individual interests within the framework of common ethnic and national interests. In effect, struggles within local-level courts in Swaziland not only provide meaning to larger political transformations, they are given meaning as manifestations of such transformations.

Context

Anthropologists have long protested against sterile collection of legal rules without consideration of context (Bohannan 1963, 1964; Gluckman 1955, 1965a; Schapera 1938). In recent studies, social context has generally been considered in legal analysis, although debate continues as to the proper balance between norm enumeration and analysis of manipulations in context (Gulliver 1979; Comaroff and Roberts 1977, 1981). Moreover, even when agreement exists that norm manipulations have been well described, some people criticize such studies for failing to address the impact of class interests. For example, Chanock (1985; see also Starr and Yngvesson 1975) has argued that early disputing studies failed to look at context in terms of relationships of power, with the result that the settlement of disputes and the invocation, use and manipulation of norms were not analysed with emphasis on the interests served by the processes. He notes that more recently disputing studies have focused upon the choices made by actors regarding selection of disputing strategies that maximized individual interests, although the power of class continues to be played down. In accordance with this proposed research priority, the Swaziland study has taken a two-pronged perspective: it examined political opposition of Swazis against colonial rule, as well as political struggles of Swazi individuals and classes (defined by birthright and gender) against one another. By focusing upon class struggles in land disputes, the study not only contributes to the 'law in action' school (Fallers 1969) which looks at interpersonal competitions in local context (Gulliver 1971), it also pursues a newer path in demonstrating individual struggles within class formations emerging in the larger socio-political context.

Change

Developers usually argue that customary law, such as expressed in land disputes, impedes change. They seem to criticize customary law as stagnant and inflexible when it does not complement their interests. Legal anthropologists have demonstrated how customary law undergoes change itself and promotes other forms of change, as power is legitimized on the local level by active users and creators, not passive recipients, of an introduced legal form (see Schapera 1969, 1970 on chief-made law). Chanock (1985: 238; see Moore 1986) agrees that African 'customary' law is actively produced, but he argues that it is currently created by each modern state and its legal form, so that scholars had better not concern themselves with the futile task of identifying the 'customary' but rather with raising questions about the kinds of interests and activities that are expressed as 'customary law'. This study of land disputes in Swaziland has investigated such interests, but it has also demonstrated that Swazi customary land law is as 'customary' today as it was in the past in the sense that it continues to be interpreted by hereditary leaders in customary forums. Nonetheless, the study proposes that this 'customary' character is evolving more rapidly in new directions than in the past – not because an imposed legal and political structure have directly defined or inhibited its operation, as Chanock (1985) demonstrates elsewhere, but more accurately, at least in the case of Swazi customary land law, because it must operate in the shadow of an imposed legal and political structure. In Swaziland, legal and political impositions have resulted in more significant changes in other areas of Swazi customary law, such as criminal law and family law. In effect, this study views 'customary law' as a slippery concept, with the consequence that it does not seek to define that which is 'customary' or to demarcate exactly processes of change, but instead to demonstrate movements in 'custom' by the example of small rule and procedural transformations that arise as continually emerging interests compete in separate cases.

In sum, throughout the book, analysis of harmony in Swazi land disputes placed questions about legal structure, context and change in a new light. First, the harmony model conveyed the overall *structure* of customary law, while analysis of individual case-by-case strategies demonstrated how ideologies are manipulated. Secondly, the harmony model illustrated the broad socio-political *context* within which interpersonal power competitions – particularly over land rights – occurred. Thirdly, the harmony model demonstrated that customary law does not necessarily impede *change*, as its critics argue, that customary law is not a well-defined body of rules but rather a body of rules reflective of individual interests at any point in time, and that customary law is not a stable body of rules but rather a body of rules continually undergoing transformations in separate cases. Harmony concepts thus were used to wed the legal (rule changes in larger historical and political structures) with the anthropological (individual behaviours in smaller social and political processes).

The nature of harmony in Swaziland

Several questions about harmony which are implicitly raised throughout this book are now dealt with systematically: What is harmony? Why, when and how do people accept or resist harmony ideologies? How is harmony used over time? and What is the relation between harmony and land disputes? In essence, what is the politics of harmony?

What is harmony?

Swazi statements about harmony point to numerous dimensions that emphasize agreement in either thought or action: consensus, unity, cooperation, compliance or docility. Swazis interpret harmony in social/political relationships when hierarchical stability and conformity are achieved. In general, they perceive harmony as synonymous with the ethnic survival of the 'Swazi Nation' in a diverse modern-day world. As a contrast, Europeans tend to perceive harmony in social/political relationships when 'egalitarian' unity and voluntary consensus are achieved.

Both sides of harmony deserve attention: one side I label 'organic' (consensus in belief, feeling or disposition) and the other I label 'control' (conformity and compliance in behaviour). Although these definitions are completely legitimate in a dictionary sense, those readers who are accustomed to think of harmony as voluntary unity in thought and behaviour may resist the harmony as 'control' dimension. Nonetheless, Swazi authorities do not split hairs over what harmoniously behaving people are really thinking: they are primarily concerned with achieving appearances of harmony. Thus, the authorities strategically use ideologies to make people think unity (organic harmony); and if they do not think it, then the authorities use coercive tactics to compel them to behave in a unified manner (control harmony). The corollary of this argument is that Swazi commoners can strategically respond to the authorities' ideologies and behavioural tactics of harmony, provided that they do not destroy appearances of social unity.

Swazis not only define harmony in terms of the end of social unity, they also define it in terms of the means used to achieve this end. When harmony ideologies aim to achieve unity through cultural/ideological consensus, Swazis generally evaluate the means positively, whereas when harmony ideologies aim to achieve unity through forced social/behavioural compliance (control), Swazis generally evaluate the means negatively. Moreover, when control harmony strategies are used to restrain/condemn an individual who threatens the social unity, they are viewed positively by the group, but when they are used to promote the narrow interests of a particular individual or class, they are viewed negatively by the group.

Harmony, and its opposite, conflict, thus take on positive or negative connotations, depending on one's perspective: one's individual and group interests. These interests are conveyed in common ideology as 'conceptions of the ideal social order'. On the one hand, Swazi authorities and some disputants arguably perceive harmony as a positive (unified, cohesive, cooperative) state of affairs in which social energies are coordinated, social solidarity is promoted and stability is produced. From this perspective, harmony serves to defend social/cultural order from outside intervention and internal disruption. At the same time, many Swazi new elites perceive harmony as a negative (oppressive) state of affairs in which social stagnation, class repression and individual resignation are promoted. On the other hand, *neither* Swazis *nor* development agents/bureaucrats tend to perceive conflict (land disputes) as a positive state of affairs in which social energies are channelled towards social/cultural advancement, while *both* Swazis and development agents/bureaucrats usually perceive conflict as a negative state of affairs in which social energies are wasted (at least such perceptions are usually acknowledged).

Why, when and how do people accept or resist harmony ideologies?

This question can be answered with reference to interactions between different social groups – the traditional elite, the new elite and commoners. It serves as a summary reformulation of two question which I have posed throughout this book: Why and how do elites propagate harmony ideologies? and When do ordinary subjects accept or resist such ideologies?

I have argued that individuals within all social groups interpret harmony in accordance with their interests, as moulded by factors of class and individual status in each dyadic social/political interaction. The traditional ruling elite use harmony to legitimate their administrative roles and validate their performances. They do so to maintain internal cohesion within the hierarchical level at which they hold power (national, chiefdom or family level) and to ward off threats of external interference, such as from land development agents, and internal interference, such as from new elites. In land dispute situations, traditional elites use harmony to contain land disputes at each hierarchical level and thereby to promote social unity: such unity justifies the continuation of the customary land tenure system and associated power structures to external power-holders and internal subordinates.

New elites also use harmony to legitimate their administrative roles and validate their performances. They do so to promote their newly emerging roles as effective agents of social and cultural ideals. They also use harmony to appear effective as land administrators. In land dispute situations, new elites, like traditional elites, use harmony to create an illusion of unity; however, in the process of creating harmony which accords with their individual and group interests, they often produce internal social conflict.

Both traditional and new elites use harmony ideologies to produce legitimacy, which in turn justifies control. When either traditional or new elites' legitimacy (i.e. control) is not threatened, individuals rely upon organic harmony to fortify in cultural terms their claims, such as over land administration, whereas when their legitimacy (i.e. control) is threatened, they rely upon control (imposed) harmony to restore through force their claims. Traditional elites base their claims on ascribed status. New elites experience problems of legitimacy and control because their achieved status does not fully support their claims; consequently, they arguably rely more heavily on control harmony strategies than do traditional elites.

Swazi commoners at the bottom of the social hierarchy strategically respond to attitudinal and behavioural expressions of harmony. They consider control issues of the authorities and their status relative to their opponents. As I demonstrated in the case analyses, they respond to harmony in each case so as to produce outcomes more favourable to them. When they perceive harmony ideologies as culturally and individually valuable – usually organic – they will abide by the principles of the ideologies. When they perceive harmony ideologies as culturally valuable but individually disadvantageous, they will strategize to achieve their own best advantage without threatening the control of the authorities. When they perceive ideologies as culturally invalid (valuable only to the authorities' personal interests) and individually disadvantageous, they will strategize to achieve their own best advantage – even if posing a challenge to the control of the authorities.

Swazi commoners accept harmony ideologies when they feel that such ideologies further the greatest social good (in the relevant social group) without significantly hindering their own interests. In addition, they may find that such ideologies are useful to them, or, when not, that they have no adequate means to resist them. They are more likely to accept ideologies conveyed by the traditional elite, who are the official bearers of culture. They usually accept organic harmony ideologies which convey accepted social ideals and aim for consensus through persuasion rather than force.

Swazi commoners resist harmony ideologies when they feel that the social good has been violated: the ideologies conveyed by the authorities conflict with their intended meaning, and thus with ideal formulations about social unity and cohesiveness. They also resist harmony ideologies when they, as individuals, will suffer severe consequences – such as loss or reduction of land rights, or when some individuals will profit unduly. Resistance may consist of open rebellion (assertion strategies), evasion (avoidance strategies) and deception.

Some classes of commoners are particularly likely to resist harmony ideologies through strategies. Women, who have probably long exercised greater land administration responsibilities than the normative socio-political structure would account for, rely upon strategies to enhance their disputing opportunities. Through use of strategies, some women are able to represent their homestead group openly at public chiefs' meetings, to argue forcefully land disputes before the Chief's Court and to make independently important decisions about land use (e.g. crops to be planted or land distribution patterns). Women who are educated and have an income can strategically take advantage of lawyers or buy land; unfortunately, the majority of women do not have these 'modern' options.

The ordinary Swazi can use inconsistencies between ideal formulations about harmony and actual behaviours as leverage against the elite. The elite are aware that commoners scrutinize their intentions and actions; they may determine their harmony strategies based on the initial disputing strategies of commoners. Thus, commoners' strategies are not always reactive; sometimes the strategies initiate confrontation, persuading the authorities to respond with harmony strategies.

The traditional elite probably most often believe that harmony ideologies serve the greatest social good, even when their own class and individual interests are simultaneously furthered. In any case, they may not always be fully conscious of their motivations in propagating harmony ideologies: they are skilled at rationalizing the social good in terms of their individual good. Commoners, too, are often persuaded that social good results from strategies of harmony, and consequently, they usually strategize within the system rather than against it. In essence, elites propagate harmony ideologies to validate their administrative powers over land, and ordinary Swazis respond in a manner which least threatens the control interests of the authorities (elite) but which achieves most effectively their immediate case interests.

How is harmony used over time?

This question can be answered with reference to processes of change. Change in ideological expressions and behavioural manifestations of harmony over time is inevitable because harmony can only define the status quo at a certain point in time and according to one person's or group's perspective. In fact, harmony is largely produced, or at least defined, through the process of conflict; thus, dispute participants make ideal statements about harmony, infusing concrete relationships and behaviours with a definition of harmony. Since harmony is constantly being propagated, it is difficult for the analyst to determine the background against which harmony is defined (i.e. the sequence of conditions). It is also difficult to determine whether specific harmony ideologies are indigenous or have been introduced, such as by colonialists or missionaries.

The conquering Dlamini clan probably relied on harmony ideologies, which bolstered such strategies of unification as inter-clan marriages, in the early stages of nation-building. They strategically used organic harmony ideologies in the context of kingship rituals (*Ncwala*) to create a social unity, mould custom and gradually forge a history. They relied on control harmony strategies, when necessary, to enforce unity. Both kinds of harmony strategies strengthened the Swazi political hierarchy, making it unusually resilient and adaptive.

In the modern-day world, in which the Swazi population has become more heterogeneous (economically and religiously), control harmony strategies have become commonplace. But organic and control strategies are interdependent and are used simultaneously during all phases of history. The Dlamini rulers and their high-ranking subordinates continue to create the illusion that Swazi unity is produced through consensus, but they continue to call upon the iron fist of forced compliance, when necessary.

Swazi traditional elites vacillate between organic and control harmony strategies: control harmony strategies cannot produce long-term legitimacy, while organic harmony strategies cannot always produce short-term social control. When used together, organic strategies produce cultural legitimacy, and control strategies complement this legitimacy with social control. Effective leaders have mastered this delicate art of balance.

The growth of economic classes, and consequently an expanded urban bureaucracy, has proved both a boon and a threat to Swazi traditional elites' reliance upon harmony ideologies. It is a boon in the sense that traditional elites can render the illusion that they alone produce consensus (organic harmony), while the bureaucrats, technocrats and civil servants – such as the police force and court officers – are left with the impersonal and dirty groundwork of forcing compliance (control harmony). At the same time, the growth of economic classes is a threat in the sense that traditional elites can no longer claim to possess exclusively the status necessary to produce organic (cultural) harmony. Their power as referents in the continual process of defining harmony has changed, and in some cases, declined.

New elites use control harmony strategies until their power/legitimacy is shored up. They calculate their best advantage; they need to rely on the cultural (organic harmony strategies), but they back up their cultural rhetoric with social control (control harmony strategies). Their harmony strategies produce a fragile image of passive local unity, but boiling beneath this image are the roots of social unrest.

Commoners interpret and respond to expressions of harmony differently in each case and over several separate hearings of the same case, according to changing circumstances and status relationships. Both traditional and new elites, in turn, must decide how to respond to disputants' strategies. Their propagation of organic harmony ideologies or harmony as control is usually based on whether their status and control is or is not threatened. This process, in which persons at the top of the hierarchy influence strategy production of those at the bottom of the hierarchy, in which persons at the bottom of the hierarchy influence strategy production of those at the top of the hierarchy, and in which persons at the same level of the hierarchy influence the strategy production of one another, renders Swazi 'politics of harmony' interactive and multi-tiered.

In effect, strategies of organic and control harmony are used in different ways (offensive and defensive) and to different degrees over time, depending on their utility to particular classes and individuals. Thus, overall strategy configurations shift in individual cases (according to the nature of the dispute and disputant relationships) and in general. What is sometimes unclear is how and by whom shifts in strategy configurations are initiated – by dissatisfied commoners or by elites seeking greater control.

What is the relation between harmony and land disputes?

The answer to this question can be answered with reference to the land dispute data. Harmony ideologies, which generally serve to downplay disruptions in land disputes, are useful to Swazi elites since they justify continuation of their land control. Harmony ideologies are also useful to ordinary Swazis since they reinforce valued cultural and social unity, which is closely linked to land use rights.

Swazi informants consistently argued that some disputes, such as those between the Central Authority and chiefs, between chiefs, and between family members, particularly threaten the intervention of outside authorities (hierarchically superior authorities), who would impose upon the internal integrity and cohesion of the particular social unit (i.e. nation, chiefdom or family). When a dispute arises within one of these social units, harmony is used to deny/downplay the dispute to outsiders and thus to contain it. For example, when the Central Authority is involved in land disputes, harmony is used to downplay the disruptiveness in order to prevent outside intervention from foreign/local development agents (Case 8) or European-influenced courts (Cases 8, 12 and 16). When chiefs are involved in land disputes, harmony is used to downplay the disruptiveness in order to prevent the interference of the Central Authority (Cases 9, 13 and 26). When family members are involved in land disputes, harmony is used to downplay the disruptiveness in order to prevent the interference of the chiefdom authorities (Cases 3, 17 and 18).

The data indicate that land disputes are also denied in situations of internal threats to the integrity and cohesion of the relevant social unit. In such cases, only some members of the social unit – particularly the elites who are concerned with maintaining their current status and control against internal challenges – rely on harmony strategies to downplay/deny disputes (Case 25). Ordinary Swazis also deny land disputes through strategies when public resolution procedures could hinder their causes (Cases 17 and 22).

In the land disputes discussed, harmony strategies were used in different ways and to different degrees. They were sometimes used to downplay/deny a dispute and sometimes to further public resolution. They were sometimes used to downplay/deny the dispute to some observers but not to other observers. Sometimes they were used to defend status interests of a few (Case 25), and sometimes to realize the interests of an entire social unit (Case 3).

Harmony and land disputes: dilemmas for African development

Harmony associated with African land disputes poses a thorny practical dilemma for development interests: how, and even if, abstract theories about harmony can be converted into concrete lay formulations, and thus into practical policy objectives regarding customary land law. The problem is that individual perceptions and interpretations influence policy formation: 'developers' will devise land tenure policy, including land dispute considerations, according to how they view harmony and conflict. However, such developers usually perceive harmony as positive and conflict as negative, despite the fact that conflict, similar to harmony, can be viewed from 'negative' and 'positive' sides.

Although both sides of harmony have been conveyed throughout this book, the dual nature of conflict needs to be re-emphasized. On the negative side, conflict about land is blamed by foreign development agencies and many Africans for causing or contributing to economic woes – such as disrupting local administration or hindering local and national development objectives. It is also blamed for causing an enormous amount of time, money and energy to be expended. Some persons who take this negative perspective adhere to policy objectives which demand alteration of the customary land tenure system and associated social/political structures.

On the positive side, land disputes can be perceived as beneficial, although this perspective is rarely taken. They can lead to a constructive 'airing out' of grievances, and produce, when properly channelled through a reasonably open and accessible dispute management system (here lies the greatest area for policy initiatives), an orderly momentum necessary for social/political change. As explained in the introduction, they can lead to new or redefined legal rules, to new or redefined legal institutions, and to new consensual understandings. In effect, land disputes are useful in that they pull apart and expose a land tenure system during the inevitable processes of change, while appearances of harmony preserve the most fundamental aspects of the system against internal and external threats. Many Africans, such as Swazis, may dislike land disputes and may be apprehensive about change, but they may realize intuitively, if not consciously, that adept use of harmony strategies in land disputes holds together the system while change is wrought from within.

Policy objectives in Swaziland, as elsewhere in Africa, need to bring out the positive rather than strictly the negative aspects of conflict. Critics of customary land tenure, rather than arguing that land disputes justify the need for outside intervention to promote land tenure changes, might realize that land disputes may permit a customary land tenure system to evolve by its own rules, at its own speed and in its own directions. In fact, African land disputes, by virtue of their predominantly political rather than economic nature, instead of broadly inhibiting development, can potentially provide one of the most significant means by which a negotiated social/political foundation for land tenure 'development' occurs.

Harmony linked with conflict, i.e. land disputes, poses a seeming conceptual contradiction. This contradiction can be resolved if critics of African customary land tenure investigate the different social/political dimensions of harmony in land disputes – both attitudinal (organic) and behavioural (control). In Swaziland, such an approach aids in explaining the internal logic of customary land dispute strategies and in comprehending their sometimes paradoxical nature: Swazis relied upon different forms of harmony to deny or downplay actual land disputes, despite the disadvantages they sometimes suffered as individuals in a hierarchical political structure, so that they might ensure cultural unity and survival in a modernizing nation.

Appendix: University of Swaziland Questionnaire Results: Women and Land Tenure

1. Q: Who can *khonta*?
   A: A married man. (70%)
   An unmarried man with his mother. (30%)
2. Q: Can an unmarried man get land?
   A: Cannot get land because a man needs land only to support a wife and children. (75%)
   Can get land for his mother. (16%)
   Can get land if he has no father or his father assists him. (9%)
3. Q: Can a woman get land?
   A: She cannot. (30%)
   She can through a son. (42%)
   She can in unusual circumstances (i.e. childlessness). (28%)
4. Q: What if a woman has no family?
   A: She will go to the chief of an area for advice or 'adoption'. (52%)
   She must get married. (4%)
   She will get her father's land. (6%)
   She will get land in her home area. (2%)
5. Q: How do non-married women (i.e. single or widowed) get land?
   A: Through a son who will *khonta* for her. (75%)
   Through inheritance from her husband. (6%)
   Through a male relative. (19%)
6. Q: Does a woman have the same rights to land as a man?
   A: Yes. (72%)
   Yes, until her son grows up and assumes responsibility. (9%)
   No, because the rights belong to her husband and sons. (19%)
7. Q: Can a woman inherit land from her husband?
   A: Yes, conditionally (eleven different 'conditions' were mentioned, such as a woman can inherit to hold land for sons). (93%)
   No. (7%)

* *Source:* Survey designed by Alice Armstrong, carried out by University of Swaziland student enumerators, and analysed by the present author.

8. Q: Can a woman inherit land from her father?
   A: Yes, if she does not have brothers or if she is not married. (63%)
   No, she must marry because only male relatives can inherit land. (37%)
9. Q: Does a woman 'own' fields?
   A: Yes. (Some respondents clarified that this actually gives long-term cultivation rights by her in-laws). (98%)
   No. (2%)
10. Q: Can a husband take away his wife's fields?
    A: No. (66%)
    Yes, under circumstances that the husband takes another wife or repudiates his wife. (34%)
11. Q: Can a woman lend out fields?
    A: No. (90%)
    Yes. (10%)
12. Q: Have any land disputes in your area involved women?
    A: Never hear of such disputes. (51%)
    Such disputes cannot exist because women do not own land. (20%)
    Yes. (unspecified). (21%)
    Yes. (specified). (8%)

Notes

Introduction

1 Several investigators have devoted attention to Swazi customary land law (tenure) (Hughes 1964a, 1964b, 1964c, 1972; Nkambule 1983), although little mention of land disputes has been made.

2 Numerous calls for customary law research in Swaziland have been made (Armstrong 1985; Meyers 1983; Nhlapo 1982). Among the few studies which have been conducted are a Judicial Commissioner's recording of principles of customary law (Fannin 1967); several legal scholars' summations of customary law (Khumalo 1977; Khoza 1975; Rubin 1963); and several anthropological analyses of the social bases of customary law (Marwick 1940; Kuper 1947a, 1947b; Hughes 1962, 1964a, 1964b, 1964c, 1972). Armstrong (1985: 2) has noted several methodological and conceptual problems of these studies: they have focused upon interviews with Swazi authorities rather than upon case observation and analysis; they have compelled Swazi informants to conceive of customary laws in hypothetical rather than real contexts; and they have implied that customary laws are static when in fact they are in a constant state of flux.

3 Throughout Africa, researchers investigating land disputes have reported problems in obtaining accurate data or even in warding off sorcery accusations and threats of expulsion.

4 On the topic of conceptual difficulties in cross-cultural analyses of land tenure relations and disputing, see Amoah 1978: 4; Bentsi-Enchill 1965: 132; Bohannan 1967: 56 and 1963: 103; Comaroff 1978a: 19; and White 1958.

5 'Developers' are defined as people who advocate land tenure changes on the grounds that such changes will increase land productivity. Radical developers propose formal transition to individual land tenure, whereas conservative developers propose more moderate and piecemeal changes in land practices.

6 Colson (1966: 7) notes that Tonga can give legal rules of land tenure, although these rules generate no model descriptive of any pattern of actual holdings.

7 Refer to discussions in Meek 1946 and Mifsud 1967 about land development in Africa.

1 Geographical, historical, political and social bases of customary land tenure relations

1 Sansom (1937) interprets a relationship between ecology and authority structures.

2 For more information, see Fair et al. 1969; Green and Fair 1969; Leistner and Smit 1969; Maasdorp 1976; Murdoch 1977.

3 For more detailed discussions of the Partition, see Doggett 1980: 30; Dyk 1971: 1; Fransman 1978a: 28; Kunene 1982a, 1982b; Mashasha 1974: 91; Matsebula 1972: 41; Nyeko 1977; Whittington and Daniel 1969: 448.

4 See Crush 1980b; Fair 1981: 29; Fransman 1978b: 65; Sallinger-McBride and Picard 1984a; Takirambudde 1983: 217–18 and n.d.: 33.

5 See de Vletter 1981: 7; Holleman 1964a: 53; Nkambule 1983: 33–4; Whittington and Daniel 1969: 450–3.

6 Tibiyo Taka Ngwane Fund (Swazi National Development Fund) was established by King Sobhuza following Independence in 1968 as an investment undertaking based on funds derived from mineral royalties. Tibiyo's revenue does not accrue to the Ministry of Finance. Moreover, it has remained under the exclusive control of the monarch and is not accountable to any other branch of the government. This system was reorganized in 1975 when funds from mineral royalties were placed under a new organization, Tisuka Taka Ngwane, and Tibiyo thereafter acted solely as an investment corporation. Davies et al. describe the economic power which has accrued to the royal family through control of Tibiyo: 'In a country with limited potential for domestic capital formation, Tibiyo has emerged as by far the most important and powerful vehicle for domestic capital accumulation' (1985: 19).

7 According to Hughes (1964c: 143–4), Swazis originally had no word which lumped all kinds of chiefs together. Rather, the three types of chiefs were clearly differentiated in terms of origins and functions.

8 This term refers to land which distances potential rivals within the royal clan from the King and also extends the control of the royal clan to different parts of the country.

9 Hughes (1964c; 1972) uses this term to refer to royals at the national capitals.

10 See Potholm (1965) for a discussion of national political developments in Swaziland.

11 See discussions of African land rights in Barrows 1973: 213; Bentsi-Enchill 1965: 132; Biebuyck 1964: 100; Bohannan 1963: 102; 1964: 142; 1967: 53; Gluckman 1955; 1965a: 89–90; 1965b; Jeppe 1980: 13; Mugambwa 1981: 83; Nkambule 1983: 37; see also Doggett 1980: 11 on Swaziland. Refer to Meek 1946 and Mifsud 1967 for comparative discussions of African land rights.

12 Since the introduction of colonial and post-Independence legislation throughout Africa, the chief's power to grant land has been seriously curtailed in some polities. For example, in Botswana, the Tribal Land Act 1968 now confers on a land board 'all the powers vested in a Chief under customary law in relation to land' (Frimpong 1986).

13 Although customary rights to land do not amount to 'ownership' in the Western sense of a private right to alienate others from the land, the term is used in the sense of a right to exclude others from the occupation and use of the land (Mifsud 1967: 9, 44–5).

14 See Njeru 1978 and Brokensha and Njeru 1977 on land adjudication in Kenya; see Wynne 1985 on Land Boards in Botswana.

15 See Barrows 1973: 12; Njeru 1978: 26; and Roberts 1970 on disruptive reforms; see Werbner 1980: 149 and Wynne 1985: 34 on the impact of Land Boards in Botswana upon traditional authority structures.

16 See critiques of Swazi Nation Land offered by Amoah 1978: 41; Daniel 1964: 235–6 and 1966a: 507; Doggett 1980: 32, 38; Fine n.d.: 13; Gina 1983: 2; Hughes 1964b: 11; Riddell and Dickerman 1986; and Whittington and Daniel 1969: 455.

17 See Amoah 1982: 5–7; Mashasha 1974: 89; and Butler 1974: 170 regarding land tenure dualism. See Butler 1974: 165–6; de Vletter 1981: 1; Doggett 1980: 35; Fair 1981: 29–30; Russell 1983: 16–17 regarding structural dualism. See de Vletter 1981: 6; Dlamini et al. 1984: 2; Maasdorp 1976: 412; and Matsebula 1982b: 2 regarding economic dualism.

18 See results of interview and questionnaire studies conducted by myself and by Alice Armstrong, as described in Chapter 5.

19 See Doggett 1980: 37–8; de Vletter 1981: 9; Hughes 1964b: 12; and Magabula 1982: 14 on Swaziland. For more information about fears throughout Africa regarding threats to traditional socio-political orders posed by changes in land use and administration, see Biebuyck 1964: 103; Comaroff 1978b: 1; Gluckman 1969: 256–7; Moore 1986: 307; Richards 1963: 270; Whittington and Daniel 1969: 453.

20 See point-by-point discussion of Doggett (1980: 41–2) on the situation prevailing in neighbouring Lesotho, where the government and populace are arguably committed to land reform.
21 See Black-Michaud (1981: 2–3) on household/homestead differentiation.
22 For a more in-depth discussion about land reforms and the impact of such reforms in Africa, see Barrows 1973; Colson 1963, 1966; Glazier 1976; Gluckman 1944; Gulliver 1958, 1963a; Mayer and Mayer 1965; Richards 1963; White 1963; Wintrob 1966.
23 The survey consisted of two parts. First, it consisted of 1,150 interviews of Swazi Nation Land homesteads (2.5 per cent of total Swazi Nation Land population) over the years 1978–9. Each interview involved administration of a questionnaire which lasted approximately two to three hours. Secondly, it involved monitoring of 87 homesteads over three months to gauge income and expenditure flows and over twelve months to observe nutritional intake.
24 Margo Russell (1985) notes that 'lack of land is rarely permanent, but occurs as a phase in the life cycle . . . The 22 per cent of the population who are not on Nation Land have the right, if they are Swazis, to acquire land there through submission to a chief. Their lack of land is thus voluntary, but they must be organised into potential homesteads to be eligible. This is true of the 5 per cent who live on freehold land as tenants.'
25 I believe, based on my case data, that a married woman's own clan members will not necessarily help her in a land dispute since her land rights are granted by her husband and his family; however, I did witness cases in which a woman's clan became involved when her husband tried to take over land that belonged to her family.
26 Despite the fact that clanship prescribes a political structure, members can upgrade their own and their clan's relative status. Thus, a wealthy, accomplished commoner can upgrade the ranking of his clan by marrying a prince's or chief's daughter, while another man can upgrade his personal standing and thereby the ranking of his clan by performing acts of diplomacy, or in the past, military prowess.
27 In my case sample, members of an age grade came before the Chief's Court with a report about a dispute between two age mates over a woman. Otherwise, I have very little evidence of age group involvement in disputes.

2 The legal structure for customary land tenure relations

1 Benda-Beckmann (1981) describes forum shopping in Indonesia, while Van Rouveroy van Nieuwaal (1981) describes how women shop for forums in marriage disputes in Togo.
2 In Part II, several cases (e.g. 8, 16 and 20), in which land disputants tried to use European-influenced courts to resolve customary land matters, are described. The disputants were usually only successful when they took a matter indirectly related to customary land rights to such courts. In Case 16, the High Court intervened to review the 'natural justice' of the case, but royal pressure apparently persuaded the judges to abandon the case.
3 See, for example, the Land Bill 1979 of Lesotho and the Tribal Land Act 1968 of Botswana.
4 A foreign-funded proposal to research Swazi customary law was rejected by Swazi authorities.
5 In this regard, see the 1986–8 USAID project report, *Changes in Agricultural Land Use: Institutional Constraints and Opportunities.*
6 Wallman (1968) argues that the Lesotho local council is now ineffective because the nature of village life has changed and too much is demanded of it, while Perry (1977) explains that it is troubled by lower attendance and by case hearings which aim at expedient disposition rather than consensus-building. A. Kuper (1970; see also 1971) reports similar observations for local councils in Botswana.
7 See, for example, the Chiefship Law 1965 in Botswana.
8 Grant (1980: 98–9; see also Silitshena 1979: 65) argues that, despite assertions that national legislation reduced the powers of chiefs following Independence, in fact, some chiefs succeeded in using new administrative agencies to their advantage.

9 Data collection proceeded according to similar models adhered to elsewhere in Africa, including other parts of Southern African (for example, Comaroff 1975, 1978a, 1978b; Comaroff and Roberts 1977, 1981; A. Kuper 1970; Roberts 1971, 1977, n.d.; Schapera 1938, 1969, 1983).

10 According to P. H. Gulliver (1969a: 14), the public aspect is critical in defining a dispute proper, but as June Starr (1978a: 122) observed, the pre-disputing stage, i.e. grievance stage, can be sufficiently complex to comprise three phases: disagreeing about facts, piling up of grievances, and seeking of resolution.

11 An extended case is derived through observation of ongoing grievances, conflicts or disputes from the time of their genesis (outside of an institutional setting such as a court) to formal processing by one or more institutions. An extended case may, in theory, comprise a series of related cases which occur over time and involve some or all of the same actors (Gulliver 1971), or one detailed case which arises repeatedly and remains unsettled after months or years (Turner 1957). In addition to being classified in dyads, extended cases may be classified in triads, which focus on the form of third party intervention (Aubert 1963: 35; Nader and Todd 1978: 8–9).

12 Dyadic relationships can be depicted as changing, such as those based on cooperative endeavours, e.g. in 'action sets' (Gulliver 1969b and 1971). They can also be depicted as relatively stable, such as those based on kinship and territory; for example, inter-family, inter-personal and inter-clan (Brokensha and Njeru 1977: 8); intra-family, intra-community, inter-community and inter-cultural (LeVine 1961: 4–5); or intra-village and inter-village (Gulliver 1958: 30).

13 English and siSwati are the official national languages. English is spoken in the Western-influenced courts (Roman-Dutch law), whereas siSwati is spoken in the customary Swazi courts.

14 I observed many cases in which litigants and witnesses spoke almost non-stop for as long as half an hour. Spectators often grumbled to me that 'such and such' had been permitted to talk about boring, seemingly inconsequential trivia.

15 Some secretaries are not fully bilingual and able to perform such functions.

16 Nearly all my informants agree that Swazi Courts and *Tinkhundla* cannot handle customary land matters, and yet my observations at Regional Administration offices indicate that Regional Administrators, *Tinkhundla* officials and Swazi Court Presidents are usually well informed about customary land disputes which come before customary chiefs and modern *Ndabazabantu*. More information about points of interface between the customary and modern authorities would probably clarify operational realities.

17 At one *Inkhundla* meeting I attended, the constituent chiefs called together their subjects to hear talks by government nurses regarding inoculation and other health concerns.

3 Two communities: arenas for land disputes

1 My inquiries into the origins of *emahambate* encountered diverse responses: some informants said that Mandanda's father and then he himself came to oversee *emahambate* as a reward for faithful service to past Kings, whereas other informants said that Mandanda was asked to oversee *emhambate* on behalf of the King because of succession and boundary disputes in the areas. My inquiries into the nature of *emahambate* encountered vague responses: most informants did not know the names of the *emahambate*, and even when I obtained a list of the *emahambate*, no informant could name all *tindvuna* who oversee them.

2 During the early part of my research, a new King was to be appointed and thus new royal villages established. Zombodze was waning in importance, gradually becoming a minor royal village, as discussed above.

3 I must convey my general impressions rather than statistical information for two reasons: first, people drifted in and out of court meetings at such a considerable rate that precise attendance

patterns could not be determined; secondly, personnel usually preferred not to provide personal information. Since my research topic was sensitive, I did not pursue such information aggressively.

4 Some people said, 'We live near the royal village and must come to the meetings often. If we were to stay home and do our own work, people might see us and think that we are disrespectful and concerned only with ourselves rather than the welfare of the community.'

5 It is unclear whether local residents were referring to Tongotongo or another Queen.

6 Although many residents described a map and plans for the community, I was never able to locate them in government ministries.

7 Kwaluseni residents referred frequently to the 'newcomers' and 'originals' councils, although I use the terms with reservation since some long-term residents attended the 'newcomers' council meetings and some new residents attended the 'originals' council meetings. In addition, I suspect that members of the 'newcomers' council would not appreciate this designation.

4 The politics of harmony: land dispute strategies

1 See discussion in Scott which describes the 'weapons of the weak' as Malaysian peasants' strategies of resistance against the ideological 'definition of the situation as seen from above'. The weak refuse to 'condone their own social and ritual marginalization...' (1985: 240).

2 In the African context, Sutherland (1981) has described how Yeyi elders selectively incorporate the style and procedure of the Tswana legal culture, including emphasis on forgiveness between parties and negotiation. In this example, harmony ideology conveys the image that the ideals of the larger and dominant legal culture are being incorporated and that local dispute management is 'working' – the consequence being that legal autonomy should be maintained.

3 Professor Laura Nader pointed out this distinction in a private conversation.

4 For additional information on Swazi land history and the current land tenure situation refer to Chapter 1. See also Bonner (1977, 1983), Crush (1977, 1980a, 1980b), Daniel (1966a, 1966b), Doggett (1980), Fair (1981), Fair and Maasdorp (1980), Fransman (1978a, 1978b), Hailey (1953), Kunene (1982a, 1982b), Kuper (1941, 1947a, 1947b, 1963), Maina (1975), Mashasha (1977), J.S.M. Matsebula (1972), M.S. Matsebula (1982a), Whittington and Daniel (1969).

5 See Roberts' (1977: 37) account of the survival of Kgatla law under contact conditions.

6 The hierarchical structure of land control described by Hughes conforms to the 'hierarchy of estates' model described by Gluckman (1969: 259) for other parts of Southern Africa; see critiques of model in Biebuyck 1964: 103; La Fontaine 1979: 96–111; and White 1958: 127.

7 See also Cohen 1966: 132; Sallinger-McBride and Picard 1984b: 32, 1984a; and Wintrob 1966: 1.

8 Anthropologists describe two kinds of land disputes: (1) those which involve social relationships within a landholding unit, and (2) those which involve political relationships between two sovereign land-holding units (Uchendu 1967: 95).

9 See Collier 1973; Gulliver 1963b; Moore 1986; and Starr and Yngvesson 1975.

10 See Fallers 1969: 204; Moore 1986; 305; Beals 1961: 28; and Wintrob 1966.

11 Gulliver (1958) provides an example of social power competitions between close kin over land use. Perry (1981) provides an example of political power competitions between Sotho chiefs over land administration; he demonstrates how some chiefs allocate land to test the status quo of land administrative powers, to construct an alternative reality of spatial and political arrangements, and to acquire prestige. For more information about the relationship between land disputes and social/political power, see also Preston-Whyte and Sibisi 1975; Starr and Yngvesson 1975: 560–1; Uchendu 1967: 94; and Van Velzen 1973: 603.

12 Brokensha and Njeru 1977, Njeru 1978 and Roberts n.d. describe similar land dispute phenomena in other parts of Africa.
13 In this regard, see Moore 1970, 1977; Roberts 1973; Roberts and Comaroff 1979; and Rosen-Prinz 1976.
14 In theory, strategies are devices according to which persons who find themselves on the weaker side of an unequal power relationship can exploit normative ambiguities, inconsistencies and conflicts to attain their situational goals (see Comaroff and Roberts 1981: 31; Hamnett 1975: 76; Mbithi 1970: 9; Moore 1986: 305; Perry 1981: 236; Starr and Yngvesson 1975: 562; and Werbner 1969: 245–6).
15 See discussion in Beals 1961: 27–8; Elias 1956: 176, 184; Hoebel 1954: 284–5; and Maine 1861: 20–3 on the use of legal fictions to overcome structural rigidities and promote new practices.

5 Land dispute cases in the Swazi hierarchy

1 The extensive literature on land tenure in Swaziland makes little mention of land disputes. Hughes discusses the historical background of boundary disputes between chiefs and cites a couple of cases (1972: 254). He also describes in hypothetical terms how a land dispute between a chief's subjects can erupt when a migrant labourer returns and tries to lay claim to his reallocated land (1972: 151–2).
2 Other relationships, such as between subjects and the Central Authority, are also relevant, but are incorporated within the subject–chief dyad since a chief commonly acts as an intermediary between his subject and the Central Authority.
3 No attempt has been made to tabulate the total number of interviews since they ranged greatly in length and depth. Some interviews consisted of several hours of intense discussion, and others consisted of a few minutes of informative but casual conversation.
4 The chief's council decided not to discuss fully this case, but rather to remand it to another court.
5 In 29 cases in the total sample, status could not be determined.
6 My informants said that most disputes involving high-ranking litigants are now referred to newer royal capitals.
7 One important land disputant dyad has been omitted from this analysis: Central Authority vs. foreign government. This dyad is too complex for consideration within this study (it involves, for example, Swazi ethnics who are resident in South Africa and desire incorporation within Swaziland). The disputant dyads of chief vs. Central Authority, or alternatively, Central Authority vs. chief, merit further study.
8 Most disputes in this sample went either to the chief's council at Zombodze or the local council at Kwaluseni. Data on disputes which went to other disputing forums were obtained from interviews.
9 Refers to the List of Cases on pp. xi–xiii for a list of dyads and cases.
10 Some of these cases are included in the data tables; others are not statistically accounted for as they were reported informally.
11 Since his family members obtained land through him, his banishment means that they must leave as well. Some informants said that his descendants may not return for some generations.
12 Village attached to an enclosure where the King's cattle are kept. The village serves as an administrative centre.
13 One might conclude that people of sufficient financial means are better able to assert and maintain their land rights.
14 Statistical data on this phenomenon cannot be compiled. Newspaper accounts report cases in which subjects withdraw allegiance to their chiefs. Several of my informants reported such cases but said that customary law prohibits them from naming their superiors in a 'disrespectful way'.

15 At the time this case occurred, the local council had not divided into two factions controlling the 'originals' and the 'newcomers' councils.
16 These suppositions must be confirmed by further research; indeed, my informants did not all agree as to the exact correlation between land disputes and powers of different types of chiefs.
17 The Western courts, which rely upon codified Roman-Dutch law and recorded cases, would demand 'hard' evidence regarding the impropriety of the authorities' manoeuvres. Therefore, the authorities' strategies aimed to downplay or disguise their manoeuvres, thus reducing the Western courts' incentives to intervene.

6 'A woman is like a field': Swazi women's land dispute strategies

1 More research is needed on the variables influencing women's actualization of presumed inheritance rights. Variables such as the presence or absence of male relatives (fathers or brothers), children (particularly sons), in-laws, co-wives and a second husband may influence the degree to which women are able to exercise potential inheritance rights.
2 Discrepancies between ideal and actual behaviour have been discussed by Freilich (1976), Harris (1974), Kay (1970), Linton (1936) and Richards (1969). Llewellyn and Hoebel (1941) differentiated between legal rules and actual behaviour. In an African case study, Abbott (1976) analysed the discrepancy between ideal cultural values and expectations regarding family structure and actual family structure reflected in interviews related to family decision-making and control of resources among the Kikuyu of Kenya. Mann (1982), Merry (1982) and Wright (1982) also examined African case studies to determine how women put ideal legal rules into practice.
3 The notion that people, when choosing a course of action, either select from a cultural pool of ideal standards or creatively develop problem-solving strategies for dealing with immediate situations (see Bailey 1969; Barth 1969) is an important aspect of the so-called 'ideal/actual' behaviour dichotomy.
4 Members of the chief's council admonished defendants on several occasions that they would sanction bad behaviour by denying access to a dispute-processing forum.

7 'How could I take my land dispute to the person with the stick?': Swazi elites' land dispute strategies

1 For more in-depth analyses, see Booth 1982, 1983a; Daniel 1982, 1983; Davies et al. 1985; Fransman 1982; Sallinger-McBride and Picard 1984b: 35; and Takirambudde 1981, 1983.
2 A faction is hereby defined as a loosely ordered group headed by a leader who has significant control over resources. A faction engages in conflict on specific occasions with a similar group over a particular issue; it aims to influence the outcome of conflict in accordance with its own interests. Factions frequently arise in situations of social change because they are better adapted to competition than other types of social groups (Boissevain 1964, 1968; Kuper 1970; Nicholas 1963, 1966; Siegal and Beals 1960).
3 It has been noted that 'throughout the colonial period the King resisted the imposition of elected councils, arguing that they were alien to the traditions of the Swazi nation' (Picard 1983: 11). In the case of Kwaluseni, it is clear that the King wanted a different kind of council to serve the unique needs of the community. The problem, as noted above, is that the King did not specify how council members were to be selected or how the council was to coordinate with the traditional hierarchy.
4 I discovered these plans in the course of my interviews in the communities.
5 For a comparative perspective on strategies which aim to augment power, see the following: Ranger 1983 on new elites' invention of tradition in Africa; Roberts 1977 and Schapera 1938, 1969 on chiefs' adaptations in Botswana; Perry 1981 on chiefs' land manipulations in Lesotho;

and Preston-Whyte and Sibisi 1975 on lineages' land manipulations among South African Zulu.

6 In this case, the authorities initially relied upon organic harmony strategies and only threatened control harmony strategies if the parties did not comply with their orders. As a contrast, in Case 11 a man was initially threatened by the authorities with force (control harmony) but was told that they would seek a peaceful solution (organic harmony) if he complied with their demands.

7 In Swaziland, chiefs often die leaving a minor heir (particularly if they married their senior wife late in life). However, succession is often not clear – even when an heir is designated. The tide of political events can result in an actual appointment of another candidate. Swazis hesitate to talk about succession because they do not want to appear to side with one or another competing faction. At Zombodze, the apparent heir was a middle-aged man, but rivalries were widely rumoured.

References

Abbott, Susan. 1976. 'Full-time Farmers and Weekend Wives: An Analysis of Altering Conjugal Roles'. *Journal of Marriage and the Family* 38, 165–74.

Amoah, P. K. A. 1978. 'Some Legal Aspects of the Customary Land Tenure Systems of Botswana, Lesotho, and Swaziland: A Comparative Study'. SWADEX 14, Workshop of Rural Environment and Development Planning in Swaziland, Ezulwini, Swaziland, 1–10 May.

Amoah, P. K. A. 1982. 'Law, Population and Development in Swaziland'. Mbabane, Swaziland: Swaziland Printing and Publishing Co.

Armstrong, Alice K. 1985. 'Legal Aspects of Land Tenure in Swaziland'. Paper prepared for USAID, Mbabane, Swaziland.

Armstrong, Alice K. and R. T. Nhlapo. 1985. *Law and the Other Sex: The Legal Position of Women in Swaziland.* Kwaluseni: University of Swaziland.

Aubert, Vilhelm. 1963. 'Competition and Descensus: Two Types of Conflict and of Conflict Resolution'. *Journal of Conflict Resolution* 7, 26–42.

Bailey, F. G. 1969. *Stratagems and Spoils: A Social Anthropology of Politics.* Oxford: Basil Blackwell.

Barnes, Carolyn. 1979. 'Background Paper on Social Factors and Government Systems for USAID's Swaziland Country Development Strategy Statement'. Mbabane, Swaziland.

Barrows, Richard L. 1973. 'Individualized Land Tenure and African Agricultural Development: Alternatives for Policy'. Paper on file at Land Tenure Center, University of Wisconsin, Madison.

Barth, Fredrik. 1969. *Political Leadership among Swat Pathans.* London School of Economics, Monograph 19.

Beals, Alan R. 1961. 'Cleavage and Internal Conflict: An Example from India'. *Journal of Conflict Resolution* 5, 27–34.

Benda-Beckman, K. von. 1981. 'Forum Shopping and Shopping Forums: Dispute Processing in a Minangkabau Village'. *Journal of Legal Pluralism* 19, 117–59.

Bendix, Reinhard. 1953. 'Social Stratification and Political Power'. In *Class, Status and Power: A Reader in Social Stratification* (Reinhard Bendix and Seymour Martin Lipset, eds.). Glencoe, Ill.: The Free Press, 596–609.

Bentsi-Enchill, Kwamena. 1965. 'Do African Systems of Land Tenure Require a Special Terminology?' *Journal of African Law* 9, 114–39.

Biebuyck, Daniel. 1963. *African Agrarian Systems.* London: Oxford University Press for the International African Institute.

Biebuyck, Daniel. 1964. 'Land Holding and Social Organization'. In *Economic*

Transition in Africa (Melville J. Herskovits and M. Harwitz, eds.). Evanston, Ill.: Northwestern University Press, 29–62.

Bishop, B. Leigh. 1979. 'Land Tenure Issues in Lesotho'. Paper on file at Land Tenure Center, University of Wisconsin, Madison.

Black-Michaud, Andrée. 1981. 'Homesteads versus Households When Collecting Socio-Economic Data'. Research Discussion Paper no. 1, Malkerns Agricultural Research Station, Malkerns, Swaziland.

Bohannan, Paul. 1963. 'Land, Tenure and Land-Tenure'. In *African Agrarian Systems* (Daniel Biebuyck, ed.). London: Oxford University Press for the International African Institute, 101–15.

Bohannan, Paul. 1964. 'Land Use, Land Tenure and Land Reform'. In *Economic Transition in Africa* (Melville J. Herskovits and M. Harwitz, eds.). Evanston, Ill.: Northwestern University Press, 133–49.

Bohannan, Paul. 1967. 'Africa's Land'. In *Tribal and Peasant Economies* (G. Dalton, ed.). New York: Doubleday, 51–60.

Boissevain, J. 1964. 'Factions, Parties and Politics in a Maltese Village'. *American Anthropologist* 66, 1275–87.

Boissevain, J. 1968. 'The Place of Non-Groups in the Social Sciences'. *Man* 3, 542–56.

Bonner, Philip. 1977. 'Classes, the Mode of Production and the State in Pre-Colonial Swaziland'. In *The Societies of Southern Africa in the 19th and 20th Centuries*, vol. 8, Collected Seminar Papers no. 22, 31–41.

Bonner, Philip. 1983. *Kings, Commoners and Concessionaires: the Evolution and Dissolution of the Nineteenth-Century Swazi State*. Johannesburg: Raven Press.

Booth, Alan R. 1982. 'The Development of the Swazi Labour Market 1900–1968'. *South African Labour Bulletin* 7, 34–57.

Booth, Alan R. 1983a. *Tradition and Change in a Southern African Kingdom*. Boulder, Colo: Westview Press.

Booth, Alan R. 1983b. 'The Homestead, the State and Migrant Labour in 20th Century Swaziland'. Paper presented at ASA Meetings, Boston, Mass.

Boserup, Ester. 1970. *Women's Role in Economic Development*. New York: St Martin's Press.

Brain, James L. 1976. 'Less than Second-Class: Women in Rural Settlement Schemes in Tanzania'. In *Women in Africa: Studies in Social and Economic Changes* (Nancy J. Hafkin and Edna G. Bay, eds.). Stanford, Calif.: Stanford University Press, 265–82.

Brokensha, David and E. H. N. Njeru. 1977. 'Some Consequences of Land Adjudication in Mbere Division, Embu'. Working Paper no. 320, Institute for Development Studies, University of Nairobi, Kenya.

Bruce, John. 1976. 'Land Reform Planning and Indigenous Tenures: A Case Study of the Tenure Chiguraf-Gwoses in Tigray Ethiopia'. Ph.D. dissertation, University of Wisconsin, Madison.

Butler, I. E. 1974. 'Local Government in Swaziland'. In *Local Government in Southern Africa* (W. B. Vosloo, D. A. Kotze and W. J. O. Jeppe, eds.). Pretoria: Acedemica, 164–82.

Chanock, Martin. 1985. *Law, Custom and Social Order: The Colonial Experience in Malawi and Zambia*. Cambridge: Cambridge University Press.

Cohen, Ronald. 1966. 'Power, Authority, and Personal Success in Islam and Bornu'. In *Political Anthropology* (Marc J. Swartz, Victor W. Turner and Arthur Tuden, eds.). Chicago: Aldine, 129–39.

Collier, Jane F. 1973. *Law and Social Change in Zinacantan*. Stanford, Calif.: Stanford University Press.

Collier, Jane F. 1974. 'Women in Politics'. In *Women, Culture and Society* (Michelle

Zimbalist Rosaldo and Louise Lamphere, eds.). Stanford, Calif.: Stanford University Press, 89–96.
Colson, E. 1963. 'Land Rights and Land Use among the Valley Tonga of the Rhodesian Federation: The Background to the Kariba Resettlement Programme'. In *African Agrarian Systems* (Daniel Biebuyck, ed.). London: Oxford University Press for the International African Institute, 137–56.
Colson, E. 1966. 'Land Law and Land Holdings Among Valley Tonga of Zambia'. *Southwestern Journal of Anthropology* 22, 1–8.
Comaroff, John. 1975. 'Talking Politics: Oratory and Authority in a Tswana Chiefdom'. In *Political Language and Oratory in Traditional Society* (Maurice Bloch, ed.). London: Academic Press, 141–61.
Comaroff, John. 1978a. 'Rules and Rulers: Political Processes in a Tswana Chiefdom.' *Man* 13, 1–20.
Comaroff, John. 1978b. 'The Transformation of Land Tenure in Barolong: On the Politics of Paraproductive Relations'. Paper presented at SSRC Conference on Land Tenure in Botswana, Satterthwaite.
Comaroff, John and Simon Roberts. 1977. 'The Invocation of Norms in Dispute Settlement: the Tswana Case'. In *Social Anthropology and Law* (I. Hamnett, ed.), ASA Monograph 14, London: Academic Press, 77–112.
Comaroff, John and Simon Roberts. 1981. *Rules and Processes*. Chicago and London: University of Chicago Press.
Coser, Lewis A. 1956. *The Functions of Social Conflict*. Glencoe, Ill.: The Free Press.
Crawford, J. R. 1969–70. 'The History and Nature of the Judicial System of Botswana, Lesotho and Swaziland – Introduction and the Superior Courts'. *South African Law Journal* 87, 76–86.
Crush, Jonathan. 1977. 'Swaziland: Development, Dependence and Interdependence'. Paper presented at Meetings of the Association of American Geographers, Salt Lake City, Utah.
Crush, Jonathan. 1980a. 'The Colonial Division of Space: The Significance of the Swaziland Land Partition'. *International Journal of African Historical Studies* 13, 71–86.
Crush, Jonathan. 1980b. 'The Genesis of Colonial Land Policy in Swaziland'. *South African Geographical Journal* 62, 73–88.
Daniel, J. B. M. 1964. 'The Swazi Rural Economy'. In *Experiment in Swaziland* (J. F. Holleman, ed.). Cape Town: Oxford University Press, 204–50.
Daniel, J. B. M. 1966a. 'Some Government Measures to Improve African Agriculture in Swaziland'. *Geographical Journal* 132, 506–15.
Daniel, J. B. M. 1966b. 'Swaziland: Some Problems of an African Rural Economy in a Developing Country'. *South African Geographical Journal* 48, 90–100.
Daniel, John. 1982. 'The Political Economy of Colonial and Post-Colonial Swaziland.' *South African Labour Bulletin* 7, 90–113.
Daniel, John. 1983. 'The South African – Swazi State Relationship: Ideological Harmony and Structural Domination'. Paper prepared for 5th Biannual Conference of the African Association of Political Science, Dakar, Senegal.
Davies, Robert H., Dave O'Meara and Sipho Dlamini. 1985. *The Kingdom of Swaziland*. London: Zed Books.
Dening, B. H. 1969. 'Local Government Trends in Swaziland'. *Journal of Administration Overseas* 8, 197–207.
de Vletter, Fion. 1981. 'Rural Development and Agricultural Dualism: A Case Study of Swaziland'. Social Science Research Unit, University of Swaziland.
de Vletter, Fion. 1984. 'The Swazi Rural Homestead: A Case Study of Subsistence

Wage Dependency and Misguided Rural Development'. Social Science Research Unit, University of Swaziland, Carnegie Conference paper no. 285.
Dlamini, E. V., N. Nkambule and V. Pungwayo. 1984. 'Proposals to Achieve a Rational National Land Use Policy'. Ministry of Agriculture and Cooperatives, Department of Research and Planning, discussion paper presented at seminar on rural development strategies for the next decade, part I.
Doggett, Clinton L. 1980. 'Land Tenure and Agricultural Development in Lesotho and Swaziland. A Comparative Analysis'. USAID Bureau for Africa, Mbabane, Swaziland.
Dyk, Stanislaus. 1971. 'The Concessions in Swaziland'. Paper on file at Deeds Office, Mbabane, Swaziland.
Elias, T. O. 1956. *The Nature of African Customary Law*. Manchester: Manchester University Press.
Evans-Pritchard, E. E. 1940. *The Nuer: A Description of the Modes of Livelihood and Political Institutions of a Nilotic People*. Oxford: Clarendon Press.
Fair, T. J. D. 1981. *Towards Balanced Spatial Development in Southern Africa*. Pretoria: Africa Institute of South Africa.
Fair, T. J. D. and G. G. Maasdorp. 1980. 'Swaziland'. In *African Perspectives* (E. B. Martin, ed.). London: Methuen, 115–35.
Fair, T. J. D., G. Murdoch and H. M. Jones. 1969. *Development in Swaziland: A Regional Analysis*. Johannesburg: Witwatersrand University Press.
Fallers, Lloyd A. 1956. *Bantu Bureaucracy*. Cambridge: Heffer.
Fallers, Lloyd A. 1969. *Law without Precedent: Legal Ideas in Action in the Courts of Colonial Busoga*. Chicago: University of Chicago Press.
Fannin, J. M. A. 1967. 'Principles of Swazi Customary Law.' Paper on file at Social Science Research Unit, University of Swaziland.
Fine, Patrick. n.d. 'Traditional Leadership and Development in Rural Swaziland.' Paper on file at Peace Corps Office, Mbabane, Swaziland.
Fransman, Martin. 1978a. 'The Colonial State and the Land Question in Swaziland, 1903–1907'. In *The Societies of Southern Africa in the 19th and 20th Century*. University of London: Institute of Commonwealth Studies, vol. 9, 27–38.
Fransman, Martin. 1978b. 'The State and Development in Swaziland, 1960–1967'. Ph.D. dissertation, Division of Development Studies, University of Sussex.
Fransman, Martin. 1982. 'Labour, Capital and the State in Swaziland, 1962–1977'. *South African Labour Bulletin* 7, 58–89.
Freilich, Morris. 1976. 'Manufacturing Culture: Man the Scientist'. In: *The Meaning of Culture* (Morris Freilich, ed.). Lexington, Mass.: Xerox College Publishers.
Frimpong, Kwame. 1986. 'The Administration of Tribal Lands in Botswana.' *Journal of African Law* 30, 51–74.
Gailey, Charles R. 1968. 'Changes in the Social Stratification of the Swazi, 1936–1967'. Ph.D. dissertation, University of South Africa.
Garbett, G. Kingsley. 1967. 'Prestige, Status, and Power in a Modern Valley Korekore Chiefdom, Rhodesia'. *Africa* 37, 307–26.
Gina, E. T. 1983. 'Constraints To Rural Development in Swaziland and Some Potential Solutions'. Paper prepared for Southern African Universities Social Science Conference on Transformation in Southern Africa, Zimbabwe.
Gina, E. T. 1984. 'The Demographic Structure of Swaziland and its Impact on Economic Development'. Paper prepared for seminar on population in Swaziland, University of Swaziland.
Glazier, Jack. 1976. 'Land Law and the Transformation of Customary Tenure: The Mbeere Case'. *Journal of African Law* 20, 39–50.

Gluckman, Max. 1940. 'The Kingdom of the Zulu of South Africa'. In *African Political Systems* (M. Fortes and E. Evans-Pritchard, eds.). London: Oxford University Press, 25–55.
Gluckman, Max. 1943. *Essays on Lozi Land and Royal Property*. Manchester: Manchester University Press.
Gluckman, Max. 1944. 'Studies in African Land Tenure'. *African Studies* 3, 14–21.
Gluckman, Max. 1955. *The Judicial Process among the Barotse of Northern Rhodesia*. Manchester: Manchester University Press.
Gluckman, Max. 1965a. *The Ideas in Barotse Jurisprudence*. New Haven, Conn. and London: Yale University Press.
Gluckman, Max. 1965b. 'Status and Rights in Land'. In *The Ideas in Barotse Jurisprudence* (ch. 5). New Haven, Conn. and London: Yale University Press.
Gluckman, Max. 1969. 'Property Rights and Status in African Traditional Law'. In *Ideas and Procedures in African Customary Law* (Max Gluckman, ed.). Oxford: Oxford University Press for the International African Institute, 252–65.
Godelier, Maurice. 1982. 'The Ideal in the Real'. In *Culture, Ideology and Politics* (Raphael Samuel and Gareth Stedman Jones, eds.). London and Boston, Mass.: Routledge & Kegan Paul, 12–38.
Grant, Sandy. 1980. 'Reduced Almost to Nothing? Chieftaincy and a Traditional Town. The Case of Linchwe II. Kgafela and Mochudi'. *Botswana Notes and Records* 12, 89–100.
Green, Edward C. 1984. 'Traditional Leadership, Community Participation and Development Education: Results and Implications of Two Surveys in Swaziland'. Paper prepared for USAID, Mbabane, Swaziland.
Green, L. P. and T. J. D. Fair. 1969. 'African Areas: Swaziland and Bechuanaland'. *Development in Africa – A Study in Regional Analysis with Special Reference to Southern Africa*. Johannesburg: Witwatersrand University Press.
Greenhouse, Carol J. 1986. *Praying for Justice: Faith, Order, and Community in an American Town*. Ithaca, N.Y. and London: Cornell University Press.
Gulliver, P. H. 1958. 'Land Tenure and Social Change among the Nyakyusa'. *East African Studies*. East African Institute of Social Research 11, Kampala.
Gulliver, P. H. 1963. 'Land Shortage, Social Change and Social Conflict in East Africa'. *Journal of Conflict Resolution* 5, 16–26.
Gulliver, P. H. 1969a. 'Case Studies of Law in Non-Western Societies'. In *Law in Culture and Society* (Laura Nader, ed.). Chicago: Aldine.
Gulliver, P. H. 1969b. 'Dispute Settlement without Courts: The Ndendeuli of Southern Tanzania'. In *Law in Culture and Society* (Laura Nader, ed.). Chicago: Aldine, 24–68.
Gulliver, P. H. 1971. *Neighbours and Networks: The Idiom of Kinship in Social Action among the Ndendeuli of Tanzania*. Berkeley: University of California Press.
Gulliver, P. H. 1979. *Disputes and Negotiations: A Cross-Cultural Perspective*. New York: Academic Press.
Hailey, Lord. 1953. *Native Administration in the British African Territories. Part V. The High Commission Territories: Basotholand, the Bechuanaland Protectorate and Swaziland*. London: HM Stationery Office for the Commonwealth Relations Office.
Hammond-Tooke, W. D. 1975. *Command or Consensus: The Development of Transkeian Local Government*. Cape Town: David Philip.
Hamnett, Ian. 1973. 'Some Problems in the Assessment of Land Shortage: A Case Study in Lesotho'. *African Affairs* 72, 37–45.
Hamnett, Ian. 1975. *Chieftainship and Legitimacy: An Anthropological Study of Executive Law in Lesotho*. London: Routledge & Kegan Paul.
Harris, Marvin. 1974. 'Why a Perfect Knowledge of All the Rules One Must Know to

Act Like a Native Cannot Lead to the Knowledge of How Natives Act'. *Journal of Anthropological Research* 30, 242–51.

Hay, Douglas, 1975. 'Property, Authority and the Criminal Law'. In *Albion's Fatal Tree: Crime and Society in Eighteenth Century England* (Douglas Hay et al., eds.). New York: Pantheon, 17–63.

Hay, Margaret Jean and Sharon Stichter. 1984. *African Women South of the Sahara*. London: Longman.

Hitchcock, Robert K. 1985. 'Sociopolitical Structure and Organization in Swaziland'. Discussion Paper no. 1, Swaziland Manpower Development Project, Ministry of Agriculture and Co-operatives, Mbabane, Swaziland.

Hoebel, Edward A. 1954. *The Law of Primitive Man: A Study in Comparative Legal Dynamics*. Cambridge, Mass.: Harvard University Press.

Holleman, J. F. 1964a. 'The Land Use Survey'. In *Experiment in Swaziland* (J. F. Holleman, ed.). Cape Town: Oxford University Press, 52–7.

Holleman, J. F. 1964b. 'Some Aspects of Agronomic Policy in Swaziland'. In *Experiment in Swaziland* (J. F. Holleman, ed.). Cape Town: Oxford University Press, 334–45.

Hughes, A. J. B. 1962. 'Some Swazi Views on Land Tenure'. *Africa* 32, 253–78.

Hughes, A. J. B. 1964a. 'Reflections on Traditional and Individual Land Tenure in Swaziland'. *Journal of Local Administration* 3, 3–13.

Hughes, A. J. B. 1964b. 'Size and Composition of Rural Homestead Groups'. In *Experiment in Swaziland* (J. F. Holleman, ed.). Cape Town: Oxford University Press, 121–31.

Hughes, A. J. B. 1964c. *Swazi Land Tenure*. Durban, South Africa: Natal University, Institute of Social Research.

Hughes, A. J. B. 1972. *Land Tenure, Land Rights, and Land Communities on Swazi Nation Land: A Discussion of Some Interrelationships between the Traditional Tenurial System and Problems of Agrarian Development*. A Monograph of the Institute for Social Research, no. 7.

Hunt, Alan. 1985. 'The Ideology of Law: Advances and Problems in Recent Applications of the Concept of Ideology to the Analysis of Law'. *Law and Society Review* 19, 11–37.

Hutcheson, A. MacGregor. 1983. 'Swaziland'. In *Africa South of the Sahara 1983–84*. 13th edn, London: Europa.

Jacob, Herbert. 1986. *Law and Politics in the United States*. Boston, Mass.: Little, Brown.

Jacobs, Susie. 1984. 'Women and Land Settlement in Zimbabwe'. *Review of African Political Economy* 27/28, 33–50.

Jeppe, W. J. O. 1980. *Bophuthatswana: Land Tenure and Development*. Cape Town: Maskew Miller.

Jones, David. 1977. *Aid and Development in Southern Africa: British Aid to Botswana, Lesotho and Swaziland*. London: Croom Helm in association with Overseas Development Institute.

Kay, Paul. 1970. 'Some Theoretical Implications of Ethnographic Semantics'. In *Current Directions in Anthropology*, Bulletin of the American Anthropological Association 3/3, 19–31.

Khoza, A. R. V. 1975. 'Swazi Law and Custom'. In *Politics and Society in Swaziland*, collection of unpublished papers, Social Science Research Unit, University of Swaziland, Kwaluseni.

Khumalo, J. A. M. 1977. *Swazi Customary Law Courts: A Supplement to Civil Practice and Procedure in All Bantu Courts in Southern Africa*. Cape Town: Juta.

Krige, E. J. 1936. *The Social System of the Zulus*. London: Longman.

Krige, E. J. 1938. 'The Place of the North-Eastern Transvaal Sotho in the South Bantu Complex'. *Africa* 11, 265–93.
Krige, E. J. and J. D. Krige. 1943. *The Realm of a Rain Queen*. London: International African Institute.
Kunene, Gerard Smanga. 1982a. 'British Colonial Policy in Swaziland: 1920–1960'. Ph.D. thesis, Dalhousie University.
Kunene, Gerard Smanga. 1982b. 'British Colonial Policy and Land Partition in Swaziland 1907–1968: Background to Partition'. Paper delivered at University of Swaziland in series 'Research in Swaziland'.
Kuper, A. 1970. *Kalahari Village Politics: An African Democracy*. Cambridge: Cambridge University Press.
Kuper, A. 1971. 'Council Structure and Decision-Making'. In *Councils in Action* (A. Richards and A. Kuper, eds.). Cambridge: Cambridge University Press, 13–28.
Kuper, Hilda. 1947a. *An African Aristocracy: Rank among the Swazi*. London: Oxford University Press for the International African Institute.
Kuper, Hilda. 1947b. *The Uniform of Colour in Swaziland: A Study of White–Black Relationships in Swaziland*. Johannesburg: Witwatersrand University Press.
Kuper, Hilda. 1963. *The Swazi: A South African Kingdom*. New York: Holt, Rinehart & Winston.
Kuper, Hilda. 1978. *Sobhuza II: Ngwenyama and King of Swaziland*. London: Gerald Duckworth.
La Fontaine, Jean. 1979. 'Land and the Political Community in Bugisu'. In *Politics in Leadership: A Comparative Perspective* (William A. Shack and Percy S. Cohen, eds.). Oxford: Clarendon Press, 95–114.
Lamphere, Louise. 1974. 'Strategies, Cooperation, and Conflict among Women in Domestic Groups'. In: *Women, Culture and Society* (Michelle Zimbalist Rosaldo and Louise Lamphere, eds.). Stanford, Calif.: Stanford University Press, 97–112.
Lamphere, Louise. 1975. 'Women and Domestic Power: Political and Economic Strategies in Domestic Groups'. In *Being Female: Reproduction, Power and Changes* (Dana Raphael, ed.). The Hague: Mouton, 117–30.
Leistner, G. M. E. and P. Smit. 1969. *Resources and Development*. Communications of the Africa Institute, no. 8, Pretoria.
Levin, Richard Michael. 1985. 'Hegemony and Crisis: Royal Power in Transition'. Ph.D. thesis, University of Liverpool.
LeVine, R. A. 1961. 'Anthropology and the Study of Conflict'. *Journal of Conflict Resolution* 5, 1–15.
Linton, Ralph. 1936. *The Study of Man*. New York: Appleton-Century-Crofts.
Llewellyn, K. N. and E. A. Hoebel. 1941. *The Cheyenne Way: Conflict and Case Law in Primitive Jurisprudence*. Norman: University of Oklahoma Press.
Maasdorp, Gavin. 1976. 'Modernization in Swaziland'. In *Contemporary Africa: Geography and Change* (C. Gregory Knight and James L. Newman, eds.). Englewood Cliffs, N.J.: Prentice-Hall, 408–22.
McFadden, Patricia. 1982. 'Women in Wage-Labour in Swaziland: A Focus on Agriculture'. *South African Labour Bulletin* 7, 140–66.
Macmillan School Atlas for Swaziland, 1986. London: Macmillan Education.
Magagula, Glenn T. 1982. 'Land Tenure and Agricultural Production in Swaziland'. Paper presented at the Workshop on Land Policy and Agricultural Development, National Institute of Development and Cultural Research, University College of Botswana.
Maina, G. Munyua. 1975. 'Land Tenure and Socio-Economic Development in Swaziland'. Paper on file at Social Science Research Unit, University of Swaziland.
Maine, Henry S. 1861. *Ancient Law*. London: Oxford University Press.

Malinowski, Bronislaw. 1926. *Crime and Custom in Savage Society*. London: Routledge & Kegan Paul.

Mann, Kristin, 1982. 'Women's Rights in Law and Practice: Marriage and Dispute Settlement in Colonial Lagos'. In *African Women and the Law: Historical Perspectives* (Margaret Jean Hay and Marcia Wright, eds.). Boston University Papers on Africa, VII, 151–71.

Marwick, Brian Allan. 1940. *The Swazi: An Ethnographic Account of the Swaziland Protectorate*. Cambridge: Cambridge University Press.

Mashasha, F. J. 1974. 'The Swazi and Land Partition (1902–1910)'. In *The Societies of Southern Africa in the 19th and 20th Centuries*, vol. 4. University of London Institute of Commonwealth Studies, collected seminar papers no. 17.

Mashasha, F. J. 1977. 'The Road to Colonialism: Concessions and the Collapse of Swazi Independence 1875–1926'. Ph.D. thesis, Oxford University.

Matsebula, J. S. M. 1972. *A History of Swaziland*. Cape Town: Longman Southern Africa.

Matsebula, M. S. 1982a. 'The Historical Origins of Swaziland's Economic Dualism and Migration'. Occasional Paper no. 8, Economics Department, University of Swaziland, Kwaluseni.

Matsebula, M. S. 1982b. 'Structural Characteristics of the Swaziland Economy'. Paper presented at Piet Southern Africa Advisory Seminar organized by Swaziland Bank Workers Union, Ezulwini, Swaziland.

Mayer, R. and I. Mayer. 1965. 'Land Law in the Making'. In *African Law: Adaptation and Development* (H. Kuper and L. Kuper, eds.). Berkeley: University of California Press, 51–78.

Mbilinyi, Marjorie J. 1972. 'The "New Woman" in Tanzania'. *Journal of Modern African Studies* 10, 57–72.

Mbithi, Philip M. 1970. 'Community Leadership and Power as Factors Affecting the Efficiency of Governmental Administrative Action: A Case Study in Rural Development Strategy'. Paper prepared for Makerere Rural Development Research Seminar.

Meek, C. K. 1937. *Law and Authority in a Nigerian Tribe*. London: Oxford University Press.

Meek, C. K. 1946. *Land Law and Custom in the Colonies*. London: Oxford University Press.

Merry, Sally Engle. 1982. 'The Articulation of Legal Spheres'. In *African Women and the Law: Historical Perspectives* (Margaret Jean Hay and Marcia Wright, eds.). Boston University Papers on Africa, VII, 68–89.

Meyers, Phillip. 1983. 'Customary Law Research Proposal'. Unpublished paper, Kwaluseni: University of Swaziland.

Mifsud, Frank M. 1967. *Customary Land Law in Africa*. Rome: Food and Agriculture Organization of the United Nations.

Ministry of Local Administration. 1978. 'Tinkhundla National Centres'. Paper submitted to SWADEV: Workshop on Rural Environment and Development Planning in Swaziland. CODEC (Ezulwini) Swaziland, Paper no. 18, 1–10 May.

Moore, Sally Falk. 1970. 'Politics, Procedure and Norms in Changing Chagga Law'. *Africa* 60, 321–44.

Moore, Sally Falk. 1977. 'Individual Interests and Organizational Structures: Dispute Settlements as "Events of Articulation"'. In *Social Anthropology and Law* (Ian Hamnett, ed.). ASA Monograph 14, London: Academic Press, 159–88.

Moore, Sally Falk. 1986. *Social Facts and Fabrications: Customary Law on Kilimanjaro 1880–1980*. Cambridge: Cambridge University Press.

Mugambwa, J. 1981. 'Land Tenure and Economic Development in Lesotho'. In

Southern Africa in Need of Law Reform (A. J. G. M. Sanders, ed.). Institute of Foreign and Comparative Law, University of South Africa, 80–90.
Mullings, Leith. 1976. 'Women and Economic Change in Africa'. In *Women in Africa: Studies in Social and Economic Change* (Nancy J. Hafkin and Edna G. Bay, eds.). Stanford, Calif.: Stanford University Press, 239–64.
Murdoch, G. 1968. *Soils and Land Capability in Swaziland.* Part III. Trends in the Rural Economy. Mbabane: Swaziland Ministry of Agriculture.
Murdoch, G. 1977. 'Past Settlement Patterns Reflected in Present Agricultural Returns and Soil Properties. Examples from Swaziland'. In *African Historical Demography*. Edinburgh, 401–4.
Nader, Laura. 1969. 'To Make the Balance'. In *Law in Culture and Society* (Laura Nader, ed.). Chicago, Ill.: Aldine, 69–91.
Nader, Laura. 1977. 'Powerlessness in Zapotec and United States Society'. In *The Anthropology of Power* (R. Fogelson and R. Adams, eds.). New York and London: Academic Press, 309–24.
Nader, Laura. 1984. 'A User Theory of Law'. *Southwestern Law Review* 38, 951–63.
Nader, Laura. 1987. 'The Crown, the Colonists, and the Course of Village Law'. In *History and Power in the Study of Law* (June Starr and Jane Collier, eds.). Ithaca, N.Y.: Cornell University Press.
Nader, Laura. 1990. *Harmony Ideology – Justice and Control in a Zapotec Mountain Village*. Stanford, Calif.: Stanford University Press.
Nader, L. and D. Serber. 1976. 'Law and the Distribution of Power'. In *The Uses of Controversy in Sociology* (L. A. Coser and O. N. Larsen, eds.). New York: The Free Press, 273–91.
Nader, Laura and Harry F. Todd, eds. 1978. *The Disputing Process – Law in Ten Societies*. New York: Columbia University Press.
Nelson, Nici, ed. 1981. *African Women in the Development Process*. Totowa, N.J.: Frank Cass.
Ngubane, Harriet. 1983. 'The Swazi Homestead'. In *The Swazi Rural Homestead* (Fion de Vletter, ed.). Social Science Research Unit, University of Swaziland, 95–122.
Nhlapo, R. T. 1982. 'Legal Duality and Multiple Judicial Organization in Swaziland: An Analysis and a Proposal'. In *The Individual under African Law* (Peter N. Takirambudde, ed.). Kwaluseni: University of Swaziland, 66–76.
Nhlapo, R. T. 1986. 'The Mixture of Civil and Customary Law in Swaziland'. Paper presented at International Academy of Comparative Law, 12th Congress, Australia.
Nicholas, R. W. 1963. 'Village Factions and Political Parties in Rural West Bengal'. *Journal of Commonwealth Political Studies* 2, 17–32.
Nicholas, R. W. 1966. 'Segmentary Factional Political Systems'. In *Political Anthropology* (Marc J. Swartz, Victor W. Turner and Arthur Tuden, eds.). Chicago: Aldine, 49–59.
Njeru, Enos Hudson Nthia. 1978. 'Land Adjudication and Its Implications for the Social Organization of the Mbere'. Research Paper no. 73, Land Tenure Center, University of Wisconsin, Madison.
Nkambule, N. M. 1983. 'A Diagnosis of Adverse Effects of Customary Land Tenure on Land Use in the Kingdom of Swaziland: Is a Land Privatisation Policy the Answer?' Master's thesis, University of Wisconsin, Madison.
Nyeko, Balam. 1977. 'African Initiatives and Responses in Colonial Swaziland: The Swazi Leaders and the Land Question, 1902–1926'. Paper presented to the International Conference on Southern African History, National University of Lesotho, Roma.
Okeyo, Achola Pala. 1980. 'Daughters of the Lakes and Rivers: Colonization and the Land Rights of Luo Women'. In *Women and Colonization: Anthropological*

Perspectives (Mona Etienne and Eleanor Leacock, eds.). New York: Praeger, 186–213.
Pala, Achola. 1976. 'African Women in Rural Development: Research Trends and Priorities'. OLC Paper no. 12, Washington, D.C., Overseas Liaison Committee, American Council on Education.
Papanek, Hanna. 1977. 'Toward Models of Development: Development Planning for Women'. *Signs: Journal of Women in Culture and Society* 3, 14–21.
Perry, J. A. G. 1977. 'Law-codes and Brokerage in a Lesotho Village'. In *Social Anthropology and Law* (Ian Hamnett, ed.). ASA Monograph 14, London: Academic Press, 189–228.
Perry, J. A. G. 1981. 'Land, Power and the Lie'. *Man* 16, 235–250.
Picard, Louis A. 1983. 'Traditionalism, the Bureaucracy and Political Development'. Paper presented at the African Studies Association Meetings, Boston, Mass.
Potholm, Christian P. 1965. *Swaziland: The Dynamics of Political Modernization.* Berkeley: University of California Press.
Preston-Whyte, Eleanor and Harriet Sibisi. 1975. 'Ethnographic Oddity or Ecological Sense? Nyuswa-Zulu Descent Groups and Land Allocation'. *African Studies* 34, 283–316.
Ranger, Terence. 1983. 'The Invention of Tradition in Colonial Africa'. In *The Invention of Tradition* (Eric Hobsbawm and Terence Ranger, eds.). Cambridge: Cambridge University Press, 211–62.
Richards, Audrey I. 1939. *Land, Labour and Diet in Northern Rhodesia.* London: Oxford University Press.
Richards, Audrey I. 1960. *East African Chiefs.* London: Faber.
Richards, Audrey I. 1963. 'Some Effects of the Introduction of Individual Freehold into Buganda'. *African Agrarian Systems* (D. Biebuyck, ed.). London: Oxford University Press for the International African Institute, 267–80.
Richards, Cara E. 1969. 'Presumed Behavior: Modification of the Ideal–Real Dichotomy'. *American Anthropologist* 71, 1115–17.
Riddell, James C. and Carol Dickerman. 1986. 'Land Tenure Profile: Swaziland'. In *Country Profiles of Land Tenure: Africa 1986.* Land Tenure Center Paper 127, 190–5.
Roberts, Simon. n.d. 'Arable Land Disputes and Administrative Change in the Kgatleng'. Paper on file at the University of Wisconsin Land Tenure Center, Madison.
Roberts, Simon. 1970. *A Restatement of the Kgatla Law of Succession to Property.* Gaborone: Government Printer.
Roberts, Simon. 1971. 'The Settlement of Family Disputes in the Kgatla Customary Courts: Some New Approaches'. *Journal of African Law* 15, 60–76.
Roberts, Simon. 1973. 'Mmatlhong's Field'. *Law in Rural Africa* 22, 1–13.
Roberts, Simon. 1977. 'Tradition and Change at Mochudi: Competing Jurisdictions in Botswana'. *African Law Studies* 17, 37–51.
Roberts, Simon and John Comaroff. 1979. 'A Chief's Decision and the Devolution of Property in a Tswana Chiefdom'. In *Politics in Leadership* (William A. Shack and Percy S. Cohen, eds.). Oxford: Clarendon Press, 115–35.
Rogers, Barbara. 1980. *The Domestication of Women: Discrimination in Developing Societies.* New York: St Martin's Press.
Rosenblum, Victor G. 1955. *Law as a Political Instrument.* New York: Random House.
Rosen-Prinz, Beth. 1976. 'Urbanization and Political Change: A Study of Urban Local Government in Swaziland'. Ph.D. dissertation, University of California, Los Angeles.
Rubin, Leslie. 1963. 'Adaptation of Traditional Law in Southern Africa'. In *The*

Development and Adaptation of Legal Systems in Africa. Interdisciplinary Colloquium in African Studies, African Studies Center, University of California.
Russell, Margo. n.d. 'The Rural Homestead in Its Context'. Research paper no. 3, Social Science Research Unit, University of Swaziland.
Russell, Margo. 1983. 'Boundaries and Structures in the Swaziland Homestead'. Research paper no. 6, Social Science Research Unit, University of Swaziland.
Russell, Margo. 1984. 'Closer Focus: A Plea for More Small-Scale Face-to-Face Interviewing in Contemporary African Social Research'. Paper presented to ARPT/CIMMYT Networkshop, Lusaka, Zambia.
Russell, Margo. 1985. 'A Report on Landlessness in Rural Swaziland'. Paper presented to the Food and Agriculture Organization. Paper on file at Social Science Research Unit, University of Swaziland.
Sachs, Carolyn and Christine Roach. 1983. *Women and Agricultural Production on Swazi Nation Land.* Office of Women in Development, USAID in Swaziland.
Sallinger-McBride, Jan and Louis A. Picard. 1984a. 'Patrons vs. Planners: The Political Contradictions of Integrated Rural Development in Swaziland'. Paper presented at African Studies Association Meetings, New Orleans.
Sallinger-McBride, Jan and Louis A. Picard, 1984b. 'Rural Development Areas in Swaziland: The Politics of Integrated Rural Development'. Revised version of paper presented at African Studies Association Meetings, New Orleans.
Sansom, Basil. 1937. 'Traditional Economic Systems' and 'Traditional Rulers and their Realms'. In *The Bantu-Speaking Peoples of Southern Africa.* London: Routledge & Kegan Paul, 135–76 and 246–83.
Schapera, Isaac. 1938. *A Handbook of Tswana Law and Custom.* London: Oxford University Press for the International African Institute.
Schapera, Isaac. 1953. *The Tswana.* Ethnographic Survey of Africa: Southern Africa, Part III. London: International African Institute.
Schapera, Isaac. 1956. *Government and Politics in Tribal Societies.* London: C. A. Watts.
Schapera, Isaac. 1969. 'Uniformity and Chief-Made Law: A Tswana Case Study'. In *Law in Culture and Society* (Laura Nader, ed.). Chicago: Aldine, 230–44.
Schapera, Isaac. 1970. *Tribal Innovators: Tswana Chiefs and Social Change, 1795–1940.* University of London: Athlone Press (New York: Humanities Press).
Schapera, Isaac. 1983. 'Tswana Concepts of Custom and Law'. *Journal of African Law* 27, 141–9.
Scott, James C. 1985. *Weapons of the Weak: Everyday Forms of Peasant Resistance.* New Haven, Conn.: Yale University Press.
Scott, Peter. 1951. 'Land Policy and the Native Population of Swaziland'. *Geographical Journal* 117, 435–47.
Shipton, Parker M. 1984. 'Strips and Patches: A Demographic Dimension in Some African Land-Holding and Political Systems'. *Man* 19, 613–34.
Shongwe, Mavela V. 1983. 'Tinkhundla: A Study of Local Government in Swaziland'. A project submitted in partial fulfilment of the requirements for the degree of Bachelor of Arts in Humanities, University of Swaziland, Kwaluseni.
Sibisi, Harriet. 1980. 'Sociological Observations on Some Aspects of Rural Development in Swaziland'. Traditional Securities and the Response to 'Modern' Economic Opportunities, Paper no. 3, Ministry of Agriculture and Cooperatives, Mbabane, Swaziland.
Siegal, J. and Alan Beals. 1960. 'Conflict and Factionalist Dispute'. *Journal of the Royal Anthropological Institute* 90, 107–17.
Silitshena, R. M. K. 1979. 'Chiefly Authority and the Organization of Space in

Botswana: Towards an Exploration of Nucleated Settlements among the Tswana'. *Botswana Notes and Records* 11, 55–67.
Simmel, George. 1955. *Conflict*. Glencoe, Ill.: The Free Press.
Stack, Carol B. 1974a. *All Our Kin: Strategies for Survival in a Black Community*. New York: Harper & Row.
Stack, Carol B. 1974b. 'Sex Roles and Survival Strategies in an Urban Black Community'. In *Women, Culture and Society* (Michelle Zimbalist Rosaldo and Louise Lamphere, eds.). Stanford, Calif.: Stanford University Press, 113–28.
Starr, June. 1978a. 'A Pre-Law Stage in Rural Turkish Disputes Negotiations'. In *Cross Examinations: Essays in Memory of Max Gluckman* (P. H. Gulliver, ed.). Leiden: E. J. Brill, 110–32.
Starr, June. 1978b. *Dispute and Settlement in Rural Turkey: An Ethnography of Law*. Leiden: E. J. Brill.
Starr, June and Barbara Yngvesson. 1975. 'Scarcity and Disputing: Zeroing in on Compromise Decisions'. *American Ethnologist* 2, 553–66.
Sumner, Colin. 1979. 'The Ideological Composition of Law'. In *Reading Ideologies: An Investigation into the Marxist Theory of Ideology and Law*. London: Academic Press, 246–85.
Sutherland, Alistair J. 1981. 'Local Level Dispute Processes in Botswana: The Yeyi Moot Encapsulated'. *Journal of African Law* 25, 94–114.
Tadesse, Zenebeworke. 1982. 'The Impact of Land Reform on Women: The Case of Ethiopia'. In *Women and Development: The Sexual Division of Labor in Rural Societies* (Lourdes Beneria, ed.). New York: Praeger, 203–22.
Takirambudde, Peter. n.d. 'A Framework for Understanding Property Legislations and Policy in Swaziland'. Paper on file at Social Science Research Unit, University of Swaziland.
Takirambudde, Peter. 1981. 'The Swaziland Contractual Regulation of Land Transactions: Trading Efficiency for Social Justice'. *Comparative and International Law Journal of Southern Africa* 14, 179–95.
Takirambudde, Peter. 1983. 'External Law and Social Structure in an African Context: An Essay about Normative Imposition and Survival in Swaziland'. *Comparative and International Law Journal of Southern Africa* 16, 209–28.
Third National Development Plan 1978/9–1982/3. Government of Swaziland.
Tinkhundla System of Government Guidelines'. n.d. Booklet for use by Tinkhundla Public Officers.
Turner, Victor. 1957. *Schism and Continuity in an African Society: A Study of Ndembu Village Life*. Manchester: Manchester University Press.
Uchendu, V. C. 1967. 'Some Issues in African Land Tenure'. *Tropical Agriculture* 44, 91–101.
Uchendu, V. C. 1971. 'The Conflict between National Land Policies and Local Sovereignty over Land in Tropical Africa'. Paper presented at the Seminar on Problems of Land Tenure in African Development, Leiden, 12–17 December 1971.
Van Rouveroy van Nieuwaal, E. A. B. 1981. 'In Search of Justice: Different Levels of Dispute Settlement among the Anufom in North Togo'. Documentary film, Afrika-Studiecentrum, Leiden, the Netherlands.
Van Velsen, J. 1967. 'The Extended-Case Method and Situational Analysis'. In *The Craft of Social Anthropology* (E. L. Epstein, ed.). London: Tavistock, 129–49.
Van Velzen, H. U. E. Thoden. 1973. 'Robinson Crusoe and Friday: Strength and Weakness of the Big Man Paradigm'. *Man* 8, 592–612.
Vincent, Joan. 1971. *African Elite: the Big Men of a Small Town*. New York: Columbia University Press.

Vincent, Joan. 1977. 'Colonial Chiefs and the Making of Class: A Case Study from Teso, Eastern Uganda'. Africa 47, 140–59.

Wallman, Sandra. 1968. 'Lesotho's Pitso: Traditional Meetings in a Modern Setting'. *Canadian Journal of African Studies* 2, 167–73.

Werbner, Richard P. 1969. 'Constitutional Ambiguities and the British Administration of Royal Careers among the Bemba of Zambia'. In *Law in Culture and Society* (Laura Nader, ed.). Chicago: Aldine, 245–72.

Werbner, Richard P. 1977. 'Small Man Politics and the Rule of Law: Centre–Periphery Relations in East-Central Botswana'. *Journal of African Law* 21, 24–39.

Werbner, Richard P. 1980. 'The Quasi-Judicial and the Experience of the Absurd: Remaking Land Law in North-eastern Botswana'. *Journal of African Law* 24, 131–51.

West, Henry W. 1971. 'Current Land Tenure Trends in Independent Countries of Africa'. Paper presented at seminar on problems of land tenure in African development, Leiden, 13–17 December 1971.

White, C. M. N. 1958. 'Terminological Confusion in African Land Tenure'. *Journal of African Administration* 10, 124–30.

White, C. M. N. 1963. 'Factors Determining the Content of African Land-Tenure Systems in Northern Rhodesia'. In *African Agrarian Systems* (D. Biebuyck, ed.). London: Oxford University Press for the International African Institute, 364–73.

Whittington, G. W. and J. B. M. Daniel. 1969. '16 Problems of Land Tenure and Ownership in Swaziland'. In *Environment and Land Use in Africa* (M. F. Thomas and G. W. Whittington, eds.). London: Methuen, 447–61.

Winter, Isobel. 1978. 'The Post-Colonial State and the Forces and Relations of Production: Swaziland'. *Review of African Political Economy* 9, 27–43.

Wintrob, Joseph W. 1966. 'The Importance of Land Tenure to Political and Economic Change in Buganda'. Paper on file at Land Tenure Center, University of Wisconsin, Madison.

Wright, Marcia. 1982. 'Justice, Women and the Social Order in Abercorn, Northeastern Rhodesia, 1897–1903'. In *African Women and the Law: Historical Perspectives* (Margaret Jean Hay and Marcia Wright, eds.). Boston University Papers on Africa, VII, 33–50.

Wynne, Susan G. 1985. 'Information Problems Involved in Partitioning the Commons for Cultivation'. Paper prepared for a conference on Common Property Resource Management, Annapolis, Maryland, 21–26 April 1985, sponsored by the Board on Science and Technology for International Development, National Academy of Sciences/National Research Council.

Youe, C. P. 1978. 'Imperial Land Policy in Swaziland and the African Response'. *Journal of Imperial and Commonwealth History* 7, 56–69.

Index

Page numbers in *italics* refer to figures, tables and maps

Index

Other books in the series

6 Labour in the South African Gold Mines, 1911–1969 *Francis Wilson*
11 Island and Tribal Art in West Africa *Rene A. Bravmann*
23 West African States: Failure and Promise: A Study in Comparative Politics *edited by John Dunn*
25 A Modern History of Tanganyika *John Iliffe*
26 A History of African Christianity 1950–1975 *Adrian Hastings*
28 The Hidden Hippopotamus: Reappraisal in African History: The Early Colonial Experience in Western Zambia *Gwyn Prins*
29 Families Divided: The Impact of Migrant Labour in Lesotho *Colin Murray*
30 Slavery, Colonialism and Economic Growth in Dahomey, 1640–1960 *Patrick Manning*
31 Kings, Commoners and Concessionaires: The Evolution and Dissolution of the Nineteenth-century Swazi State *Philip Bonner*
32 Oral Poetry and Somali Nationalism: The Case of Sayyid Mahammad Abdille Hasan *Said S. Samatar*
33 The Political Economy of Pondoland 1860–1930: Production, Labour, Migrancy and Chiefs in Rural South Africa *William Beinart*
34 Volkskapitalisme: Class, Capital and Ideology in the Development of Afrikaner Nationalism 1934–1948 *Dan O'Meara*
35 The Settler Economies: Studies in the Economic History of Kenya and Rhodesia 1900–1963 *Paul Mosley*
36 Transformations in Slavery: A History of Slavery in Africa *Paul E. Lovejoy*
37 Amilcar Cabral: Revolutionary Leadership and People's War *Patrick Chabal*
38 Essays on the Political Economy of Rural Africa *Robert H. Bates*
39 Ijeshas and Nigerians: The Incorporation of a Yoruba Kingdom, 1890s–1970s *J. D. Y. Peel*
40 Black People and the South African War 1899–1902 *Peter Warwick*
42 Industrialisation and Trade Union Organisation in South Africa 1924–55 *Jon Lewis*
43 The Rising of the Red Shawls: A Revolt in Madagascar 1895–1899 *Stephen Ellis*
45 Law, Custom and Social Order: The Colonial Experience in Malawi and Zambia *Martin Chanock*
46 Salt of the Desert Sun: A History of Salt Production and Trade in the Central Sudan *Paul E. Lovejoy*
47 Marrying Well: Marriage, Status and Social Change among the Educated Elite in Colonial Lagos *Kristin Mann*
48 Language and Colonial Power: The Appropriation of Swahili in the Former Belgian Congo, 1880–1938 *Johannes Fabian*
49 The Shell Money of the Slave Trade *Jan Hogendorn and Marion Johnson*

50 Political Domination in Africa: Reflections on the Limits of Power *edited by Patrick Chabal*
51 The Southern Marches of Imperial Ethiopia: Essays in History and Social Anthropology *edited by Donald Donham and Wendy James*
52 Islam and Urban Labor in Northern Nigeria: The Making of a Muslim Working Class *Paul M. Lubeck*
53 Horn and Crescent: Cultural Change and Traditional Islam on the East African Coast, 500–1900 *Randall L. Pouwels*
54 Capital and Labour on the Kimberley Diamond Fields 1871–1890 *Robert Vicat Turrell*
55 National and Class Conflict in the Horn of Africa *John Markakis*
56 Democracy and Prebendal Politics in Nigeria: The Rise and Fall of the Second Republic *Richard A. Joseph*
57 Entrepreneurs and Parasites: The Struggle for Indigenous Capitalism in Zaire *Janet McGaffey*
58 The African Poor: A History *John Iliffe*
59 Palm Oil and Protest: An Economic History of the Ngwa Region, South-eastern Nigeria, 1800–1980 *Susan M. Martin*
60 France and Islam in West Africa, 1860–1960 *Christopher Harrison*
61 Transformation and Continuity in Revolutionary Ethiopia *Christopher Clapham*
62 Prelude to the Mahdiyya: Peasants and Traders in the Shendi Region, 1821–1885 *Anders Bjørkelo*
63 Wa and the Wala: Islam and Polity in Northwestern Ghana *Ivor Wilks*
64 Bankole-Bright and Politics in Colonial Sierra Leone: The Passing of the 'Krio Era', 1919–1958 *Akintola Wyse*
65 Contemporary West African States *Donald Cruise O'Brien, John Dunn and Richard Rathbone*
66 The Oromo of Ethiopia: A History, 1570–1860 *Mohammed Hassen*
67 Slavery and African Life: Occidental, Oriental and African Slave Trades *Patrick Manning*
68 Abraham Esau's War: A Black South African War in the Cape, 1899–1902 *Bill Nasson*